Max-Planck-Institut für ausländisches
öffentliches Recht und Völkerrecht

Beiträge zum ausländischen öffentlichen Recht und Völkerrecht

Begründet von Viktor Bruns

Herausgegeben von
Rudolf Bernhardt · Karl Doehring
Jochen Abr. Frowein

Band 93

Rudolf Bernhardt · John Anthony Jolowicz (Eds.)

International Enforcement of Human Rights

Reports submitted to the Colloquium of the
International Association of Legal Science
Heidelberg, 28 – 30 August 1985

Appendix
Texts of Selected Universal and
Regional Human Rights Instruments

Springer-Verlag Berlin Heidelberg New York
London Paris Tokyo

Library of Congress Cataloging-in-Publication Data: International Association of Legal Science. Colloquium (1985 : Heidelberg, Germany) International enforcement of human rights. (Beiträge zum ausländischen öffentlichen Recht und Völkerrecht ; Bd. 93) Includes index. 1. Civil rights (International law)–Congresses. I. Bernhardt, Rudolf, 1925– . II. Jolowicz, J. A. (John Anthony). III. Title. IV. Series. K3239.6 1985 341.4'81 87-4700.

ISBN-13: 978-3-642-71921-9 e-ISBN-13: 978-3-642-71919-6
DOI: 10.1007/978-3-642-71919-6

(U.S.)

Softcover reprint of the hardcover 1st edition 1987

2142/3130-543210

Preface

The International Association of Legal Science organized, in 1985, a colloquium on the International Enforcement of Human Rights. The meeting took place from August 28–30, in Heidelberg, on the premises of the Max Planck Society for the Advancement of Sciences. Professor *André Tunc,* President of the Association, presided. The undersigned acted, respectively, as General Rapporteur for the colloquium and as Director of Scientific Work of the Association.

The present volume contains the reports submitted to the colloqium. In addition, a paper on Approaches to Human Rights in Asia, written by Mrs. *Yamane,* is included. The reports were discussed by the participants during the meeting. (See the list of participants on page 159). The discussion was not recorded and is not here summarized.

RUDOLF BERNHARDT JOHN ANTHONY JOLOWICZ

This volume owes its appearance to Professor *Bernhardt* and to his colleagues of the Max Planck Institute in Heidelberg. That fact cannot, however, be allowed to prevent it from containing an acknowledgment of a debt of gratitude owed by the International Association of Legal Science. As Director of Scientific Work of the Association at the time of the colloquium, I therefore gladly take this opportunity to make two observations. First, it should be known to readers of this volume that discussion at the working sessions of the colloquium was lively and well-informed and that each session had to be terminated for lack of time, not for lack of contributions; this is sufficient evidence in itself of the colloquium's success. Secondly, this success was due not only to the excellence of the reports here reproduced, but also and above all to the scholarship and skill of Professor *Bernhardt* himself, as General Reporter and as organiser of the colloquium, to his and his colleagues' kindness and hospitality to the participants, and to the work of the German Association of Comparative Law. To them all I express, both personally and on behalf of the International Association, our warmest thanks.

JOHN ANTHONY JOLOWICZ

Contents

The International Bill of Rights: The Universal Declaration and the Covenants

LOUIS HENKIN

This report addresses what has come to be called the International Bill of Rights – the Universal Declaration and the two comprehensive International Covenants – and its part in the international enforcement of human rights. Like others I assume that the Colloquium, and therefore this report, should address international enforcement in its largest sense, to include not only means to compel or induce compliance with norms but all the various international efforts to promote the enjoyment and improve the condition of human rights in the world today.

After a word of background, I shall introduce, identify and describe the three international instruments; indicate their history since promulgation; appraise their contribution and significance. It may be desirable also to put these instruments in the context of the International Human Rights movement and relate them to other elements in the Human Rights program of the United Nations.

Antecedents

International concern with human rights is a contemporary development, dating largely from the Second World War. Traditionally, the international political system, and therefore international law, considered what we now call human rights to be a matter of domestic, not international, concern. This international lack of interest in human rights was often expressed in two overlapping propositions: the individual was not a subject of international law; and how a state treated its own inhabitants was its own affair. That tradition no doubt reflected the prevailing conception of the limited domain of international law. It may have been also a reflection of the prevailing morality: since human rights were not highly respected in most countries, since governments were not moved to refrain from inhumanity at home, they could not be expected to care more for the human condition elsewhere.

The contemporary international concern with human rights, however, is not wholly without antecedent. States that sent persons and goods abroad during the age of mercantilism came to insist on an international standard of justice which other states were obligated to honor in respect of foreign nationals and their property. The idea of rights that grew in the 17th and 18th centuries in England, France, and the American colonies, and then in the United States, leaped across borders and seas and permeated international relations. In the 19th century, a burgeoning international morality led to the abolition of slavery and the international prohibition of slave trade, and later to efforts to make war less inhumane. Because some governments identified with some inhabitants of other states, usually from affinities of religion or ethnicity, international protection of minorities, by various means including a series of treaties, was seen as necessary to reduce international tension and to prevent war. The spread of various versions of socialism, and early manifestations of the welfare state, led to organized international efforts to improve the social and economic conditions of working people, culminating in the International Labor Organization and its various programs including a network of international conventions.

The International Human Rights movement as we know it began during the Second World War. President Franklin Roosevelt gave it famous expression in 1941 when he proclaimed the Four Freedoms, which became aims of World War II. Increasing awareness of Hitler's unspeakable enormities confirmed international determination to establish some measure of international responsibility for the condition of human beings everywhere. The result was the inclusion of charges of crimes against humanity in the Nuremberg Charter and the incorporation of human rights provisions in the U.N. Charter.

The Nuremberg Charter addressed the past; the U.N. Charter looked to the future. The Nuremberg Charter judged the actions of the leaders of Nazi Germany; the U.N. Charter planned and legislated for all states, including the victorious Allies, even the Great Powers. It was perhaps not surprising, however, that while states were prepared to declare the need to assert some international responsibility for human rights, they were reluctant to break radically with the traditional assumptions and attitudes of international law and politics that human rights were domestic matters. They were not eager to impose on all states, and assume for themselves, firm and explicit undertakings to respect the human rights of their own inhabitants, and to establish international institutions to enforce such obligations. Although a few small states urged the addition to the Charter of an International Bill of Rights, in the end the steps taken were modest. The Charter established the promotion of human rights as one of the purposes of the United Nations. The Economic and Social Council was directed to set up a commission for the promotion of human rights. In Articles 55 and 56, states pledged to take joint and separate action in cooperation with the U.N. Organization, for the achievement of the U.N. purpose of promoting human rights.

The significance of the pledge which the Charter demanded of members was not clear or agreed when the Charter was drafted; it is not clear or agreed now. In effect, the development and articulation of less ambiguous and more specific human rights undertakings were postponed to a later day and a different forum.

The International Human Rights movement pressed on, but differences of opinion emerged as to the best means for promoting human rights. There was disagreement in particular as to whether it was desirable to seek binding international human rights norms. Some questioned whether such norms could be developed in a system of sovereign states with diverse political institutions and cultural values, whether any declared values could be effectively established in an international system that was decentralized and lacked institutions to compel or induce compliance. The result was a decision to seek, at least as a first step, not a binding international human rights agreement but a universal declaration of human rights.

The Universal Declaration of Human Rights

What became the Universal Declaration was the work of the Human Rights Commission established by the Economic and Social Council of the U.N. General Assembly. It bears the imprint of great personages of the time – Eleanor Roosevelt, René Cassin, Charles Malik and others. The rhetoric of its preamble is ringing and the thirty substantive articles that follow have become the heart of the International Bill of Rights.

To students of the historic development of the idea of rights, to those acquainted with the United States Declaration of Independence and the U.S. Bill of Rights, the French Declaration of the Rights of Man and the Citizen, and their English antecedents, most of the provisions of the Universal Declaration are familiar. Unlike the earlier instruments, however, the Universal Declaration, addressed to a universal audience, eschews building rights on any philosophical foundation and grounds them rather in general appeals to values of freedom, justice and peace, in faith in the dignity and worth of the human person, in commitment to social progress and better standards of life in larger freedom.

Some political philosophy is implicit, of course, in the idea of rights. It is a limited but powerful idea. It insists that state authority in respect of its own inhabitants is not absolute, that every human being has a minimum hard core of rights against his/her society. It implies, of course, that government may not abuse its inhabitants by various forms of tyranny or repression. But it implies also limitations even on *bona fide,* benign governments acting in the public interest. These, too, must respect a minimum of individual autonomy and freedom.

The catalogue of rights in the Declaration is not a lowest common denominator of national practices; it is a comprehensive enumeration of all rights that were deemed to be implicit in or required for human dignity, "a common standard of achievement", high but one within reach of all societies. Most of the substantive provisions of the Declaration follow those of Western bills of rights, though the Declaration includes a number of rights which they had not made explicit, perhaps because they took them for granted, such as the right to be recognized as a person before the law or to marry and found a family. The rights recognized in the Universal Declaration include: the right to life, liberty and security of the person; freedom from slavery or servitude; freedom from torture or cruel, inhuman or degrading treatment or punishment; recognition as a person before the law; equality before the law and equal protection of the law; a right to an effective remedy for violations of fundamental rights; freedom from arbitrary arrest, detention or exile; fair and public trial for persons charged with crime, with guarantees necessary for one's defense; the presumption of innocence; conviction only according to law, and freedom from the application of *ex post facto* law; freedom from arbitrary interference with privacy, family, home or correspondence, and legal protection against such interference; freedom of movement and residence within a country, the right to leave any country, and the right to seek asylum; the right to a nationality and not to be arbitrarily deprived of one's nationality, and the right to change one's nationality; the right to marry and found a family, and equality of men and women in marriage and its dissolution; the right to own property and not to be arbitrarily deprived of it; freedom of thought, conscience and religion, freedom of opinion and expression, assembly and association. The Universal Declaration also includes some political rights, for example the right to take part in government and the right to have equal access to the public service, which are accepted as being human rights for every person but only in relation to "his country" (Art. 21 (1), (2)). (Compare the right of everyone to return "to his country", Art. 13 (2)).

These rights are familiar developments of the idea of rights reflected in eighteenth century bills of rights. The Universal Declaration, however, added a new series of rights. Drawing on nineteenth century ideas of socialism, and on non-socialist commitments to what has come to be called the welfare state, the Declaration also includes certain "economic and social rights", notably, the right to social security; the right to work, to free choice of employment and protection against unemployment, to just remuneration and equal pay for equal work, and the right to join a trade union; the right to rest and leisure; to a standard of living adequate for oneself and one's family; the right to education, which at elementary levels must be free and compulsory; the right to participate freely in cultural life and to enjoy protection for one's scientific, literary or artistic productions.

The rights set forth in the Declaration are not subject to "distinctions of any kind, such as race, colour, sex, language, religion, political or other opinion, national or social origin, property, birth or other status" (Art. 2). But rights are not absolute. Art. 29 (2) provides: "In the exercise of his rights and freedoms, everyone shall be subject only to such limitations as are determined by law solely for the purposes of securing due recognition and respect for the rights and freedoms of others and of meeting the just requirements of morality, public order and the general welfare in a democratic society".

The Declaration was adopted by the U.N. General Assembly on December 10, 1948. (A day earlier, the Assembly had adopted the Convention on the Prevention and Punishment of the Crime of Genocide). The Declaration was adopted without dissent, though eight states abstained. In the intervening years the Universal Declaration became truly universal. The principal abstainers, the Communist states of Europe, expressly approved the Declaration in 1975 in the Final Act of the Conference on Security and Cooperation in Europe (the Helsinki accord).

The Universal Declaration has been repeatedly approved by innumerable resolutions supported by virtually all states. Although the Declaration was followed by numerous international covenants and conventions, it remains the principal catalogue of human rights and the principal articulation of the international human rights idea.

The Jurisprudential Character of the Universal Declaration

There can be little doubt that, when drafted and promulgated, the Universal Declaration was not generally seen as a binding agreement. It was adopted by a deliberative not a legislative body. It is called a "declaration", not a convention, covenant, or other designation commonly used for binding international agreements. It does not purport to be an agreement or to bind all or any states. It was not designed or prepared for adherence by individual states. The General Assembly purported to proclaim the Declaration only

> "as a common standard of achievement for all peoples and all nations, to the end that every individual and every organ of society, keeping this Declaration constantly in mind, shall strive by teaching and education to promote respect for these rights and freedoms and by progressive measures, national and international, to secure their universal and effective recognition and observance . . .".

In effect, the international community adopted a standard and asked each member state to take that standard to heart, and to proceed to take any necessary measures to assure that the standard would be honored within its jurisdiction. Implementation of the Declaration was to be the responsibility of each state through its domestic institutions and laws.

From the beginning, however, there were some who claimed greater jurisprudential status for the Declaration. Some saw it as giving content to the pledge by members in the U.N. Charter, "to take joint and separate action" to promote respect for human rights, so that when the Declaration was adopted it became the legal obligation of every U.N. member to honor it. Others saw the adoption of the Declaration, and its subsequent invocation in various forms, as constituting state practice combining with other actions to form customary law of human rights. At the least, it was commonly recognized that, as a solemn declaration adopted by the U.N. General Assembly without dissent, the Universal Declaration had some mandatory character.

Today, few governments (or scholars) would insist that a violation of *any* provision of the Declaration was a violation of international law; most states (and scholars) would agree that failure to respect *some* of the provisions of the Declaration would constitute a violation of international law. The United Nations apparently acted on that legal assumption when it took various measures in respect of violations of human rights by governments that had adhered to no international human rights agreement (other than making the pledge in U.N. Charter), e.g., the numerous resolutions against *apartheid* in the Republic of South Africa, or the modest procedure for considering some private complaints of "consistent patterns of gross violations", pursuant to Resolution 1503 of the Economic and Social Council.

If the jurisprudential character of the Declaration remains controversial, no one would doubt its significance as the principal articulation of the international human rights idea and the authoritative enumeration of universally recognized human rights. As such, its contribution to the enforcement of human rights is unquestionable and unparalleled. The Universal Declaration has been the principal conduit for bringing the idea of human rights into the life of many nations: it is expressly referred to in state constitutions; its provisions are adopted or adapted in others. It is the source of numerous international covenants and conventions. It is commonly and universally invoked as a standard of justice and freedom. It ranks with the U.N. Charter as one of the most celebrated and most respected international instruments of our time.

The International Covenants

After the Universal Declaration was adopted, there were various views as to how best to secure its "universal and effective recognition and observance". Although some continued to insist that a binding international law of human rights was neither desirable nor feasible, the view that prevailed was that the Declaration should be converted into an international human rights covenant that would clearly be of binding character in international law.

It took the nations of the world eighteen years to complete that task. In part, the long delay was a tribute to respect for law: states that were prepared readily to vote for a declaration that was deemed to be only hortatory were reluctant to accept the same terms in a legally binding instrument. Even though states would be free not to adhere to an international human rights covenant, many were reluctant to have the community of states develop an international law of human rights to which they could not adhere, or by whose light their behavior could be adjudged to be deficient. Also, the drafting of a legally binding instrument inevitably took longer: law required greater precision and qualification than did a mere declaration. In international agreements states wished to spell out not only their obligations but the limits of and the limitations on those obligations.

There were other kinds of reasons for the delay. International legislation became more complicated as, due to the proliferation of new states, the number of states participating in the process multiplied nearly three-fold. And the new states, soon acquiring the appellation and character of a "Third World", brought new attitudes (and some new principles) into the international human rights movement. They sought to obtain the attractive mantle of human rights for their struggle to end colonialism and to assert their sovereignty over their natural recources. They sought international support for their struggle for modernization and development. They put their stress on the new rights, the economic and social rights that appear later in the Universal Declaration. For their part, developed North Atlantic states, while they had acquiesced in recognizing economic and social benefits as human rights and including them in the Universal Declaration, were reluctant to undertake international legal obligations to implement such rights. Economic and social rights were essentially aspirations only. Neither these rights nor the obligation to respect them, they argued, can be defined with legal precision, and undertakings to realize them are not enforceable. International attempts to treat them as legal rights would only dilute the standards established in respect of the traditional civil and political freedoms and immunities and attenuate the obligations of states to respect and ensure them.

As a result of these differences, the Universal Declaration was bifurcated into two distinct and different covenants, a Covenant on Civil and Political Rights, and another Covenant on Economic, Social, and Cultural Rights. Over the objection of the more developed states, which questioned the relevance and propriety of such provisions in covenants on human rights, both Covenants begin with the right of peoples to self-determination and to sovereignty over their natural resources. Then the two covenants go different ways.

In the Covenant on Civil and Political Rights states undertake to respect and ensure the rights recognized by the Covenant for all persons subject to their jurisdiction and to enact any laws and adopt any other measures necessary to that end. The rights recognized in the Covenant, following the first twenty-one articles of the Universal Declaration, generally spell out the same rights in greater detail and sometimes with qualifications. Unlike the Declaration, however, the Covenant includes a right not to be imprisoned for debt, and makes special mention of the rights of children and of minorities; it also requires states to prohibit propaganda for war or incitement to racial hatred. On the other hand, the right to enjoy private property and not to be arbitrarily deprived of one's property, found in Art. 17 of the Universal Declaration, is missing from the Covenant. That omission doubtless was not a rejection of the essential right but was the result of sharp disagreement as to the scope and definition of the right, and perhaps a spill-over of the controversy, particularly intense during those years, over the protection of properties of foreign nationals.

The Covenant also spells out permissible limitations on particular rights when necessary for national security, public order (*ordre public*), public health and morals or the rights and freedoms of others. Art. 4 permits derogation from most (not all) rights in time of proclaimed public emergency which threatens the life of the nation, to the extent strictly required by the exigencies of the situation.

Unlike the Declaration, the Covenant, since it created legal obligations, addressed the need to provide measures for their enforcement. International law generally, we know, is enforced "horizontally" by other states, rather than by a superior authority with coercive power. States are induced to comply with their undertakings by the fear of the consequences of violation, notably the expected reaction of the state victim and, in respect of some norms, of other states, of international institutions, of world opinion. Even a multilateral agreement with many parties tends to be a series of bilateral arrangements with each state concerned to assure compliance with the agreement in respect of its own interests. An international human rights agreement, however, tends to become a series of parallel unilateral undertakings. The real victims of a violation are the inhabitants of the violating state, not some other state or its nationals. While in legal principle every state party is a promisee and entitled to request compliance by any other state party, ordinarily no other state has any interest in doing so and is especially reluctant to demand compliance or threaten sanctions for violation at the expense of its friendly relations and diplomatic capital.

It has been necessary, therefore, to develop special "enforcement machinery", that would monitor compliance and bring to bear international influence and world opinion so as to help deter or terminate violations. The International Covenant on Civil and Political Rights established a Human Rights Committee of experts as its principal monitoring body. Within one year of adherence to the Covenant, and thereafter upon request, states parties are required to report to the Committee on measures taken to give effect to the rights recognized in the Covenant. The Committee studies these reports and transmits them with appropriate "general comments" to all states parties, and may transmit these comments also to the Economic and Social Council. In addition, member states may, if they wish, declare that they agree to be subject to complaints to the Committee by other state parties (Art. 41). Under a separate, optional protocol to the Covenant, member states may agree to submit to communications – complaints – to the Committee lodged against them by or on behalf of private persons claiming to be victims of violation.

As of January 1, 1987, 86 states have become parties to the International Covenant on Civil and Political Rights, some with varying reservations. Parties include states from every region and of every ideology, among them members of NATO and of the Soviet Bloc. A remarkable exception is the United States. The United States has a good record of respect for human rights and has an effective constitutional system for enforcing them, but to date the U.S. Government, and particularly the U.S. Senate, has been unwilling to accept international obligations, scrutiny and enforcement in respect of the human rights of its inhabitants. To my deep regret, there seems to be little prospect of change in that attitude, which reflects, I think, strong sentiments of unilateralism and of resistance to external "legislation" and "governance".

Of the 86 states parties to the Covenant 38 – fewer than half – have also adhered to the Optional Protocol, submitting to complaints by alleged victims before the Human Rights Committee. These states are presumably confident of the human rights condition in their countries; they lie in different regions, some states of Western and Northern Europe, smaller Latin American countries, a few African States. Some states of Western Europe – the Federal Republic of Germany, the United Kingdom – are not represented, perhaps because they are parties to the European Convention which has its own enforcement system. No member of the Communist bloc has adhered to the Protocol.

Contrary to original expectations, states have been even more reluctant to inject human rights into their relations with other countries than to submit to international consideration of complaints by their inhabitants. As compared with 38 states parties to the Protocol, only 18 states have made declarations under Article 41 agreeing that the Human Rights Committee may receive complaints against them from other states parties. States that have made such declarations include eleven from Western and Northern Europe, and a scattering of others.

Selected Issues under the Civil and Political Rights Covenant

a) Self-determination and sovereignty over resources

An identical Art. 1, declaring the right of peoples to self-determination and to their natural wealth and resources, was added at the front of each covenant. There was no attempt to integrate that provision into the scheme of either Covenant. The obligation of each state under Art. 2 of the Covenant on Civil and Political Rights to respect and to ensure the rights recognized by the Covenant for persons subject to its jurisdiction does not readily apply to the people's right to self-determination or to its sovereignty over its national resources. Arguably, a state is required to respect and ensure self-determination for a minority people subject to its jurisdiction; a state is perhaps required to respect and ensure the sovereign rights of all its people to their natural resources, for example by refraining from alienating those resources to foreign governments or entities. If, as has been suggested, the right to self-determination includes "internal self-determination", *i.e.,* the right of self-government and of individual participation in self-government, the obligation of the state to respect and ensure such rights would supplement the explicit obligations to that end in Art. 25 of the Covenant.

b) The character of state obligations

The obligation of a state party to respect recognized rights seems unambiguous and has raised few issues. The government and its officials, and all others who act for the state, must not violate any of the enumerated rights, for example by torturing someone or arbitrarily detaining him. But a state party is obligated also "to ensure" the recognized rights. That seems to imply that the rights recognized are not merely rights against government (as are rights under the U.S. Constitution, for example), but also against other persons. The state's obligation to ensure those rights requires it to maintain laws and institutions to assure that one person will not detain or torture another.

Different states may fulfill their obligations under Art. 2 in different ways. Some may incorporate the Covenant into their domestic law; some may assure compliance with the Covenant by other provisions in their own Constitution or laws; some may need to do nothing additional, because they have the necessary laws and institutions already in place. The obligation of a state party is to ensure compliance; the means for doing so are not prescribed, but they must be adequate.

c) Limitations on rights

No rights under the covenant are described as absolute, but only some rights are expressly declared to be subject to limitations. While the terms in which permissible limitations are couched differ somewhat, they essentially include national security, public order, health and morals. These terms are not defined, but the history of the negotiations suggests that national security means security against external enemies. Public order is defined in part by the parenthetical reference to the French term *ordre public,* which suggests that states may limit rights not only to the extent necessary to assure against public disorder, but also to meet other public needs. But the concept of *ordre public* has traditional limits and it is not to be interpreted so broadly as to swallow up individual rights. The limitation must be "necessary" for the ends indicated, and necessity must be shown, not merely alleged.

d) Legal rights for the individual

The Covenant on Civil and Political Rights recognizes the human rights indicated, and states parties to the Covenant undertake to respect and ensure them. The rights recognized are presumably "rights" in some moral order; by recognizing those moral rights and undertaking to respect and ensure them, states are in effect undertaking to convert these moral rights into legal rights in their domestic laws and jurisprudence. Whether the Covenant gives the individual legal rights under international law is debatable and may depend on the ambiguities of the conception of "rights". The more "conservative" view is that the obligations undertaken by a state party run to other state parties; the individual is only a third party beneficiary. Where the state, by adhering to the Protocol, has also agreed to be subject to private complaints, there is a stronger argument that the individual has been given both rights and remedies under international law; at least, the individual can claim an international right to this particular remedy. Some states have provided some remedy under their domestic law for individual victims of a violation of human rights by another state. For the United States, see, e.g., *Filartiga* v. *Pena-Irala,* 630 F.2d 876 (2d. Cir. 1980).

e) Interpreting the Covenant

In general, the Covenants should be interpreted in the light of their spirit and purpose – to maximize the enjoyment of individual rights. The circumstances in which there may be derogation from rights under Art. 4, and the limitations on rights permissible for national security and other public interests, should be strictly construed. And while a state party's obligations are, in the first instance, for the state to determine, they are international obligations to other parties, and the interpretation and application of these obligations are questions of international law and matters of international concern, not of domestic concern only.

The experience under the Covenant is still limited and there has been little authoritative interpretation of the Covenant, though the "jurisprudence" of the Human Rights Committee is growing steadily. The Committee has in effect entered a number of official judgments applying the Covenant, in "views" expressed pursuant to the Protocol, and some interpretations of the Covenant are implied in "general comments" of the Committee. Individual members of the Committee also have frequently indicated views, which are entitled to respect. To a large extent, the terms of the Covenant on Civil and Political Rights parallel those in the European Convention and the American Convention, and interpretation by the commissions and courts under those conventions provide guidance that should be given weight in interpreting the Covenant. Pertinent national jurisprudence in countries committed to human rights is not immaterial.

f) Issues in interpretation

The meaning of various provisions of the Covenant was the subject of debate during the course of its development, and other issues of interpretation have been raised since. Some points are worth brief mention.

1. The Covenant does not outlaw capital punishment, but forbids its imposition on pregnant women and for crimes committed by persons under 18 years of age. States are encouraged to abolish capital punishment; and it has been suggested that under the Covenant states parties that have abolished capital punishment may not reintroduce it.

An effort to define the right to life as "from conception" – presumably to require the state to outlaw abortion – was rejected during the negotiations of the Covenant. (The phrase "from conception" is included in the American Convention).

2. The Covenant forbids detention if it is "arbitrary". While some sought to interpret that term as meaning "unlawful", the prevailing view was that detention can be arbitrary even if it is in accordance with law, when the law supporting detention is itself unjust or if detention is unjust in the circumstances. For violation of a law that does not itself contravene the Covenant, a person may be detained in accordance with due process of law as conceived in humane systems of criminal justice and punishment.

3. Freedom of conscience and religion is protected, including the right to change one's religion.

4. The covenant requires states to prohibit propaganda for war, as well as advocacy of national, religious or racial hatred that constitutes incitement to discrimination, hostility or violence. This was included over objections that such prohibition would violate freedom of press or speech. It has been suggested that the provision would be consistent with enlightened definitions of freedom of expression if it is interpreted as requiring prohibition not of mere advocacy but of incitement to action which the state is permitted (or required) to prohibit under the Covenant.

5. Art. 25 recognizes the right of every citizen to participate in government, to vote and to hold office. It was written so as to make it possible for states with different conceptions of democracy to adhere to it, but the Covenant requirement is satisfied only if elections are genuine and voting is

universal, and are such as to guarantee the free expression of the will of the electors.

6. Freedom from discrimination on invidious grounds in the enjoyment of any of the rights recognized by the Covenant is expressly provided in Art. 3, and equality and non-discrimination are also expressly required in respect of protections for children (Art. 24). In addition, the Covenant requires states to provide the equal protection of the law (Art. 26). That provision forbids invidious discrimination even in respects that are not otherwise denials of rights, e.g., in the grant of some benefit or privilege, or in the application of general laws or police regulations.

The Optional Protocol

A state that adheres to the Optional Protocol to the Covenant recognizes the competence of the Human Rights Committee "to receive and consider communications" from individuals subject to that state's jurisdiction who claim to be victims of a violation by the state of any of the rights set forth in the Covenant. The Committee must consider a communication inadmissible if it is anonymous, or if the Committee considers it to be an abuse of the right of submitting communications, or incompatible with the Covenant. The Committee will not consider a communication if the individual has not exhausted available domestic remedies, or if the matter is being examined under another procedure of international investigation or settlement.

The Committee brings the communication to the attention of the state party alleged to be violating the Covenant, and the state is required to submit within six months "written explanations and statements clarifying the matter and the remedy, if any, that may have been taken by that state". The Committee examines communications in closed meetings, then forwards "its views" to the state party and to the individual.

Since the Committee began work under the Protocol in 1977, it has had more than 200 communications, but a large number were declared inadmissible; the Committee expressed its views in only a fraction of the cases. In those views the Committee has considered such issues as whether the author of the communication qualified as the victim or representative of the victim; whether the alleged victim was "subject to the jurisdiction" of the state party for purposes of the Covenant and the Protocol; whether the Committee was precluded because the complainant had not exhausted domestic remedies. In addressing the substance of claims of violation, the Committee has found violations of the right to life, to be free from torture or arbitrary detention, and from improprieties in the criminal process or in the punishment imposed; the right to leave one's country (violated by refusal to renew the victim's passport), of freedom of expression and religion, the right to family life, and other rights.

The Contribution of the Covenant to Human Rights Enforcement

The contribution of the Covenant on Civil and Political Rights to the enforcement of human rights is difficult to appraise. Half the states of the world have adhered to the Covenant, thereby confirming the legitimacy of international concern with human rights and establishing the international human rights standards. One cannot prove but one is probably warranted in concluding that the Covenant has had some deterrent influence on the behavior of states parties, and perhaps also on states generally.

The enforcement machinery of the Covenant on Civil and Political Rights is, by standards of developed legal systems, primitive. Unilateral reporting tends to be incomplete and self-serving. The Committee's consideration of state reports is a subject of some continuing controversy within the Committee, with Western experts on the Committee tending to be more probing, and representatives of Communist states resisting scrutiny as being beyond the Committee's jurisdiction, intrusive, and invading the sovereignty of states. The Committee cannot issue judgments but only make "general comments" and the degree of specificity of such general comments is also sometimes a subject of controversy.

The optional program under Art. 41 for complaint to the Committee by states parties has not developed. Complaints under that program can be made only by a state that has declared its acceptance of the procedure and only against another declaring state. The states that have filed declarations under Art. 41 tend to have good human rights records. Even if a declaring state has deemed another declaring state to be guilty of significant violations, it has apparently not seen fit to expend its political good will by bringing a complaint on behalf of inhabitants of another country.

On the other hand, in cases under the Protocol, the Committee expresses "views" that are in effect judgments. Clearly, the Committee has helped enforce human rights in these cases, and in some instances the state charged has changed its ways to prevent violation in the future. It is plausible to assume also that the findings and interpretations of the Committee in actions under the Protocol, even more than its "general comments" on state reports, exert a deterrent influence and contribute to the effectiveness of the Covenant.

The Covenant on Economic, Social and Cultural Rights

A discussion of international "enforcement of human rights" strongly suggests that the reference is to civil and political rights. But economic and social rights are also an integral part of the contemporary idea of human rights and of the Universal Declaration, and most states wanted such rights, too, to be recognized and converted into legally binding obligations. The decision to deal with them in a separate covenant, however, reflected the recognition that there were significant differences between these and civil-political rights, which required different dispositions, not least as to means of international enforcement.

In this Covenant, too, states recognize the indicated benefits as human rights, but, perhaps significantly, individual provisions are couched as obligations of the State to recognize the right rather than as a statement of the individual's entitlement. A few of the provisions of the Covenant are undertakings to respect freedoms – the right to choose one's work, to join a trade union – and these can be respected and ensured in the same way as civil and political rights under the other Covenant. Most of the provisions in this Covenant entail commitments by the state to recognize rights to economic and social benefits, generally requiring societal programs to realize them.

In general, the Covenant follows and expands the analogous provisions of the Universal Declaration. To the right to join a trade union, the Covenant adds a right to strike (subject to domestic law) and rights for the trade union to function freely. The various other rights – to food, clothing, health care, education – are also spelled out more fully, and programs are suggested for realizing them.

In the Covenant on Civil and Political Rights states undertake to respect and ensure those rights; in the Covenant on Economic, Social, and Cultural Rights states undertake to "take steps" to achieve the rights recognized in the Covenant "progressively", to the "maximum of available resources". There are no provisions for derogation from these rights; in general, limitations on the rights are expressed in terms different from those used in the other Covenant: "the State may subject such rights only to such limitations as are determined by law only in so far as this may be compatible with the nature of these rights and solely for the purpose of promoting the general welfare in a democratic society" (Art. 4). Although none was originally provided, a special body, comparable to the Human Rights Committee, was established in 1985 to promote or induce compliance with this Covenant. Members are required to report on measures taken and progress achieved to the Economic and Social Council of the United Nations, and copies of the reports may go also to relevant U.N. Specialized Agencies.

As of January 1, 1987, the Covenant on Economic, Social and Cultural Rights has been adhered to by 89 states. Enforcement of the Covenant has not raised significant issues. Some of the rights in the Covenant are also "negative" rights, freedoms, like those in the Covenant on Civil and Political Rights. It should not be difficult to determine whether a state is denying a person the opportunity to "gain his living by work which he freely chooses or accepts" (Art. 6); or to join a trade union of his choice; or "the freedom indispensable for scientific research and creative activity" (Art. 15); or whether the state is abridging the right of a trade union to "function freely" (Art. 8). It should not be difficult to determine that there has been forbidden discrimination on invidious grounds in respect of remuneration for work or the enjoyment of welfare benefits. As regards the bulk of the Covenant, however, enforcement is not the issue, because compliance is not the issue. It is difficult to define the state's obligation to achieve "an adequate standard of living" or particular welfare rights, and difficult to show that the state is not taking the necessary steps to comply with that obligation, or is not doing so "to the maximum of its available resources". It is arguable that a state is violating that obligation if resources are not available for social needs because the state invests in armaments beyond any plausible need of national security, or in large "modernization" programs unrelated to any production that contributes to the standard of living of present generations, but such an argument has hardly been made and is not likely to be heeded.

It is difficult, therefore, to develop means for enforcing these obligations, or even for enhancing the influence of world opinion in respect of such obligations. The Covenant provides for reports to the Economic and Social Council, but these reports seem to serve largely to support requests for aid for developing countries. That ensuring the economic and social rights of a state's inhabitants is an international obligation, that the Covenant provides that the state party shall take steps to meet these obligations "individually and through international assistance and co-operation", may contribute marginally to the success of these efforts.

The difference in the character of rights and in procedures for enforcing them may account also for less attention to the terms of this Convention, and fewer issues of interpretation and application. There has been some disagreement as to the meaning of the right to work. The dominant view is that it protects the freedom to seek and to engage in work of one's own choice; some have insisted that it requires the state also to provide full employment, and that a state that tolerates unemployment violates the Covenant. There may be disagreement as to whether the right of developing states to deny "economic rights" to non-nationals (Art. 2(3)) permits such discrimination in respect of trade union rights, or the freedom of scientific research. It may be argued that under Art. 2(1) a state party to the Covenant has undertaken obligations not only to take steps to realize the human rights of its own citizens, but also to provide "international assistance and cooperation" so that other states parties may realize those rights for their citizens, but few states would accept that interpretation.

Unlike the Covenant on Civil and Political rights, this Covenant, in largest part, serves not as a deterrent but as commitment, and reinforces the Universal Declaration as a statement of that commitment. It tends to confirm the status of economic-social rights as human rights having parity (not priority) in competition with civil-political rights, though the claim that one may have to sacrifice civil-political rights to realize economic-social rights is generally unpersuasive if not patently false. The Covenant provides an additional argument for international cooperation to make it possible for poor states to help realize these human rights for their inhabitants.

U.N. Human Rights Activities

The instruments I have discussed were developed as part of the U.N. program to promote human rights. They were prepared under the aegis of the United Nations and are implemented under its auspices. The Human Rights Committee which monitors the Covenant on Civil and Political Rights reports to the U.N. General Assembly, and receives supporting services from the United Nations Secretariat. States parties to the Covenant on Economic, Social and Cultural Rights report to the U.N. Economic and Social Council. United Nations organs frequently refer to these instruments and urge compliance with them. But the covenants are international agreements like any others and their obligations are upon states parties, not on U.N. members generally. The Human Rights Committee is a treaty organ created by the parties, not a U.N. body controlled by or responsible to U.N. organs. Insofar as the U.N. General Assembly or the Economic and Social Council receive reports on the operation of the Covenants, that is a part voluntarily given to those organs by the states parties to the Covenants and voluntarily accepted by those organs. The Committee to monitor the Covenant on Economic, Social and Cultural Rights is a later creation by the Economic and Social Council not by the parties to the Covernant.

The Covenants and the Declaration are only part of the U.N. rights program. The U.N. has also promoted numerous other human rights conventions on specialized subjects, such as the Convention on the Prevention and Punishment of the Crime of Genocide, the Convention on the Elimination of All Forms of Racial Discrimination, the Convention on the Political Rights of Women. Like the comprehensive covenants, these conventions, and others prepared under the auspices of U.N. Specialized Agencies (the International Labour Organization, UNESCO), create obligations only for states parties, though such agreements have also contributed to the development of some customary law of human rights.

There have also been important efforts by the United Nations to promote respect for human rights universally and without regard to special treaty undertakings. The pledge which U.N. members make in the Charter to promote respect for human rights individually and in cooperation with the U.N. has provided a basis for U.N. actions to induce respect for human rights by U.N. members even if they are not party to the Covenants or other human rights conventions. The Human Rights Commission, a subsidiary of the Economic and Social Council (not to be confused with the Human Rights Committee created by the Covenant on Civil and Political Rights) has assumed some authority deriving from the U.N. Charter to induce respect for human rights. Pursuant to a resolution of the Economic and Social Council, a working group of a Subcommission of the Commission may receive communications alleging "consistent patterns of gross violations" of human rights, and the Human Rights Commission has taken small steps to persuade those governments and others to eliminate violations. The United Nations General Assembly itself has considered some charges of gross violations – notably *apartheid* – and had adopted resolutions condemning violations, calling for their termination, recommending actions against the Republic of South Africa and other violators. Even the Security Council has acted to enforce human rights, as when violations of human rights by the Republic of South Africa were deemed to create a threat to international peace and security.

Efforts to establish a U.N. High Commissioner for Human Rights have not succeeded to date.

Together the Declaration and the two Covenants are the International Bill of Rights. They have established human rights as the political idea of our time, perhaps the only idea which is universally accepted. They have ended the traditional dogma that how a state treats its own inhabitants is its own business and made the condition of human rights everywhere the concern of all. They have launched a new field of international law which includes some binding obligations for all states, whether pursuant to the U.N. Charter or as customary law, and comprehensive additional obligations for the many states that are parties to the covenants. They have promoted additional conventions on specific rights. For states parties to the Covenant on Civil and Political Rights a developing "enforcement machinery" through the Human Rights Committee helps induce compliance, and that Committee joins other bodies under other international instruments – e.g., the Committee on the Elimination of Racial Discrimination, the commissions and courts under the European and American Conventions – in developing human rights jurisprudence and procedures. (The Committee created in 1985 to monitor the Covenant on Economic, Social and Cultural Rights may play a similar role). They provide a legal basis for the efforts of non-governmental organizations and of national and international organs of communication to promote respect for human rights. They inspire all efforts to mobilize world opinion to establish human rights universally and render gross violations of human rights anywhere unacceptable. If ideas matter, if law reflects and also influences how states behave, these international instruments must be contributing significantly to improving the condition of human rights in the world today.

The rights recognized and promoted by the Universal Declaration and the two international covenants are sometimes characterized as the two first generations of rights. Since those instruments were concluded, other rights have been suggested – the right to peace, to development, to a healthy environment. Some have questioned whether these are really individual human rights, which a person can claim against one's own society, and whether a state can meaningfully undertake to respect and ensure them. To date, these have not been incorporated in international instruments like the Declaration or the Covenants. Whether or not they may be in the future, it does not question their importance to insist that they must be seen as supplementary: they ought not supersede or limit the human rights enshrined in the Declaration and the Covenants or reduce the obligations of states under that International Bill of Rights.

In Europe, the human rights idea has served as a focus for greater political integration of like-minded states; in other regions, too, human rights programs may serve some common political goals. The human rights idea that has received universal acceptance is much more modest. It does not see human rights necessarily as, or as part of, an embracing political philosophy. It does not insist that human rights is the only "good" or even the paramount value. It does not insist that the human rights idea is a complete way to the good society, rejecting other paths – community, love, friendship, charity. What the human rights idea insists on is that in modern society respect for human rights is an indispensable minimum for a civilized world. Particularly in large, urban, industrial society, where community and love cannot prevail, human rights is the universal "floor" on which all aspirations for human society, including peace, human development, a healthy environment, prosperity, must be built.

International Protection of Human Rights

Soviet Report

V. A. TUMANOV

1. The Soviet concept regards international law as a major factor for the promotion of the consistent development and actual realization by all States of the institution of human and civil rights and freedoms, all of which are essential for the progressive development of the present era. Ever since the provision which calls for "promoting and encouraging respect for human rights and for fundamental freedoms" was incorporated in the United Nations Charter and since it has become a rule of international law, the protection of human rights has been one of the main functions of international law.

2. In what way does contemporary international law perform this function? This involves, first and foremost, the drafting of general recommendations specifying what rights and fundamental freedoms should be universally observed and exercised without distinction as to race, sex, language, or religion. Having assumed the form of international agreements on human rights (declarations, pacts, conventions, etc.), these recommendations place States under legal obligation to provide and effectively protect an appropriate set of rights. The most comprehensive agreements of this kind are the Covenants on Human Rights approved by the United Nations General Assembly in 1966, namely, the Covenant on Civil and Political Rights and the Covenant on Economic, Social and Cultural Rights.

This raises the problem of implementation, *i.e.,* legislative and other measures taken by States to implement the provisions of international agreements. Even though it is not the immediate topic of our symposium, this problem is in many respects closely interwoven with the problem under consideration, that is, international enforcement of human rights.

3. It should be emphasized at the very outset (as has been done in the General Rapporteur's memorandum) that it is primarily the State that must guarantee respect for fundamental human rights. The actual regulation and protection of human rights and freedoms is an internal affair of each State, being carried out in keeping with the operation of its domestic law. A dif-

ferent approach would contravene the principle of sovereignty, therefore all the important instruments concerning human rights which have been drafted within the framework of the United Nations, including the foregoing covenants, expressly provide that the legislative regulation, implementation and protection of human rights shall be the internal affair of every State. The "invasion" of the sphere of human rights by international law regulations "does not mean that human rights are regulated by international law directly, nor that they have ceased to be a primarily internal affair of the State" (*G. I. Tunkin,* Theory of International Law (Moscow 1970), p. 93).

It follows from the foregoing that it is implementation, interpreted as the State's activity, that serves as the basic and principal means of putting into effect international legal enactments designed to promote and enhance respect for human rights. The more comprehensive and efficient is the State's activity (legislative, administrative, judicial, etc.) aimed at realizing international legal enactments, the less is the need to use any other ways and means of putting them into practice.

4. Comparison of Soviet legislation with main international instruments dealing with human rights reveals that the former, both in its doctrine and practices, attaches great importance to an explicit and consistent implementation of international legal enactments. One convincing proof is the USSR Constitution of 1977, which, in the 37 articles comprising its second section "State and the Individual", outlines a broad range of social, economic, civil and political rights, as well as guarantees ensuring the implementation of most of them. Along with incorporation of international legal enactments in domestic legislation, the Soviet doctrine and practice do not rule out the possibility of applying the norms of international treaties as directly effective law.

5. Another way in which international law performs its function of human rights protection involves the creation of a special international mechanism for verifying the implementation by States of their international obligations concerning human rights. The international Covenants on Human Rights (another example is the International Convention on the Elimination of All Forms of Racial Discrimination) make it incumbent upon the participating States to submit reports on the implementation of recommendations contained in these agreements for consideration by international bodies and committees, including those which were established specifically for this purpose (e.g., the International Human Rights Committee mandated by the Covenant on Civil and Political Rights). Reports considered at the Committee's open sessions contain data on the measures that have been taken by the State concerned to put into effect the rights mentioned in the Covenant, "the progress that has been made in the exercise of these rights", as well as factors hampering the realization of the Covenant's provisions. The Committee has considered reports submitted by Denmark, Finland, Cyprus, Hungary, Czechoslovakia, Syria, the USSR, Sweden, and others. This is one

of the actually operating international mechanisms for verifying the implementation by States of their international obligations concerning human rights. Such verification, however, by no means implies to possibility of any enforcement. This is no more than a review of the results of implementation and its possible promotion.

6. The principal mechanism of human rights protection by international law may be summarized in the following formula: "regulation – ratification – implementation – control". Certainly international law has also some other possibilities, as indicated in Professor *Bernhardt's* general report. These include, for example, activities of international organizations and decisions of international courts.

Moreover, the concept of "the international protection of human rights" is larger than their protection by international law, since the first one includes possibilities outside of the law. For example: In our time the consistent observance by all States of the human rights and fundamental freedoms universally recognized by international law is one of the guiding principles of progressive world public opinion and world legal consciousness. The influence of this non-juridical factor in terms of the protection of human rights is quite considerable.

7. Therefore the General Rapporteur was right to consider the problem in a broader context. However, the expression "enforcement" is less successfully compared with "protection" or "defence", since enforcement might be interpreted as including forceful measures, which are not consonant with the foregoing universally recognized provision, *i.e.,* that the determination of a citizen's legal status is first and foremost the competence of the sovereign State concerned, which is not likely to tolerate "enforcement" directed against it and will, with good reason, qualify it as a violation of the principle of non-interference in the internal affairs of States. When the issue of enforcement is dealt with in this fashion regarding the activities of existing and proposed international bodies (for instance, the proposed post of the United Nations Commissioner for Human Rights), the possibility of interference by third States charging that a particular State is failing to observe its obligations concerning human rights (humanitarian intervention) is all the more unacceptable.

8. A different stand on this issue can only be adopted in the case of massive and gross violations of human rights being committed on such a vast scale as to endanger world peace and security. Here it is possible to see a possibility for enforcement in the forms that are peculiar to international law (e.g., consideration by an international body without the State's consent, adoption of resolutions condemning the State's actions, etc.). Such an action, however, would not imply a recognition or development of the institution of human rights; rather, the application of these enforcement mechanisms will in effect contribute to eradicating the deeds which are qualified by international law as international crimes (aggression, genocide, apartheid, etc.). In

such cases, it would be more logical to speak not of "international enforcement of human rights" but of "international enforcement directed against international crimes".

9. In the Covenants on Human Rights and other international instruments, the norms concerning human rights are formulated in general terms. They are in essence models of given human rights, properly denoted by the term "standard of human rights". Such general formulas are inevitable, because it is only in this way that one can take account of the economic, political, ideological, cultural and other differences that influence the contents and interpretation of the human rights and freedoms of the same name in countries belonging to different social systems or differing from one another by their levels of development.

The Covenants on Human Rights point out that the human rights they envisage "cannot be the object of any restrictions", but this provision, aimed at achieving their most complete implementation, should in no way be taken as a denial of the fact that in different social conditions, identical human rights and freedoms may not necessarily be adequate in every respect. This happens not because in one case the government restricts these rights and freedoms, while in another it does not, but rather because of objective socio-economic, historical and other reasons. Thus, for instance, the interpretation and contents of the right to work, as well as the place and share of the system of socio-economic rights in socialist societies substantially differ from those in capitalist societies. This gives rise to considerable, but not insurmountable difficulties in the course of implementation, evident during evaluations during which States' fulfilment of their commitments is verified. One can easily imagine the difficulties that would arise because of this circumstance should human rights be "enforced".

10. Our epoch has seen enhanced influence of international law on domestic law and legal order. This has been caused not by an expansion of any enforcement arrangements available to international law, but by the latter's growing moral and political authority, which in turn stems from the progressive development of international law on a general democratic basis. The more tangible and comprehensive the contribution of international law to the consolidation of world peace and security, peaceful coexistence of States with different social systems, the right of peoples to life and social progress and termination of the arms race, the higher will be its authority and prestige, and the more effective will be the fulfilment of its main functions, including the one which is aimed at "promoting and encouraging respect for human rights and for fundamental freedoms".

The Enforcement of Human Rights and Peoples' Rights: Observations on their Reciprocal Relations

KARL JOSEF PARTSCH

I.

Louis Henkin raised an important question at the end of his paper for this Colloquium: the relationship between individual human rights and the rights characterized as "human rights of the third generation", namely the rights to peace and solidarity, and to development and environment. One can have grave doubts whether this concept of "generations of rights" is well-founded. One of the main characteristics is that a new generation takes the place of the former, that the aims and scopes of the former generation fade away and are replaced by new wishes and aspirations. Apparently *Louis Henkin* does not share this concept for the reciprocal relationship between these categories of rights; a new generation would never be satisfied with a supplementary role. Even for those who fully agree with his conclusions, however, the danger exists that the partisans of these new rights may interpret them as realizations of the "purposes and principles of the United Nations" and deduce from them limitations of traditional human rights, applying Art. 19 para. 3 of the Universal Declaration.

II.

The very impressive report of *E. R. Mbaya* on the Banjul Charter of the OAU on Human and Peoples' Rights raises the problem of the relationship between these categories of rights. He has clearly indicated which rights are considered to be Peoples' Rights in this instrument. He has treated them as a separate category to be distinguished from civil and political rights and also from social, economic and cultural rights. He lays strongest emphasis on the right to development, conceived in this Charter as one of the Peoples' Rights – not as an individual right – together with the rights to self-determination, to peace and to environment. He has avoided mixing them with human rights – quite different from the Director General of UNESCO who not only expressed the view that human rights and peoples' rights are "equal", without saying whether they are equal in value or in character, but also tried to bring peoples' rights under the concept of human rights, using the term "Peoples' Rights *as* Human Rights". These views were not shared, however, by the members of the organization. They expressly recognized that a dialectical link existed between these two categories of rights [1]. Their relationship had still to be defined and it would be necessary to give some thought to this problem in future.

III.

It is not helpful to distinguish between rights contained in international instruments of a legally binding character and those only claimed in recommendations of UN organs. The main right of peoples, namely the right to self-determination, is guaranteed in common Art. 1 of the two Covenants. The relations between this provision and the rights and freedoms contained in Parts III of the Covenants raise problems similar to those which exist between peoples' rights and human rights in general.

It is sometimes recalled that in early national instruments (*i.e.,* the American Declaration of Independence, the French Declaration of the Rights of Men and Citizens) peoples' rights appear together with human rights. Though this cannot be denied, it does not help to define their characters and to determine the functions these different categories of rights fulfill in a legal order.

The question has been raised whether conflicts between human rights and peoples' rights can occur at all, because both are based on the idea of the sovereignty of the people and have only different addressees, exercising their effects on different levels. Peoples' rights create obligations for States, while human rights are addressed to individuals.

The first argument is highly debatable, at least in the domestic field. Human rights have clearly the function of limiting the free exercise of State sovereignty in the interest of justice, even in States based on the will of the people. Their recognition limits the absolute power of parliament.

---

[1] The Director General's Draft Medium Term Plan (1984–1989) Doc. 4 AC/4 contained in Chapter XIII "Peace, International Understanding, *Peoples' Rights and Human Rights"* in para. 13063 (sentence 2) the request: "Particular prominence will be given *to the principle of the equality* of human rights, and the rights of peoples". The General Conference (Fourth Extraordinary Session Paris 1982) changed the title of Chapter XIII to read: "Peace, International Understanding, *Human Rights and Peoples' Rights"* and replaced sentence 2 by the following text: "It (*i.e.* the subprogramme) will *inter alia* aim at developing the thinking that has already begun on the concept of the rights of peoples, its contents and scope, and on the dialectical links between individual rights and the rights of peoples" (Second Medium Term Plan [1984–1989] Doc. 4 XC/4 *approved*) (emphasis added). – This was the starting point of the discussions on the subject.

The international protection of human rights is largely exercised by imposing obligations on States to respect the rights of their citizens and only exceptionally reaches them directly. It is furthermore unavoidable that the powers conferred by peoples' rights to a community can only be fully exercised by encroaching upon the individual rights of its members. In this way the old problem of the compatibility of the international protection of human rights with the principle of State sovereignty is raised.

There are multifold doctrines to solve this problem. Some of them lead to weaken or even to deny the concept of sovereignty in the interest of the international protection of the individual and also of groups. This idea may even lead to the transformation of the international order into a supranational or transnational order. Others – more traditional or realistic – maintain the doctrine of sovereignty while recognizing only certain limitations. It does not seem necessary to discuss here the different solutions in view of the fact that all of these doctrines recognize a dialectical link, a relation of reciprocal tension between the idea of sovereignty and the international protection of human rights.

It is therefore sufficient to determine the place where the concept of peoples' rights is located in the system of law. Is it an emanation of the doctrine of State sovereignty and closely connected with it? Is it legitimate to regard peoples' rights as belonging to human rights – only the other side of the same coin, as has been said?

The attempt to find an answer to these questions in the African Charter is not made with the intention to criticize this important instrument. It is evident that in this region a strong need exists to emphasize national identity and unity in view of the special conditions under which the members of the OAU attained their independence.

IV.

First, the term "peoples" needs to be clarified. This term may be used either for an ethnic or cultural group or for a community organized within a State and forming its citizens. Thus, the United Nations Charter begins with the words: "We, the poeples of the United Nations" and continues: "our Governments ... have agreed ...". Here, as in other international instruments, "people" means nothing else than a nation, the citizens of established States. In the same document the term "peoples" is also used for those communities which "have not yet attained a full measure of self-government" and are either protected under Chapter XI or XII of the Charter.

These two forms of communities – citizens of established States and inhabitants of non self-governing and trust territories – also enjoy fully the right of self-determination under common Art. 1 of the two Covenants. In order to avoid a conflict with the principles of territorial integrity and political unity of a sovereign State, there is attributed to the territories mentioned above "a status separate and distinct from the State administering them" (Declaration on Friendly Relations of 1970). To other communities, which could also be regarded as "peoples", *inter alia* ethnic minorities within a State, such status is not conceded. They only enjoy the minor rights mentioned in Art. 27 of the Covenant on Civil and Political Rights. An attempt of secession from their home State is punishable under national law.

The African Charter closely follows these concepts. It not only confirms the right to self-determination of the citizens of OAU member States but also of "colonized or oppressed peoples" in Africa (Art. 20 para. 2). The right freely to determine political status and to pursue economic and social development is guaranteed "according to the policy they [the "peoples"] have freely chosen". It could be argued that, thereby, the door is left open to grant the right of self-determination also to other communities. In view of the strong guarantees for the sovereign rights of the member States of the OAU in its Charter, it seems highly improbable that this could happen.

From the text of the guarantees of the rights to development (Art. 22), to peace and security (Art. 23) and to environment (Art. 24) which constitute the other peoples' rights, no argument can be drawn for a different definition of the term "people".

It results from this investigation that *"Peoples" are the citizens of an established State and the inhabitants of non-self-governing and trust territories.* Other communities forming only a minority within a State are not covered.

V.

The right to self-determination – the main form of "Peoples' Rights" – has a human rights aspect and at the same time an aspect of State sovereignty. Its field of application is essentially determined by State sovereignty.

Compared with the very strong and detailed provisions on State sovereignty in the 1963 Charter of the OAU (Art. 3 paras. 1–3) the catalogue of "Peoples' Rights" in the Banjul Charter begins with a rather modest affirmation of the equality of peoples (Art. 19). The word "sovereignty" or "sovereign equality" does not appear; not even the State is mentioned. The provision, according to its wording, could be applied to ethnic communities within a State without their own statehood.

Art. 20 on the right to self-determination – largely following the text of common Art. 1 of the Covenants – does not confirm such an interpretation. It has already been mentioned that there is a significant addition referring to the policy they have freely chosen. The choice of a policy is a matter performed by a State and a free choice is equivalent to the exercise of State sovereignty. Thus, the sovereignty aspect is dominant, even though the word does not appear.

A similar approach can be found in the article concerning economic self-determination (Art. 21). Though the frequently used term "permanent sovereignty over national resources" is not used, the practical consequences of such power are indicated: "In case of spoliation the dispossessed people shall have the right to the lawful recovery of its property as well as to an appropriate compensation" (Art. 21 para. 2). This provision is apparently meant to revise transfers of property which occurred during the colonial regime. Since the country gained independence and an "economic co-operation based on mutual respect" was established, other principles apply (Art. 21 para. 3). Such co-operation apparently justifies legalization of investment treaties with a far reaching protection of foreign investors. An equal exchange shall take place and there shall apply "the principles of international law" instead of the "provisions of appropriate laws", according to Art. 14 of the Charter on the protection of property.

The fundamental change from "spoliation" to "co-operation based on mutual respect" is brought about by the attainment of national independence and sovereignty. Under this aspect the protection of a human right, namely property, varies.

VI.

When in the African Charter rules for the exercise of political and economic self-determination are formulated, the aspect of State sovereignty dominates and prevails over the human rights aspect.

When examining the dialectical link between State sovereignty and human rights it shall be appropriate to consider "Peoples' Rights" as an emanation of State sovereignty and not as an element of the international protection of human rights. The fact that not only States but also the inhabitants of non-self-governing and trust territories are regarded as legitimate beneficiaries of "Peoples' Rights" is a specific political problem which has certainly to be taken into account. This extension is also based upon and justified by the idea of sovereignty.

The European Convention on Human Rights

FRANCIS G. JACOBS

Introduction

This report focuses on the ways in which the European Convention on Human Rights can be "enforced". Part I deals with enforcement by international institutions, the aspect which is of the greatest significance in the context of the European Convention. Part II deals, far more briefly, with enforcement by national means, which has proved less significant in practice.

By way of basic information about the Convention, it is perhaps sufficient to recall that the Convention (done at Rome, 4 November 1950) has been ratified by all twenty-one member States of the Council of Europe[1]. It sets out and "defines" certain rights, in Arts. 2 to 18, and provides machinery for their enforcement as described in Part I of this report.

Four Protocols provide for certain additional rights: the First Protocol (Paris, 20 March 1952), the Fourth Protocol (Strasbourg, 16 September 1963), the Sixth Protocol (Strasbourg, 28 April 1983) and the Seventh Protocol (Strasbourg, 22 November 1984). The Second, Third, Fifth and Eighth Protocols are procedural, and their effect is considered where appropriate below.

The present report does not seek to deal with the rights protected by the Convention and Protocols, although some account is given of the approach adopted by the Court to the interpretation of the Convention.

It deals principally with the Convention machinery, and in particular with recent developments in the practice of the Convention organs, the Commission, Court and Committee of Ministers.

---

[1] Austria, Belgium, Cyprus, Denmark, France, Federal Republic of Germany, Greece, Iceland, Ireland, Italy, Liechtenstein, Luxembourg, Malta, Netherlands, Norway, Portugal, Spain, Sweden, Switzerland, Turkey, United Kingdom.

Part I. Enforcement by international institutions

There are, broadly speaking, two kinds of procedure for supervising the obligations of States under human rights instruments. One is the reporting system whereby States submit reports on the implementation of their obligations: those reports are examined by an international body. The other is a judicial or similar procedure, whereby cases may be referred to an international judicial or quasi-judicial body.

The European Convention provides for both types of procedure. However the reporting system is much more rudimentary in the Convention itself, being set out in a single Article which appears, as if by an afterthought, towards the end of the Convention, in a Section which contains miscellaneous provisions and the final clauses of the Convention. The reporting system has also been little developed in the history of the Convention.

It is proposed to deal first, therefore, with the machinery which the Convention establishes for dealing with cases: and in particular with the European Commission and Court of Human Rights, established by Art. 19 of the Convention "to ensure the observance of the engagements undertaken by the High Contracting Parties in the present Convention".

The *European Commission of Human Rights* consists of a number of members equal to that of the Contracting Parties (Art. 20), elected (normally for a period of six years) [1a] by the Committee of Ministers of the Council of Europe, pursuant to Art. 21 of the Convention, from a list of names drawn up in the Assembly. In practice, when a vacancy occurs in respect of a given State, the group of parliamentarians from that State puts forward three candidates, of whom at least two must be its nationals; and in practice the Government is normally able to influence the nomination of candidates. No qualifications for membership of the Commission are laid down in the Convention, which provides only that members shall sit in their individual capacity (Art. 23). The election of Government officials has generally not been regarded as appropriate [2] and most members of the Commission, although nationals of the State in respect of which they were elected, hold independent judicial or academic legal appointments in their own countries.

An amendment to Art. 21 of the Convention, introduced by the Eighth Protocol, will require, when it enters into force, that candidates "shall be of high moral character and must either possess the qualifications required for appointment to high judicial office or be persons of recognised competence in national or international law". An amendment to Art. 23 will require that

---

[1a] See Art. 22 of the Convention.

[2] The principal exception concerns Sweden. It is perhaps surprising that Sweden, a State which takes particular pride in its stance on human rights, has had on two separate occasions, as members of the Commission, senior Foreign Ministry officials.

members of the Commission, during their term of office, shall not hold any position which is incompatible with their independence and impartiality.

The work of the Commission is part-time; it holds six regular sessions a year in Strasbourg, with occasional special sessions there or elsewhere as necessary; under its Rules of Procedure certain tasks may be performed by delegates or rapporteurs. The Commission, which held its first session in July 1955, deals with about 500 applications a year, compared with about 100 in the first years of the Convention.

In addition, a large number of provisional files, often entailing considerable correspondence, is opened every year by the Commission's secretariat; such files do not always result in an application being registered.

Even so, the figures alone probably under-state the increase in the Commission's work-load, since the recent case-law shows a great increase in the variety and complexity of the cases brought, and since many more cases are now the subject of more substantial argument – reflecting in part a higher proportion of legally represented applicants. In addition, a much higher proportion of cases has been found admissible and required examination on the merits.

As indicated below, changes in the Commission's procedure have been effected to meet the increasing demands of its case-load, and further innovations are under way. In particular, an amendment to Art. 20 of the Convention, introduced by the Eighth Protocol will, when it enters into force, permit the Commission to set up Chambers, each composed of at least seven members. The Chambers will be competent to examine applications submitted under Art. 25 of the Convention which can be dealt with on the basis of the established case-law or which raise no serious questions affecting the interpretation or application of the Convention. The Commission will also be empowered to set up committees, each composed of at least three members, which will be competent, acting unanimously, to declare inadmissible or strike from its list of cases applications submitted under Art. 25, when such a decision can be taken without further examination.

Because of the part-time character of the Commission and its heavy case-load, the Commission's secretariat has an important role. The secretariat is provided by the Secretary General of the Council of Europe and its members are qualified lawyers from the Member States, engaged as full-time officials of the Council, with a supporting administrative and clerical staff. Its main functions are to conduct correspondence with applicants and governments, to organise the Commission's sessions, to prepare cases for examination, to advise the Commission on questions of national law and the law of the Convention, and to assist members of the Commission in the drafting of its decisions and reports. The practice has been for a case to be assigned, as it comes in, to a member of the secretariat, who will prepare the case for the Commission, discuss it with the rapporteur, and attend sessions of the Commission whenever the case is being examined. The quality of the Commission's work, and its effectiveness, necessarily depend in part on the quality of its secretariat.

Examination of admissibility

Examination of the admissibility of applications is one of the principal tasks of the Commission. It is clear from the preparatory work of the Convention that the role of the Commission was envisaged as a screen or filter to sift the expected mass of individual applications, and indeed it is obvious that such an *organe de filtrage* was necessary in a system which was to be open to the world at large, without formality or expense.

It follows that the stage of admissibility is crucial in the working of the Convention. Quite apart from the interpretation of the rules concerning the conditions of admissibility, a simple and flexible procedure must be devised so that the Commission is not submerged by the number of applications, while at the same time it can be ready to take the necessary action on the isolated complaint, not immediately distinguishable from many others, which requires thorough investigation. The following brief account of the procedure on admissibility must be read with these considerations in mind.

Procedure before the Commission in the examination of admissibility is primarily in writing. Art. 25 (1), which refers to petitions addressed to the Secretary General of the Council of Europe, clearly envisages that the application which institutes proceedings before the Commission should be made in writing. Most applications originate in a letter to the Commission's Secretary setting out the complaint, and there are no special requirements as to form.

Applications may be made either by the applicant in person, or by a lawyer acting under a power of attorney. An applicant may be assisted or represented by a barrister, solicitor, professor of law, or any other lawyer approved by the Commission. While the official languages of the Commission are English and French, applicants are regularly allowed to use certain other languages.

An application should state the applicant's name and that of the respondent government, the object of the claim, as far as possible the provision of the Convention alleged to have been violated, and a statement of the facts and arguments on which the applicant relies. In particular, the application should include information showing that it satisfies the conditions laid down in Art. 26 regarding exhaustion of domestic remedies and observance of the six months rule. To facilitate the applicant's task, he is normally sent an application form by the secretariat of the Commission, but he may submit other documents instead or in addition.

Before the Commission's Rules of Procedure were amended in 1973, individual applications were first referred to a group of three members for a preliminary examination of admissibility, and the group's report was then submitted to the Commission.

If the group of three members unanimously reported that the application appeared to be admissible, it was communicated directly to the respondent government for written observations on admissibility. In any other case, the Commission, taking account of the group's report, could either itself communicate the application or declare it inadmissible without communicating it; in fact, a substantial majority of individual applications was never referred to the respondent government.

When an application was referred to the government, its observations were sent to the applicant for his reply. There would then be a further examination by a group of three before the Commission decided on admissibility.

'Group of three' procedure was replaced in 1973 by a more flexible rapporteur system. Under this system, a report on the admissibility of an application is submitted by a single member acting as rapporteur. He may request relevant information on matters connected with the application, from the applicant or the government, and sends any information so obtained from the government to the applicant for comments. In any event the application is examined by the plenary Commission; but after the entry into force of the Eighth Protocol certain cases will be able, as mentioned above, to be delegated to a Chamber or to a committee of three members.

The Commission, if it does not decide at that stage that the application is inadmissible, may either itself request further information from the applicant or the government, or formally ask the government for its written observations on admissibility.

Before deciding upon the admissibility of the application the Commission may invite the parties to submit further observations, either in writing or at an oral hearing. With a view to shortening the proceedings, the Commission's recent practice shows a tendency to avoid an oral hearing at the stage of admissibility, but a case will not be declared admissible without a hearing if the respondent government objects.

Art. 33 of the Convention provides that the Commission should meet in camera. Consequently, no information relating to proceedings before the Commission may be made available to the public or the Press. The secrecy of the proceedings has been criticised but may in some cases protect both the applicant and the respondent government from harmful publicity. Further, secrecy may facilitate a subsequent friendly settlement, since a government's incentive to settle a case might be reduced by publicity. However, the Commission's more important decisions on admissibility, and its reports, are generally published, and press communiqués on cases of public interest are released from time to time. This does not entitle the parties to the proceedings to disclose further information. Publicity by the applicant might in some circumstances be regarded by the Commission as constituting an abuse of the right of petition.

The decision of the Commission on the admissibility of an application is normally final and there is no possibility of appeal. However, if an application is declared admissible, it is open to the Commission, under Art. 29, subsequently to reject the application if it finds, in the course of its examination of the merits, that one of the grounds of inadmissibility has been established. Such a decision can only be taken unanimously; but on the entry into force of the Eighth Protocol will be capable of being taken by a two-thirds majority. Art. 29 gives the Commission the power to examine at any stage of the proceedings on the merits, *ex officio* and irrespective of any pleas by the parties, the question whether or not one of the grounds provided for in Art. 27 has been established.

If the application is referred to the Court, it is possible that the Court may take a different view on the question of admissibility.

If, on the other hand, the application is declared inadmissible by the Commission, the applicant has no means of challenging this decision. He may, however, submit a new application if it contains any relevant new information. If it contains no such new information, but is substantially the same as the previous application, it will be inadmissible on that ground.

There are no fees or charges for applications to the Commission, the expenses of the Commission and the Court being met, under Art. 58 of the Convention, by the Council of Europe. Under the Addendum to the Rules of Procedure, the Commission may grant an applicant free legal aid at any stage of the proceedings after the respondent government's observations on admissibility have been received. The applicant must submit a certified declaration of means, showing that he has not sufficient means to meet his costs. Legal aid may be granted to cover the applicant's lawyer's fees, on a scale fixed by the Commission's Secretary, and also other necessary expenses.

The procedure for inter-State cases is broadly similar to that outlined above. However, under Rule 44, any inter-State case is automatically communicated at once to the respondent government for its observations on admissibility.

The Commission has no power under the Convention to order interim or interlocutory measures to safeguard the position of the parties pending a final decision. However, in urgent cases – for example, where there is a possibility of immediate expulsion which might raise an issue under Art. 3 – the Commission may informally notify the respondent government not to take steps which might prejudice the outcome of the case.

Freedom to correspond with the Commission, even in the case of persons in detention whose correspondence is normally subject to control, is protected by Art. 25 (1) of the Convention and by the European Agreement relating to persons participating in proceedings of the European Commission and Court of Human Rights.

Subsequent proceedings before the Commission

If the Commission finds an application admissible, it ascertains the facts and tries to reach a friendly settlement. Should this attempt fail, the Commission draws up a report containing both a statement of the facts and an opinion as to whether the facts found disclose a breach by the respondent State of its obligations under the Convention. The report is transmitted to the Committee of Ministers of the Council of Europe, whereupon the case may be brought before the Court, within three months, by the Commission and/or by any Contracting State concerned. If this does not occur, the Committee of Ministers decides whether there has been a violation of the Convention.

The *European Court of Human Rights* consists of a number of judges equal to that of member States of the Council of Europe (currently twenty-one). No two judges may be nationals of the same State.

The judges are elected by the Assembly (normally for a period of nine years) from a list of persons nominated by member States of the Council of Europe; they may be re-elected. The judges sit on the Court in their individual capacity and they enjoy full independence in the discharge of their duties. This is nowhere specified in the Convention, as it is in the case of the Commission (Art. 23), since independence is deemed to be inherent in the judicial function.

The Court elects its President and Vice-President. The Court's members receive an allowance for each day of duty and its expenses are borne by the Council of Europe. The Court is assisted by a registry coming under its direct control. The Court itself elects its Registrar and Deputy Registrar after having consulted the Secretary General of the Council of Europe. The other officials in the registry are appointed by the Secretary General with the agreement of the President or the Registrar.

The Convention provides that the Court shall draw up its own rules and shall determine its own procedure[3]. The initial Rules of Court, which were adopted in 1959 and were modified over the years on several points, were completely revised on 24 November 1982. The new text, which makes substantial alterations especially in the position of the applicant before the Court, took effect on 1 January 1983 for cases brought before the Court after that date[4].

---

[3] Art. 55 of the Convention. The Court's autonomy in this respect may be contrasted with the position of the Court of Justice of the European Communities, whose rules of procedure require the unanimous approval of the Council (Art. 188 of the EEC Treaty), a requirement which may help to explain why the latter Court's rules are very broadly drawn and rarely revised: see *W. H. Godwin,* Yearbook of European Law 3 (1983), p. 453–454.

[4] See *P. Mahoney,* Developments in the procedure of the European Court of Human Rights: the revised Rules of Court, Yearbook of European Law 1983, p. 127.

The Court has been bold in adopting rules for which there is no clear basis in the Convention itself. Thus, whilst the Convention provides that cases shall be heard by a Chamber, the Rules of Court, as mentioned below, empower the plenary Court to sit, and that power has been not infrequently exercised. It is, however, plainly desirable (and perhaps not objectionable to governments) that important cases should be heard by the plenary Court, even if, with all judges sitting, the tribunal may become somewhat unwieldy. The Court has also been adventurous, and has encountered some opposition from governments, in progressively extending the role of the individual applicant in proceedings before it, as described below.

The jurisdiction of the Court in contentious matters extends to all cases concerning the interpretation and application of the Convention. It can, however, be exercised only with regard to States which have either declared that they recognise it as compulsory *ipso facto* or given their consent to a particular case being referred to the Court. To date, nineteen States have accepted the Court's compulsory jurisdiction, namely, all member States of the Council of Europe except Malta and Turkey.

For the consideration of each case brought before it, the Court sits in a chamber of seven judges including, as *ex officio* members, the President or the Vice-President and the judge who is a national of any State Party concerned. If the "national" judge is unable to sit or withdraws, or if there is none, the State in question is entitled to appoint a member of the Court (an elected judge of a different nationality) or a person from outside the Court (an *ad hoc* judge). The names of the other judges are chosen by lot by the President before the opening of the case. When the Eighth Protocol enters into force, a chamber will consist of nine judges.

The Chamber thus constituted may, or must, under certain conditions, relinquish jurisdiction in favour of the plenary Court, and this course has frequently been followed: in some cases, even after the oral hearing [5].

The first stage of the procedure is generally written, although exceptions to this rule are not uncommon: memorials and other documents are filed with the Court's registry in the order and time-limits laid down by the President. The Commission's report, which is transmitted to the Court, will generally provide a very full basis for the Court's proceedings, setting out the Commission's findings of fact, a full summary of the submissions of the applicant and of the respondent government, and the Commission's own reasoning and conclusions on the legal issues raised, as well as the opinion on whether the Convention has in any respects been breached. The Court itself normally invites the applicant and the government to submit written me-

---

[5] See e.g. The *Sunday Times* case, Judgment of 26 April 1979, para. 7: however, the Court obtained the agreement of the Government and of the Delegates of the Commission that no further oral hearings were necessary. Presumably, in a case to which the present Rules applied, the Court would consult the applicant as well.

morials at the same time: the need for a full exchange of written pleadings is obviated by the Commission's report. Once the case is ready for hearing, the President fixes the date of the opening of the oral proceedings which, in principle, are public.

The State or States concerned are parties to the case. The Commission also takes part and appoints one or more of its members as Delegates for this purpose, but it does not appear as a party. After a case has been brought before the Court, the Commission's main function becomes to assist the Court; as "defender of the public interest", it is associated with the proceedings in order to enlighten the Court.

The Convention does not empower individual applicants to refer a case to the Court or to appear before it as parties. To permit an applicant to refer his case to the Court would require an amendment to the Convention and would be contrary to the intentions of the authors of the Convention who devised the system so as to restrict access to the Court to the Commission and to the States. However the applicant's position has been substantially improved in recent years by the greater willingness of the Commission, as described below, to refer cases to the Court.

The Convention also precludes the applicant, once his case is referred, from appearing before the Court as a party. However the applicant's position in this respect has been developed by the Court's own Rules and practice. One of the former Rules of Court permitted the Delegates of the Commission to have the assistance of any person of their choice. This provision was interpreted by the Court as permitting the Commission to be assisted by the applicant's own lawyer [6], or by the applicant himself. The Commission's Delegates subsequently availed themselves of this option on several occasions.

A similar provision still appears in the 1983 Rules of Court but they have at the same time introduced an important innovation: once a case has been referred to the Court by a Government or the Commission, the applicant may express the wish to take part in the proceedings. If he does so, he has broadly the same position before the Court as the State. He has in principle to be represented by a lawyer and, where the applicant has been granted legal aid in connection with the representation of his case before the Commission, the grant continues in force before the Court. Otherwise the President of the Court may, under certain conditions, at any time grant legal aid at the applicant's request.

The President may, in the interest of the proper administration of justice, invite or grant leave to a Contracting State which is not a party to the proceedings to submit written comments within a time-limit and on issues which he shall specify. He may also extend such an invitation or grant such

[6] *Vagrancy* case, Judgment of 18 November 1970.

leave to a person concerned other than the applicant. To date, the President has permitted recourse to this procedure in two instances, but has refused two other requests for leave.

The Court decides all disputes regarding its jurisdiction. By majority vote, it gives final judgments which are binding on the States concerned and whose execution is supervised by the Committee of Ministers.

Where judgment does not represent in whole or in part the unanimous opinion of the judges who heard the case, each judge is entitled to deliver a separate opinion, concurring or dissenting.

If the Court has found a violation, it is empowered under Art. 50 of the Convention to afford "just satisfaction" to the injured party.

There have been rulings on this issue in thirty-nine cases. "Just satisfaction" of a pecuniary nature was granted in thirty-four of those cases: the amounts awarded (ranging from 100 Dutch guilders for Mr. Engel to some 1 150 000 Swedish crowns for the Sporrong Estate), represented, depending on the case, compensation for loss (pecuniary or non-pecuniary) and reimbursement of costs and expenses (notably lawyers' fees). However, in several cases the Court has held that the finding of a violation of the rights of the applicant amounted in itself to adequate "just satisfaction" in respect of the whole or part of the claims put forward: while frequently reimbursing costs, the Court has frequently rejected other claims for compensation.

Perhaps the most significant development in the Convention system in recent years has been the increasing readiness of the Commission to refer cases to the Court, as reflected in the following figures, and the consequent development in the case-law of the Court.

Taking into account several judgments concerning questions of jurisdiction or procedure, the Court has up till now delivered 121 judgments, the total being made up as follows: one in 1960, two in 1961, one in 1962, one in 1967, three in 1968, two in 1969, two in 1970, two in 1971, two in 1972, one in 1973, one in 1974, two in 1975, six in 1976, five in 1978, five in 1979, seven in 1980, seven in 1981, eleven in 1982, fifteen in 1983, eighteen in 1984, eleven in 1985 and sixteen in 1986.

The increasing readiness of the Commission to refer cases to the Court has had a number of important consequences.

In the first place, it has led to a greater measure of judicial formalism. In place of the somewhat more practical, less formal, and perhaps in some cases more political approach of the Commission and the Committee of Ministers, the developing role of the Court has led to a more strictly normative approach. The Convention has become more of a legal instrument: a development for which the States Parties may not have been ready in the earlier years, but which is perhaps more appropriate today. The decreasing role of the Committee of Ministers is also a welcome development, given that it is obviously not well equipped to take a final decision on the issue of breach of the Convention[7].

A further development of great importance has been the emergence of a substantial body of case-law, which is largely coherent, carefully argued, and increasingly demonstrates a dynamic, "teleological" approach to the interpretation of the Convention. This approach can best be illustrated by a selective survey of some leading judgments of the past ten years.

Recent trends in the case-law of the Court

Perhaps the guiding theme in the Court's recent approach to the Convention is that, for the Court, "the Convention is a living instrument" which "must be interpreted in the light of present-day conditions"[8]. Thus, for example, in the *Tyrer* case, the Court "cannot but be influenced by the developments and commonly accepted standards in the penal policy of the member States of the Council of Europe in this field"[9].

A notable illustration of the Court's approach to interpretation is provided by the *Golder* case[10], which raised the issue of the scope of Art. 6 (1) of the Convention, and in particular whether Art. 6 (1) guaranteed a right of access to the courts. Golder, a convicted prisoner serving his sentence in England, was identified by a prison officer's statement as having taken part in a serious disturbance in the prison and as having assaulted the officer. Golder, in an attempt to clear his name, sought but was refused permission to consult a solicitor with a view to taking civil proceedings for libel against the prison officer.

The United Kingdom Government submitted that Art. 6 (1) does not confer a right of access to the courts, but confers only a right, in any proceedings that might be instituted, to a hearing that is fair and in accordance with the other requirements of the paragraph: a submission that finds some support particularly in the English text. The Commission, however, having set out at length in its report the principles of interpretation which it considered applicable to the Convention, was unanimously of the opinion that Art. 6 (1) guarantees a right of access to the courts, and that there are no inherent limitations on the right of a convicted prisoner to institute proceedings and for this purpose to have unrestricted access to a lawyer.

The issue was therefore squarely before the Court. The Court was prepared to consider, as did the Government and the Commission, that it should be guided by the principles of interpretation set out in Art. 31 to 33

---

[7] See below, p. 48.

[8] *Tyrer* case, Judgment of 25 April 1978, para. 31.

[9] *Tyrer* case, *loc. cit.*

[10] Judgment of 21 February 1975. The issue was previously before the Commission in the *Knechtl* case, which was terminated by a friendly settlement: see *F. G. Jacobs,* The European Convention on Human Rights (1975), p. 90.

of the Vienna Convention on the Law of Treaties. It states that

"That Convention has not yet entered into force and it specifies, at Article 4, that it will not be retroactive, but its Articles 31 to 33 enunciate in essence generally accepted principles of international law to which the Court has already referred on occasion. In this respect, for the interpretation of the European Convention account is to be taken of those Articles subject, where appropriate, to 'any relevant rules of the organisation' – the Council of Europe – within which it has been adopted (Article 5 of the Vienna Convention).
In the way in which it is presented in the 'general rule' in Article 31 of the Vienna Convention, the process of interpretation of a treaty is a unity, a single combined operation: this rule, closely integrated, places on the same footing the various elements enumerated in the four paragraphs of the Article" [11].

Applying those principles, the Court reached the conclusion that Art. 6 (1) did guarantee the right of access to the courts. It had regard, among other things, to the following elements: the terms of Art. 6 (1) – the French text being clearer on this point than the English text; the relationship between Art. 6 (1) and other provisions of the Convention; the preamble to the Convention, and in particular its reference to the "rule of law"; the "general principles of law recognised by civilised nations" [12]; and the consequences of the alternative interpretations; here the Court stated

"Were Article 6 (1) to be understood as concerning exclusively the conduct of an action which had already been initiated before a court, a Contracting State could, without acting in breach of that text, do away with its courts, or take away their jurisdiction to determine certain classes of civil actions and entrust it to organs dependent on the Government. Such assumptions, indissociable from a danger of arbitrary power, would have serious consequences which are repugnant to the aforementioned principles and which the Court cannot overlook . . .
It would be inconceivable, in the opinion of the Court, that Article 6 (1) should describe in detail the procedural guarantees afforded to parties in a pending lawsuit and should not first protect that which alone makes it in fact possible to benefit from such guarantees, that is, access to a court. The fair, public and expeditious characteristics of judicial proceedings are of no value at all if there are no judicial proceedings.
Taking all the preceding considerations together, it follows that the right of access constitutes an element which is inherent in the right stated by

---

[11] Paras. 29–30.

[12] Art. 38 (1) (c) of the Statute of the International Court of Justice; such general principles were included in "any relevant rules of international law applicable in the relations between the parties" (Art. 31 (3) (c) of the Vienna Convention).

Article 6 (1). This is not an extensive interpretation forcing new obligations on the Contracting States: it is based on the very terms of the first sentence of Article 6 (1) read in its context and having regard to the object and purpose of the Convention, a lawmaking treaty, and to general principles of law.

The Court thus reaches the conclusion, without needing to resort to 'supplementary means of interpretation' as envisaged at Article 32 of the Vienna Convention, that Article 6 (1) secures to everyone the right to have any claim relating to his civil rights and obligations brought before a court or tribunal. In this way the Article embodies the 'right to a court', of which the right of access, that is the right to institute proceedings before courts in civil matters, constitutes one aspect only. To this are added the guarantees laid down by Article 6 (1) as regards both the organisation and composition of the court, and the conduct of the proceedings. In sum, the whole makes up the right to a fair hearing."

The Court went on, however, to accept that the right of access to the courts is not absolute: there is room for "implied limitations", although it found none applicable in the present case.

The *Airey* case[13] also demonstrates the practical approach of the Court in relation to the same issue of access to the courts. At the time of the case, legal aid was not available in Ireland for the purpose of seeking a judicial separation, nor indeed for any civil matters. Could this amount to a denial of access to a court? The Court held that in practice it could.

Mrs. Airey was unable to obtain a decree of judicial separation; in Ireland such a decree was obtainable only in the High Court and she was unable to obtain legal representation, in the absence of legal aid and not being in a financial position to meet the costs herself. The Court rejected the Government's contention that she did have access to the court because she could act in person.

In reaching the conclusion the Court recalled the principle that "the Convention is intended to guarantee not rights that are theoretical or illusory but rights that are practical and effective[14]". It had regard to the complexity of the procedure in question, the difficulties of proof, and the fact that "marital disputes often entail an emotional involvement that is scarcely compatible with the degree of objectivity required by advocacy in court"[15]. Hence it was most improbable that a person in Mrs. Airey's position could effectively present her own case. This was confirmed by the fact that in every one of the judicial separation proceedings initiated in Ireland in the seven preceding years, the petitioner had without exception been represented by a

[13] Judgment of 9 October 1979.
[14] Para. 24.
[15] *Ibid.*

lawyer[16]. Accordingly Mrs. Airey did not have an effective right of access to the court.

The judgment in the *Airey* case is also of particular interest on the relationship between different provisions of the Convention: a restrictive interpretation of one provision cannot be derived from an express provision elsewhere. The Convention expressly provides for free legal aid in Art. 6 (3) (c) which relates to criminal proceedings and is itself subject to limitations. But the Court rejected the Government's contention that, in consequence, no right to legal aid could be derived from Art. 6 (1). On the other hand the Court accepted that there was no obligation on the State to provide free legal aid for every dispute relating to a 'civil right'[17].

The Court's evolutionary approach to the interpretation is strikingly illustrated by a number of recent cases on Art. 8, such as *Dudgeon*[18] and *Marckx*[19] dealing respectively with privacy and family life.

In the *Marckx* case the applicants, Paula Marckx (an unmarried woman) and her infant daughter Alexandra, complained that certain aspects of Belgian legislation infringed Art. 8 of the Convention: in particular, an unmarried mother and her 'illegitimate' child suffered certain disadvantages in relation to the manner of establishing affiliation, the extent of the child's family relationships, and the property rights of the child and of her mother.

The earlier case-law had suggested that Art. 8 merely required the State to abstain from such interferences with the rights protected by Art. 8 (1) as were not justified under Art. 8 (2).

The evolution in the Court's approach can be seen in the following passage:

> "By proclaiming in paragraph 1 the right to respect for family life, Article 8 signifies firstly that the State cannot interfere with the exercise of that right otherwise than in accordance with the strict conditions set out in paragraph 2. As the Court stated in the 'Belgian Linguistic' case, the object of the Article is 'essentially' that of protecting the individual against arbitrary interference by the public authorities . . . Nevertheless, it does not merely compel the State to abstain from such interference: in addition to this primarily negative undertaking, there may be positive obligations inherent in an effective 'respect' for family life.
>
> This means, amongst other things, that when the State determines in its domestic legal system the regime applicable to certain family ties such as those between an unmarried mother and her child, it must act in a manner calculated to allow those concerned to lead a normal family life. As

[16] *Ibid.*
[17] Para. 626.
[18] Judgment of 22 October 1981.
[19] Judgment of 13 June 1979.

envisaged by Article 8, respect for family life implies in particular, in the Court's view, the existence in domestic law of legal safeguards that render possible as from the moment of birth the child's integration in his family. In this connection, the State has a choice of various means, but a law that fails to satisfy this requirement violates paragraph 1 of Article 8 without there being any call to examine it under paragraph 2"[20].

Thus, Art. 8, as well as imposing a purely negative obligation not to interfere, is read as also imposing positive obligations.

It is also significant that, where the positive obligation imposed by Art. 8 (1) is not respected, the Court finds it unnecessary to consider whether any justification is available under Art. 8 (2)[21].

Several other features of the Court's approach in the *Marckx* case are worthy of mention.

First, the Court accepted (following the Commission's case-law in this respect) that Art. 8, in guaranteeing the right to respect for family life, makes no distinction between the 'legitimate' and the 'illegitimate' family[22]. In addition to other arguments, the Court was ready to rely upon a resolution of the Committee of Ministers of the Council of Europe (adopted outside the field of the Convention), which regarded the single woman and her child as one form of family no less than others[23].

Secondly, the Court expressly recognized that the Convention must be given an interpretation different from that which might have been appropriate when the Convention was drafted.

"It is true that, at the time when the Convention of 4 November 1950 was drafted, it was regarded as permissible and normal in many European countries to draw a distinction in this area between the 'illegitimate' and the 'legitimate' family. However, the Court recalls that this Convention must be interpreted in the light of present-day conditions . . . In the instant case, the Court cannot but be struck by the fact that the domestic law of the great majority of the member States of the Council of Europe has evolved and is continuing to evolve, in company with the relevant international instruments, towards full juridical recognition of the maxim 'mater semper certa est'"[24].

---

[20] Para. 31.

[21] See *P. J. Duffy,* The protection of privacy, family life and other rights under Article 8 of the European Convention on Human Rights, Yearbook of European Law 2 (1982), p. 191 at 200.

[22] Para. 31.

[23] Resolution (70) 15 of 15 May 1970 on the social protection of unmarried mothers and their children; Judgment, para. 31.

[24] Para. 41.

Thirdly, and as a consequence of its recognition of the evolutionary character of the Convention, the Court proceeded to rule that the principle of legal certainty listed the temporal effect of its Judgment and dispensed the Belgian authorities from applying the Judgment to events ante-dating the Judgment. 'On this question', the Court held:

> "reliance has to be placed on two general principles of law which were recently recalled by the Court of Justice of the European Communities: 'the practical consequences of any judicial decision must be carefully taken into account', but 'it would be impossible to go so far as to diminish the objectivity of the law and compromise its future application on the ground of the possible repercussions which might result, as regards the past, from such a judicial decision' (8 April 1976, Defrenne v. Sabena, Reports 1976, p. 480). The European Court of Human Rights interprets the Convention in the light of present-day conditions but it is not unaware that differences of treatment between 'illegitimate' and 'legitimate' children, for example in the matter of patrimonial rights, were for many years regarded as permissible and normal in a large number of Contracting States (see, *mutatis mutandis,* paragraph 41 above). Evolution towards equality has been slow and reliance on the Convention to accelerate this evolution was apparently contemplated at a rather late stage. As recently as 22 December 1967, the Commission rejected under Article 27 § 2 – and rejected *de plano* (Rule 45 § 3 (a) of its then Rules of Procedure) – another application (no. 2775/67) which challenged Articles 757 and 908 of the Belgian Civil Code; the Commission does not seem to have been confronted with the issue again until 1974 (application no. 6833/74 of Paula and Alexandra Marckx). Having regard to all these circumstances, the principle of legal certainty, which is necessarily inherent in the law of the Convention as in Community law, dispenses the Belgian State from re-opening legal acts or situations that antedate the delivery of the present judgment. Moreover, a similar solution is found in certain Contracting States having a constitutional court: their public law limits the retroactive effect of those decisions of that court that annul legislation"[25].

But the ruling of the Court of Justice of the European Communities in the *Defrenne* case was itself extremely controversial on precisely this point[26]. The recognition of such a limit on the effect of the Judgment is similarly open to criticism, and such a criticism was made by Judge Pinheiro Farinha, dissenting on this point[27]. He considered that it was not for the Court to

---

[25] Para. 58.

[26] See e.g. *M. Waelbroeck,* May the Court of Justice limit the retrospective operation of its Judgments?, Yearbook of European Law 1 (1981), p. 115.

[27] Partly Dissenting Opinion of Judge Pinheiro Farinha, para. 4.

state whether the law it has declared applies to cases other than the case decided. It was primarily for the Belgian national courts to decide questions raised by domestic legislation on part, present and future facts. It is they who, as appropriate, must apply the rules of *res judicata,* limitation and so forth in order to ensure the stability of existing situations.

It will be apparent that citation of the cases of *Golder, Airey* and *Marckx* as illustrations, which could be multiplied, of the Court's approach over the past ten years does not imply unreserved approval of the recent case-law. The significant point is precisely that while both the Commission and the Court displayed understandable caution in their early years, the Convention has now reached fruition and the recent case-law is perhaps as likely to be criticised for being too "progressive" as for being too cautious.

Having gained, and hitherto retained, a degree of confidence on the part of States, essential in a system based on voluntary acceptance of their jurisdiction, the Commission and Court have apparently felt free to adopt a more expansive approach.

The Committee of Ministers

Certain important functions are assigned under the Convention, not to the independent bodies established by the Convention (the European Commission and Court of Human Rights) but to the principal political organ of the Council of Europe, the Committee of Ministers.

As well as supervising the execution of judgments of the Court, a task considered above, the Committee of Ministers has the function, under Art. 32 of the Convention, of deciding the question of violation in cases not referred to the Court. Since States have been reluctant to refer cases to the Court, the individual applicant cannot do so, and the Commission was for many years unwilling to do so, most cases, until recently, went for final decision to the Committee of Ministers.

The Committee of Ministers, the governmental organ under the Statute of the Council of Europe, consists of the Ministers for Foreign Affairs of the Member States. In practice the Foreign Ministers meet twice a year; at other sessions they are represented by Deputies meeting regularly (and often resident) in Strasbourg. The Committee, which normally sits in private, assisted by the Secretary General, is the executive body of the Council of Europe. In addition to its functions under the Convention, it also has powers in relation to human rights under the Statute of the Council of Europe.

The principal functions of the Committee of Ministers under the Convention are, first, to decide the question of violation in cases not referred to the Court; secondly, to supervise the execution of its own decisions and of the judgments of the Court.

Art. 32 (1) of the Convention provides that:

"If the question is not referred to the Court in accordance with Article 48 of this Convention within a period of three months from the date of the transmission of the Report to the Committee of Ministers, the Committee of Ministers shall decide by a majority of two-thirds of the members entitled to sit on the Committee whether there has been a violation of the Convention."

In deciding whether there has been a violation, the Committee of Ministers acts in a judicial capacity. The Rules adopted by the Committee of Ministers for the application of Art. 32 of the Convention[28] make provision for further proceedings. Further, Art. 1 (3) of the European Agreement relating to persons participating in proceedings of the European Commission and Court of Human Rights[29] extends the provisions of the Agreement to proceedings before the Committee of Ministers under Art. 32. But the Rules adopted by the Committee of Ministers are hardly adequate and the Committee is not equipped to carry out the tasks envisaged by the Convention[30].

In practice, it has normally followed the majority opinion in the Commission and there are no separate proceedings in the Committee to investigate the merits of the case. An unfortunate precedent was set by the *Fourons* case, concerning the linguistic regulations applicable to teaching in the area of Les Fourons in Belgium. The Commission was unanimously of the opinion, in a report transmitted to the Committee of Ministers in 1971, that the Belgian legislation infringed Art. 2 of the First Protocol in conjunction with Art. 14 of the Convention. The Committee of Ministers' Resolution merely 'takes note' of the Commission's opinion; takes note of new provisions introduced in Belgium after the adoption of the Commission's report; and 'decides in consequence that no further action is called for in this case'[31]. The Resolution thus conflicts with the express duty of the Committee of Ministers under Art. 32 (1) to decide whether there has been a violation of the Convention. The correct course would have been to decide that there had been a violation but that the situation had been remedied by the measures subsequently introduced.

Similarly in the case of *Eggs* v. *Switzerland,* where the Swiss Government had amended the law in order to bring it into line with the Convention, the Committee of Ministers confined itself to referring to the opinion of the Commission, without itself taking a decision[32]. It would be preferable in such a case for the Committee to adhere strictly to Art. 32 of the Convention

---

[28] Collected Texts (1979), p. 501.

[29] Collected Texts (1979), p. 201.

[30] The Appendix to the Rules (p. 503) itself states that the Committee "is not well equipped to take evidence, etc. and ought not normally to undertake such tasks".

[31] Resolution DH (74) 1 of 30 April 1974.

[32] Resolution DH (79) 7 of 19 October 1979.

and to decide that there had been a violation of the Convention but that, since the legislation in issue had been amended, no further measures were necessary[33]. This was the procedure adopted in the second *Vagrancy* case[34], in the *Kiss* case[35] and in the *Hilton* case[36].

Still less satisfactory is the situation where the requisite two-thirds majority cannot be attained, so that the Committee of Ministers is precluded from expressing a view on whether any further measures are necessary. This was the position in the *Huber* case[37], where the Committee of Ministers, having recorded that the two-thirds majority had not been attained, decided that no further action was called for, in the *East African Asians* case[38], and most recently in *Dores and Silveira* v. *Portugal*[39], in which the Commission had been unanimously of the opinion that there had been a breach of Art. 6 (1) of the Convention.

If the Committee of Ministers finds a violation, it prescribes a period during which the State concerned must take the measures prescribed by its decision (Art. 32 (2)); if the State fails to comply, the Committee decides what effect should be given to its original decision and publishes the Commission's report (Art. 32 (3)). There is no provision for publication of the report in other cases referred to the Committee of Ministers or to the Court, but the general practice has been to publish the reports. The Parties to the Convention undertake to regard as binding decisions taken under Art. 32.

The reporting system

As mentioned above, the Convention's reporting system is rudimentary. This is true not only of the Convention provisions, but also to some extent of their manner of implementation.

Art. 57 of the Convention, the sole relevant provision, is very brief. It states:

> "On receipt of a request from the Secretary-General of the Council of Europe any High Contracting Party shall furnish an explanation of the manner in which its internal law ensures the effective implementation of any of the provisions of this Convention".

---

[33] A view supported by *P. van Dijk/G. J. H. van Hoof*, Theory and Practice of the European Convention on Human Rights (1984), p. 169.

[34] Resolution DH (72) 1 of 16 October 1972.

[35] Resolution DH (78) 3 of 19 April 1978.

[36] Resolution DH (79) 3 of 24 April 1979.

[37] Resolution DH (75) 2 of 15 April 1975; see *H. Golsong*, EuGrZ 1975, p. 448; *A. Morgan*, Human Rights Review 1976, p. 157.

[38] Resolution DH (77) 2 of 21 October 1977; see *A. Drzemczewski*, Modern Law Review 1978, p. 337.

[39] Resolution DH (85) 7 of 11 April 1985.

Many questions of fundamental scope are left unanswered by the Article: to mention but three, how frequently may the Secretary General request information; may he address requests only to all States, or to one or more alone[40]; and may he act exclusively on his own initiative or only after some degree of consultation with the Committee of Ministers[41]? On the last question, the then Secretary General went firmly on record in 1964 stating that

> "The Secretary General in making a request under Article 57 is acting on his own responsibility and at his own discretion, in virtue of powers conferred upon him by the Convention independently of any powers he may have in virtue of the Statute of the Council of Europe. His power under Article 57 is not subject to control or instruction[42]."

However the exclusivity of the Secretary General's powers under Art. 57 has recently, it is understood, been debated in the Committee of Ministers. The question is of some constitutional importance but the answer, it is suggested, cannot reasonably be in doubt. It seems clear both from the terms and from the structure of the Convention that the Committee of Ministers has no formal role in the Art. 57 inquiry and that the Secretary General does indeed have an independent role. Confirmation of that view can be found in the *travaux préparatoires* since the United Kingdom's proposal for what became Art. 57, itself based on the draft U.N. Covenant, would have provided that the Secretary General could act only on the authority of a resolution of the Consultative Assembly of the Council of Europe, a qualification which was excised by the Committee of Experts[43].

Art. 57 has been used infrequently, and the manner of its use is open to criticism. It was not used at all for over ten years, the first request being made in 1964. That request was extraordinarily broad, all States being asked to explain the way in which their internal law ensured the effective implementation of the Convention. The States' replies varied predictably both in their scope and in their value. There appears to have been no follow-up to the inquiry.

In 1970 the inquiry went to the opposite extreme and was of very narrow scope, being limited to Art. 5 (5) of the Convention; while in 1975 information was requested on the implementation of Arts. 8, 9, 10 and 11. On the

---

[40] But although the French text may be ambiguous on this point («Toute Haute Partie Contractante . . .»), the English text ("any High Contracting Party") seems more clear. Similarly the question raised by *K. Vasak,* La Convention européenne des Droits de l'Homme (1964), p. 223, whether requests must extend to *all* the provisions of the Convention does not arise on the English text.

[41] See *W. Pahr,* Etude fonctionnelle des organes européens de protection internationale des droits de l'homme, Revue des Droits de l'Homme 1969, p. 199.

[42] Statement by the Secretary General of 29 August 1964, Collected Texts (1979), p. 913.

[43] *Vasak, op. cit.* (note 40) n. 11, p. 222.

most recent occasion, some two years ago, a more elaborate questionnaire was devised which it seems provoked some resistance from Governments and led them to query the exclusivity of the Secretary General's powers as mentioned above.

A variety of factors probably explains the unsatisfactory experience with Art. 57. First there is the inadequacy of the Convention itself in failing to regulate the purposes and procedures of the reporting system. As has been seen, the Convention leaves many crucial questions entirely unanswered. Moreover, the defects in the Convention could not easily be remedied by the Secretary General having regard to his relatively weak position in relation to the Member States, both politically and legally: in the latter respect, it is significant that he is not an organ either of the Council of Europe[44] or of the Convention itself[45]. Nonetheless the services of the Council of Europe are also open to criticism for the weak and unimaginative use made of the system.

The failure to develop the reporting system is also attributable to the success and effectiveness of judicial control and the acceptance of the optional control machinery by the great majority of Contracting States. These developments have undoubtedly lessened the need for a more systematic use of the reporting system.

Finally, account must be taken of the proliferation of reporting systems in other international human rights instruments to which many States Parties to the Convention are also subject: see for example Arts. 22 and 23 of the Constitution of the International Labour Organisation, Art. 9 of the Convention on the Elimination of All Forms of Racial Discrimination, Arts. 40 *et seq.* of the International Covenant on Civil and Political Rights, Arts. 16 *et seq.* of the International Covenant on Economic, Social and Cultural Rights and Art. 21 of the European Social Charter. In view of such a proliferation of reporting obligations, it is perhaps not surprising that under the Convention the principal developments have occurred in the Commission and Court whose procedures are almost unique.

Part II. Enforcement of human rights by national means

It is well established that in some countries the ratification of a treaty on the international plane does not make that treaty automatically part of domestic law. Where a treaty does become part of domestic law, doubts may still arise whether it is "directly applicable" or "self-executing".

---

[44] In contrast to the Secretariat of the United Nations, one of its "principal organs": Art. 7 (1) of the Charter.

[45] *Vasak, op. cit.* (note 40) n. 11, takes the view that the Secretary General is an organ of the Convention.

The European Convention has the status of domestic law in only two-thirds of the twenty-one states party to the Convention. The seven parties where the Convention does not have the status of domestic law are the four Scandinavian countries (Denmark, Iceland, Norway and Sweden), Ireland, Malta and the United Kingdom [46].

Perhaps this political reality influenced the European Court of Human Rights to hold, despite strong evidence to the contrary in the Convention's negotiating history, that the Convention itself imposes no obligation to incorporate the Convention into domestic law. Art. 1 of the Convention provides that "the High Contracting Parties *shall secure* to everyone within their jurisdiction the rights and freedoms defined in Section I of this Convention", but in the case of *Ireland* v. *United Kingdom* the Court was prepared to hold only that:

> "By substituting the words 'shall secure' for the words 'undertake to secure' in the text of Article 1, the drafters of the Convention also intended to make it clear that the rights and freedoms set out in Section I would be directly secured to anyone within the jurisdiction of the Contracting States. That intention finds a particularly faithful reflection in those instances where the Convention has been incorporated into domestic law" [47].

Yet, to be fully effective, it is clear that implementation of the Convention does require some form of incorporation.

As the Court has indicated, the scope of the obligations of States Parties perhaps emerges more clearly from the terms of Art. 13 of the Convention than from Art. 1: Art. 13 provides that

> "Everyone whose rights and freedoms are set forth in this Convention are violated shall have an effective remedy before a national authority notwithstanding that the violation has been committed by persons acting in an official capacity."

Although the Court has held that neither Art. 13 nor the Convention in general lays down for States Parties any given manner for ensuring within their internal law the effective implementation of the Convention, the Court has interpreted Art. 13 as requiring that, where an individual has an arguable claim to be the victim of a violation of the rights set forth in the Convention, he must have a remedy before a national authority which can both decide his claim and, if appropriate, afford redress. While such an authority need not be a judicial authority, its powers and the guarantees which it affords are relevant in determining whether the remedy before it is effective.

---

[46] See generally *A. Z. Drzemczewski,* European Human Rights Convention in Domestic Law (1983).

[47] Judgment of 18 January 1978, para. 239.

And the Convention does not merely oblige the higher authorities of the States Parties to observe for their own part the rights and freedoms it embodies: those authorities must also prevent or remedy any breach at subordinate levels.

In its Judgment of 28 May 1985 in the *Case of Abdulazziz and others,* the Court held that since the Convention did not have the force of law in the United Kingdom, the applicants had no remedy available to them and there was thus a breach of Art. 13 [48]. It seems therefore possible to argue that a State which has not incorporated the Convention will necessarily be in breach of Art. 13 and that Art. 13 therefore indirectly requires States to incorporate the Convention.

"Subsidiary" character of the Convention procedures

The European Court of Human Rights has on a number of occasions stressed the subsidiary character of the Convention procedures, emphasising the primary role of the guarantees which the States Parties themselves are required to provide, especially under Art. 1 and Art. 13 [49].

The subsidiary character of the Convention procedures is demonstrated, in particular, by Art. 26 of the Convention, which requires the prior exhaustion of domestic remedies as a condition of access to the Strasbourg machinery. Art. 26, which both reflects and embodies generally recognised rules of international law, thus imposes a stringent requirement on potential applicants.

The subsidiary character of the Convention procedures has also been treated by the Convention bodies, perhaps more controversially, as limiting the scope of their scrutiny of the decisions of the national authorities. The Commission and Court have taken the view that it is not their function to substitute themselves for the national authorities, but rather to consider only whether the national authorities had sufficient grounds for taking the decision in question, or, as it has sometimes been expressed, whether the national authorities have exceeded the "margin of appreciation" which is, on this view, left to them under the Convention [50].

---

[48] Judgment of 28 May 1985.

[49] See *M.-A. Eissen,* La Cour européenne des droits de l'homme, Bulletin Cassin, October 1983, 13, p. 54, n. 154.

[50] *van Dijk/van Hoof, op. cit.* (note 33) n. 4, p. 427 *et seq.* and references at p. 429, n. 237.

The Status of the Convention in domestic law

Despite the Court's emphasis on the primary role of the national authorities in securing respect for human rights, it cannot be claimed that the status of the Convention in the domestic law of the member States of the Council of Europe is at all satisfactory.

Although all twenty-one member States are parties to the Convention, the status of the Convention is in some countries non-existent, and in many others obscure. Exactly one-third of the States have not incorporated the Convention into domestic law: as mentioned above, these are the four Scandinavian countries (Denmark, Iceland, Norway, Sweden), Ireland, Malta and the United Kingdom. At most, in those countries, the courts can make use of a rule of statutory interpretation to the effect that, in the absence of express indications to the contrary, domestic law should be interpreted so as to be in conformity with the international obligations of the State. Apart from the fact that the Convention may be overridden if there is an express indication of a different intention, the true weakness here results from the fact that the Convention appears very rarely to have been invoked and applied as a guide to statutory interpretation. Domestic courts have often taken refuge in the alleged generality and vagueness of the Convention's provisions and, especially in the United Kingdom, have paid little attention to the Convention jurisprudence[51]. Similarly the executive and the legislature, in promoting and enacting legislation, have paid insufficient regard to the Convention and have sometimes been content to await a verdict from Strasbourg before making the necessary changes in their domestic law – and even then, only such changes as appeared strictly necessary: a doctrine of minimal response. On the credit side, it must however be acknowledged that States have generally made some response to adverse rulings[52].

In the remaining fourteen member States where the Convention does have the status of domestic law there remains considerable uncertainty as to the precise status of the Convention's norms in the constitutional hierarchy; there is uncertainty as to which of those norms are directly applicable; and there seem again to be relatively few cases in which reliance on the Convention has proved of decisive importance in resolving a dispute. This is perhaps not altogether surprising in those countries whose domestic constitution or legislation provides adequate protection for human rights: but even in those countries the possibilities of using the Convention case-law to enlarge the scope of domestic provisions appear to have been little used. The author of the most exhaustive study of the Convention's status in domestic

---

[51] *F. G. Jacobs,* Towards a United Kingdom Bill of Rights, University of Michigan Journal of Law Reform 1984, p. 29.

[52] See *Eissen, op. cit.* (note 49) n. 19, p. 66 *et seq.*

law has reached the conclusion that, although the incorporation of the Convention's substantive provisions may be deemed desirable, of much greater significance appears to be the acceptance of the right of individual petition and of the compulsory jurisdiction of the Court[53]. But that conclusion may itself reflect the fact that the national courts have generally failed to take sufficient account of the development of the substantive provisions in the case-law of the Court.

The general conclusion which suggests itself is that the "national" role of the Convention has been as limited as its international and institutional development has been innovative and profound.

---

[53] *Drzemczewski, op. cit.* (note 46) n. 17, p. 191.

Implementation in the Inter-American Human Rights System

THOMAS BUERGENTHAL

I. Introduction

This paper considers the international enforcement aspects of the inter-American system for the protection of human rights[1]. That system has two distinct legal bases or sources with overlapping enforcement mechanisms. One has its legal basis in the Charter of the Organization of American States, the other in the American Convention on Human Rights (Pact of San José).

The institutions established to enforce the rights the system protects are the Inter-American Commission on Human Rights and the Inter-American Court of Human Rights. The Commission assumed its functions in 1960 as an institution of the OAS Charter-based system[2]. With the entry into force in 1978 of the American Convention on Human Rights, the Commission also became a Convention organ[3]. Now it exercises dual functions: those derived from the OAS Charter and those conferred on it by the Convention. The Inter-American Court of Human Rights came into being with the entry into force of the Convention[4]. Although it is primarily a Convention organ,

---

[1] On this subject generally, see *Buergenthal,* The Inter-American System for the Protection of Human Rights, in: T. Meron, Human Rights in International Law: Legal and Policy Issues 439 (1984); *Trindade,* The Evolution of the Organization of American States (OAS) System of Human Rights Protection: An Appraisal, 25 German Yearbook of International Law 498 (1982); *Gros Espiell,* Organisation des Etats Americains (OEA), in: Vasak, Les Dimensions Internationales des Droits de l'Homme 600 (1978); *Frowein,* The American and European Conventions on Human Rights: A Comparison, 1 Human Rights L.J. 44 (1980).

[2] See *Farer & Rowles,* The Inter-American Commission on Human Rights, in: J. Tuttle, International Human Rights Law and Practice, 47 (1978).

[3] See *Volio,* The Inter-American Commission on Human Rights, 30 The American University Law Review 65 (1980); *Buergenthal, supra* note 1, at 452.

[4] *Kokott,* Der Interamerikanische Gerichtshof für Menschenrechte und seine bisherige Praxis, 44 Zeitschrift für ausländisches öffentliches Recht und Völkerrecht 806 (1984); *Buergenthal,* The Inter-American Court of Human Rights, 76 The American Journal of International Law 231 (1982); *Dunschee de Abranches,* The Inter-American Court of Human Rights, 30 The American University Law Review 79 (1980).

the Court's jurisdiction extends in certain circumstances also to the interpretation of the human rights provisions of treaties other than the Convention, including the human rights provisions of the OAS Charter [5].

Although the powers of the Commission differ significantly depending upon whether it acts as a Convention organ or as a Charter organ, the distinction is often blurred in practice [6]. This is true especially in cases involving a Member State of the OAS which is also a party to the Convention. Here the Commission usually relies on its dual authority, sometimes with considerable success [7].

In addition to the Commission and the Court, which might be described as the specialized organs of the inter-American human rights system, one other institution – the OAS General Assembly – plays an important enforcement role. The Assembly is the principal organ of the Organization whose human rights powers have their source both in the OAS Charter and in the Convention.

II. The inter-American system: substantive rights

A. The Convention

The American Convention on Human Rights was opened for signature on November 20, 1969 and entered into force on July 18, 1978. By 1985, 19 OAS Member States out of 31 had ratified the treaty. These states are: Argentina, Barbados, Bolivia, Colombia, Costa Rica, Dominican Republic, Ecuador, El Salvador, Grenada, Guatemala, Haiti, Honduras, Jamaica, Mexico, Nicaragua, Panama, Peru, Uruguay and Venezuela. Missing from the list are Brazil, the United States, Paraguay, Chile, Surinam and the remaining English speaking Caribbean nations.

---

[5] See generally, *Gros Espiell,* Sobre la Interpretación de las Palabras 'O de Otros Tratados Concernientes a la Protección de los Derechos Humanos en los Estados Americanos' en el Artículo 64 de la Convención Americana sobre Derechos Humanos, in: Inter-American Court of Human Rights, Series B: Pleadings, Oral Arguments and Documents, No. 1, at 49 (1983); *Buergenthal,* The Advisory Practice of the Inter-American Human Rights Court, 79 The American Journal of International Law 1 (1985).

[6] *Aguilar,* Procedimiento que debe aplicar la Comisión Interamericana de Derechos Humanos en el examen de las Peticiones o Comunicaciones Individuales sobre Presuntas Violaciones de Derechos Humanos, in: Inter-American Commission on Human Rights, Human Rights in the Americas 199 (1984).

[7] *Moyer & Padilla,* Executions in Guatemala as Decreed by the Courts of Special Jurisdiction in 1982–1983, in: Inter-American Commission on Human Rights, Human Rights in the Americas 280 (1984).

The Convention guarantees some two dozen broad categories of civil and political rights. These include the following: the right to juridicial personality; right to life; right to humane treatment; freedom from slavery; right to personal liberty; right to a fair trial; freedom from *ex post facto* laws; right to compensation for miscarriage of justice; right to privacy; freedom of conscience and religion; freedom of thought and expression; right of reply; right of assembly; freedom of association; rights of the family; right to a name; rights of the child; right to nationality; right to property; freedom of movement and residence; right to participate in government; right to equal protection of the law; and right to judicial protection. These guarantees are supplemented by a broad non-discrimination clause and an undertaking by the States Parties to take progressive measures for "the full realization of the rights implicit in the economic, social, educational, scientific, and cultural standards set forth in the Charter of the Organization of American States as amended by the Protocol of Buenos Aires" [8].

Art. 27 allows the States Parties to derogate from their obligations under the Convention "in time of war, public danger, or other emergency that threatens [their] independence or security" [9]. Derogation is not permitted, however, from the application of the more basic human rights proclaimed in the treaty [10]. The catalog of non-derogable rights is longer than that of other human rights treaties, possibly because the right of derogation authorized by Art. 27 (1) appears to be more liberal since it may be invoked not only in time of war and other comparable situations, but also in an emergency that "threatens the . . . security of a State Party" [11].

The Convention also contains a so-called federal clause, which enables a federal state to assume more limited obligations by binding itself only in relation to matters over which it "exercises legislative and judicial jurisdiction" [12]. It should also be noted that Art. 1 (2) of the Convention declares that "for the purposes of this Convention, 'person' means every human

---

[8] American Convention on Human Rights [hereinafter cited as Convention], Art. 26. The OAS is currently considering the draft of a treaty dealing with economic, social and cultural rights. See Preliminary Draft Additional Protocol to the American Convention on Human Rights, OEA/SER.P/AG doc. 1656/83, p. 17, 4 Human Rights L.J. 467 (1983). For the text of the Convention and all other OAS human rights instruments, see the Handbook of Existing Rules Pertaining to Human Rights in the Inter-American System [hereinafter cited as Handbook], which is published jointly by the Inter-American Court and Commission and periodically brought up to date.

[9] Convention, Art. 27 (1).

[10] Convention, Art. 27 (2).

[11] But see the convincing argument for a more restrictive application by *Grossman,* Algunas Consideraciones sobre el Regimen de Situaciones de Excepción Bajo la Convención Americana sobre Derechos Humanos, in: Inter-American Commission on Human Rights, Human Rights in the Americas 121, 125–126 (1984).

[12] Convention, Art. 28 (1).

being". This language indicates that the rights guaranteed by the Convention do not protect corporations or other juridical persons as such. But to the extent that an injury to a corporation or association might be deemed to violate the rights of an individual under the Convention, a claim thereunder would have to be recognized.

The States Parties to the Convention have an obligation not only "to respect" the rights guaranteed in the Convention, but also "to ensure" the free and full exercise of these rights [13]. Hence, the treaty imposes both positive and negative duties: a state has the obligation not to violate the rights which the Convention guarantees and it is required to adopt whatever measures may be necessary and reasonable under the circumstances "to ensure" the full enjoyment of these rights.

B. The OAS Charter

The Charter of the Organization of American States was opened for signature in Bogotá, Colombia, in 1948 and entered into force in 1951. It was amended in 1967 by the Protocol of Buenos Aires, which entered into force in 1970 [14]. Prior to its amendment, the OAS Charter contained two principal human rights provisions. The first, retained in the amended Charter as Art. 3 (j), declares that "The American States reaffirm the following principles: ... (j) The American States proclaim the fundamental rights of the individual without distinction as to race, nationality, creed, or sex". The second provision, now Art. 16, provides that "each State has the right to develop its cultural, political, and economic life freely and naturally. In this free development, the State shall respect the rights of the individual and the principles of universal morality". Although the 1948 OAS Charter did not define the meaning of "the fundamental rights of the individual", the very diplomatic conference that drafted the Charter also proclaimed the American Declaration of the Rights and Duties of Man [15]. Adopted in the form of a non-binding conference resolution consisting of 38 articles, this instrument enumerates a catalog of basic civil, political, economic, social and cultural rights as well as duties of the individual.

When the Inter-American Commission on Human Rights was established in 1960, the Statute adopted for it by OAS Council charged the Commission with the task of promoting the human rights proclaimed in the Declaration. The normative character of the Declaration was significantly strengthened by the entry into force of the Protocol of Buenos Aires, which

---

[13] Convention, Art. 1 (1).

[14] See generally, *Buergenthal,* The Revised OAS Charter and Protection of Human Rights, 69 The American Journal of International Law 828 (1975); *Trindade, supra* note 1, at 499–505.

[15] For the Text, see Handbook, *supra* note 8.

transformed the Declaration into an instrument embodying the authoritative interpretation of the meaning of "the fundamental rights of the individual" as that phrase is understood in Art. 3 (j) [16]. The rights proclaimed in the American Declaration, it should be noted, resemble the catalog of rights contained in the Universal Declaration of Human Rights.

III. The institutions of the inter-American system

A. The Commission

1. *Its Powers in General*

The Inter-American Commission on Human Rights consists of seven members elected in their individual capacities by the OAS General Assembly for a term of four years. The Commission is both an OAS organ and a Convention organ. As OAS organ, its "principal function" is "to promote the observance and protection of human rights and to serve as a consultative organ of the Organization in these matters" [17]. As Convention organ, the Commission's function is "to take action on petitions and other communications pursuant to its authority under the provisions of Articles 44 through 51" of the Convention [18].

Here it should be noted that the OAS Charter specifies that "the structure, competence, and procedure" of the Commission shall be determined by the Convention [19]. To give effect to this provision, the Convention, in Art. 41, spells out the Commission's functions in relation to all OAS Member States, on the one hand, and the States Parties to the Convention, on the other. Art. 41 of the Convention reads as follows:

> "The main function of the Commission shall be to promote respect for and defense of human rights. In the exercise of its mandate, it shall have the following functions and powers:
> a. to develop an awareness of human rights among the peoples of the Americas;
> b. to make recommendations to the governments of the member states, when it considers such action advisable, for the adoption of progressive measures in favor of human rights within the framework of their domestic law and constitutional provisions as well as appropriate measures to further the observance of those rights;

---

[16] See *Buergenthal, supra* note 14; *Shelton,* Abortion and the Right to Life in the Inter-American System: The Case of 'Baby Boy', 2 Human Rights L.J. 309, 312–313 (1981).

[17] OAS Charter, Art. 112 (1).

[18] Convention, Art. 41 (f).

[19] OAS Charter, Art. 112 (2).

c. to prepare such studies or reports as it considers advisable in the performance of its duties;
d. to request the governments of the member states to supply it with information on the measures adopted by them in matters of human rights;
e. to respond, through the General Secretariat of the Organization of American States, to inquiries made by the member states on matters related to human rights and, within the limits of its possibilities, to provide those states with the advisory services they request;
f. to take action on petitions and other communications pursuant to its authority under the provisions of Articles 44 through 51 of this Convention; and
g. to submit an annual report to the General Assembly of the Organization of American States."

This provision assigns to the Commission a number of different tasks. First, Art. 41 (a) confers on it very extensive powers relating to the promotion of human rights. This provision and the authority granted in subparas. (c) and (e) require the Commission to support hemisphere-wide education and research programs devoted to human rights. Second, Art. 41 (b), (c), (d) and (g), read together, empower the Commission to take a variety of measures to prevent violations of human rights by any OAS Member State, whether or not it has ratified the Convention. Since exercise of these functions is not tied to the complaint machinery established under the Convention, the Commission is here free to act on its own motion without any specific request or petition[20]. Third, Art. 41 (f) empowers the Commission to examine petitions and communications charging the States Parties with violations of their obligations under the Convention[21]. In performing this task, the Commission exercises investigatory, conciliation and quasi-judicial functions[22].

The Statute of the Commission[23], adopted by the OAS General Assembly in 1979, implements Art. 41 of the Convention and clarifies the Commission's powers in relation to any OAS Member State[24], the States Parties to the Convention[25] and those OAS Member States that have not ratified it[26]. The here applicable normative regime is described in Art. 1 (2) of the Statute, which reads as follows:

---

[20] *García Amador*, Atribuciones de la Comisión Interamericana de Derechos Humanos en relación con los Estados Miembros de la OEA que no son Partes en la Convención de 1969, in: Inter-American Commission on Human Rights, Human Rights in the Americas 177 (1984); *Buergenthal, supra* note 1.

[21] *Aguilar, supra* note 6.

[22] *Buergenthal, supra* note 1, at 454.

[23] The Statute of the Commission is reprinted in Handbook, *supra* note 8.

[24] Commission Statute, Art. 18.

[25] Commission Statute, Art. 19.

[26] Commission Statute, Art. 20.

"For purposes of the present Statute, human rights are understood to be:
(a) the rights set forth in the American Convention on Human Rights, in relation to the States Parties thereto;
(b) the rights set forth in the American Declaration of the Rights and Duties of Man, in relation to the other Member States."

As far as OAS Member States in general are concerned, the Statute empowers the Commission to prepare human rights studies and reports, to request governments to provide it with information, to submit an annual report to the OAS General Assembly on its activities and "to conduct on-site observations in a state, with the consent or at the invitation of the government in question"[27]. In relation to the parties to the Convention, the Statute merely reiterates the powers of the Commission to deal with petitions and communications charging violations of the Convention[28]. Art. 20 of the Statute rounds out this grant of power in the following terms:

"In relation to those Member States of the Organization that are not Parties to the American Convention on Human Rights, the Commission shall have the following powers, in addition to those designated in Article 18:
a. to pay particular attention to the observance of the human rights referred to in Articles I, II, III, IV, XVIII, XXV, and XXVI of the American Declaration of the Rights and Duties of Man;
b. to examine communications submitted to it and any other available information, to address the government of any Member State not a Party to the Convention for information deemed pertinent by this Commission, and to make recommendations to it, when it finds this appropriate, in order to bring about more effective observance of fundamental human rights; and
c. to verify, as a prior condition to the exercise of the powers granted under subparagraph b. above, whether the domestic legal procedures and remedies of each Member State not a Party to the Convention have been duly applied and exhausted."

As these provisions of the Statute of the Commission indicate, the Commission enjoys very broad powers. In dealing with a State Party to the Convention, for example, the Commission is not limited to the petition procedures prescribed in the Convention. It may, in addition, invoke the powers it has as a Charter-organ. As such, the Commission may exercise the authority the Statute confers on it in relation to all OAS Member States, enabling it, *inter alia,* to initiate country studies, which are investigations of the human rights situation in a particular country, without going through the formal

---

[27] Commission Statute, Art. 18 (g).
[28] Commission Statute, Art. 19.

petition procedure[29]. Moreover, Art. 20 (b) of the Statute authorizes the Commission to establish a petition system applicable to states that have not ratified the Convention. It has enabled the Commission to handle individual petitions charging violations of the Declaration in much the same way it deals with petitions filed under the Convention[30].

2. *Individual Petitions and Inter-State Complaints*

a) Under the Convention

The American Convention stipulates that by becoming a party to it, a state accepts *ipso facto* the jurisdiction of the Commission to deal with private complaints lodged against that state[31]. The Commission may deal with so-called inter-state complaints – complaints filed by one State Party against another – only if both states, in addition to ratifying the Convention, have recognized the inter-state jurisdiction of the Commission[32]. The American Convention thus reverses the approach utilized by the European Convention and other human rights treaties, which establish an optional individual petition system and a mandatory inter-state complaint procedure. Moreover, unlike the European Convention, for example, the American Convention does not limit the right to file private petitions only to victims of violations, providing instead that:

> "Any person or group of persons, or any nongovernmental entity legally recognized in one or more member states of the Organization, may lodge petitions with the Commission containing denunciations or complaints of violations of this Convention by a State Party"[33].

The admissibility of a petition is conditioned on (a) the exhaustion of domestic remedies "in accordance with the generally recognized principles of international law", and (b) the requirement that the petition be submitted to the Commission within a period of six months from the date on which the victim of the alleged violation was notified of the final domestic judgment in his case[34]. But these requirements do not prevent the admissibility of a

---

[29] The type of country studies that the Commission has carried out are described in Inter-American Commission on Human Rights, Ten Years of Activities 1971–1981, 251–311 (1982) and in its annual reports to the OAS General Assembly.

[30] Commission, Rules of Procedure, Art. 52 Handbook, *supra* note 8. See generally, *Norris,* The Individual Petition Procedure of the Inter-American System for the Protection of Human Rights, in: H. Hannum, Guide to International Human Rights Practice 198 (1984).

[31] Convention, Art. 44.

[32] Convention, Art. 45.

[33] Convention, Art. 44.

[34] Convention, Art. 46 (1).

petition whenever it can be shown that

> "a. the domestic legislation of the state concerned does not afford due process of law for the protection of the right or rights that have allegedly been violated;
> b. the party alleging violation of his rights has been denied access to the remedies under domestic law or has been prevented from exhausting them; or
> c. there has been unwarranted delay in rendering a final judgment under the aforementioned remedies" [35].

The Commission's rules of procedure provide, moreover, that the respondent government has the burden of demonstrating the non-exhaustion of available domestic remedies if the complaint alleges that it was impossible to comply with the exhaustion requirement [36].

In dealing with complaints that are not rejected as inadmissible at the outset of the proceedings, the Commission examines the allegations, seeks information from the government concerned, investigates the facts, and may hold hearings in which both the government and the petitioners participate. The Commission must also "place itself at the disposal of the parties concerned with a view to reaching a friendly settlement of the matter on the basis of respect for the human rights recognized" in the Convention [37]. If a friendly settlement is obtained, the Commission must prepare a report, describing the facts of the case and how it was resolved [38]. This report is transmitted by the Commission to the General Assembly of the OAS "for publication".

If the parties are unable to reach a friendly settlement, the Commission must draw up a report setting out the facts that have emerged from its investigation and the conclusions it has reached about the case [39]. This report, which may also include whatever recommendations the Commission wishes to make regarding the resolution of the dispute, is transmitted to the states concerned. If the report contains recommendations for action by the state, it has three months within which to comply with or react to them. During that period, the case may also be referred to the Inter-American Court of Human Rights by the Commission or a "state concerned" [40]; private parties have no standing to refer a case to the Court.

---

[35] Convention, Art. 46 (2).

[36] Commission, Rules of Procedure, Art. 37 (3).

[37] Convention, Art. 48 (f).

[38] Convention, Art. 49.

[39] Convention, Art. 50.

[40] Convention, Art. 61. It is not clear what is meant by the expression "state concerned". The Court has not as yet dealt with this issue, which would require it to resolve certain contradictions in the language of Arts. 51 and 61 of the Convention. For a discussion of this problem, see *Buergenthal, supra* note 1, at 462.

If a case has not been referred to the Court or settled by the parties, "the Commission may, by the vote of an absolute majority of its members, set forth its opinion and conclusions concerning the question submitted for its consideration"[41]. If the Commission decides to adopt this report – and it is under no obligation to do so in all cases – it must set out its "recommendations" and "prescribe a period within which the state is to take the measures that are incumbent upon it to remedy the situation examined"[42]. Once this period has expired, it "shall decide by a vote of an absolute majority of its members whether the state has taken adequate measures and whether to publish its report"[43]. This last decision concludes the Commission proceedings in the case.

The Commission's rules of procedure permit it to make its final report part of its annual report to the OAS General Assembly. This rule, which does not prevent the publication of the report as a separate document as well, gets the case on the agenda of the General Assembly where the state's failure to comply with the Commission's recommendations may be discussed and acted upon. Since an OAS Assembly debate may give rise to adverse publicity, governments take seriously the threat of the publication of a critical report by the Commission as well as any condemnatory resolution the Assembly might adopt with regard to a case. Here it should be noted, however, that individual cases have thus far not produced any OAS General Assembly action.

Inter-state communications may be dealt with by the Commission only if the applicant and respondent states have recognized the jurisdiction of the Commission to receive such cases[44]. A state may recognize this jurisdiction on an *ad hoc* basis for a specific case or in general[45]. Approximately one half of the countries which have ratified the Convention have made the requisite general declaration, but not inter-state case has to date been filed with the Commission. All other admissibility requirements for inter-state applications are in all respects the same as those prescribed for individual petitions. Thus, unlike the European Convention which imposes more stringent admissibility requirements on individuals, the American Convention treats both types of complaints in an identical fashion, assuming, of course, that both states parties to a dispute have accepted the jurisdiction of the Commission[46].

---

[41] Convention, Art. 51 (1).
[42] Convention, Art. 51 (2).
[43] Convention, Art. 51 (3).
[44] Convention, Art. 45.
[45] Convention, Art. 45 (1) and 45 (3).
[46] Convention, Arts. 46 and 47.

b) Under the OAS Charter

Art. 20 of the Statute of the Commission, which was adopted by the OAS General Assembly in 1979, pursuant to its OAS Charter authority, empowers the Commission to deal with communications charging states that are not parties to the Convention with violations of human rights [47]. The Commission processes these cases in much the same fashion as it does petitions filed under the Convention [48]. The only difference that applies comes into play at the final stages of the proceedings. Unlike the two reports the Commission must prepare in cases brought to it under the Convention [49], only one report, denominated a "final decision", is drawn up in connection with communications involving non-State Parties. It may contain, in addition to the facts and conclusions, any recommendations the Commission deems advisable and a deadline for their implementation [50]. If a state does not comply with these recommendations, the Commission may publish the decision, be it in its annual report to the OAS General Assembly, as a separate document, or both [51].

A communication brought against a non-State Party cannot be referred to the Court as a contentious case, because the tribunal's contentious jurisdiction extends only to cases involving States Parties to the Convention which have accepted its jurisdiction [52]. But since any OAS Member State, whether or not it is a party to the Convention, may request an advisory opinion from the Court [53], it is not inconceivable that a non-State Party, deemed by the Commission to have violated its human rights obligations under the OAS Charter, might seek an advisory opinion on some of the legal issues forming the basis of the Commission's determination. The Commission or the OAS General Assembly also have the right to request advisory opinions [54] and might do so in cases in which the Court lacks contentious jurisdiction. The General Assembly has thus far not availed itself of this power, and the Commission has done so in only one case [55]. That case involved a State Party, however, which had not recognized the Court's jurisdiction.

---

[47] See *García Amador, supra* note 20.

[48] Commission, Rules of Procedure, Art. 52.

[49] Convention, Arts. 50 and 51.

[50] Commission, Rules of Procedure, Art. 53 (1).

[51] Commission, Rules of Procedure, Arts. 53 (3) and 53 (4).

[52] Convention, Art. 62.

[53] Convention, Art. 64.

[54] *Ibid.*

[55] Restrictions to the Death Penalty (Arts. 4 (2) and 4 (4) American Convention on Human Rights), Advisory Opinion No. OC-3/83 of September 8, 1983 [hereinafter cited as Advisory Opinion on the Death Penalty], Inter-American Court of Human Rights, Ser. A: Judgments and Opinions, No. 3 (1983). On this case, see the interesting article by *Moyer* and *Padilla, supra* note 7.

3. *Country Studies and On-Site Investigations*

Art. 18(c) of the Statute of the Commission, which applies to all OAS Member States and not only States Parties to the Convention, empowers it "to prepare such studies or reports as it considers advisable for the performance of its duties". This provision is amplified by Art. 18(g), which authorizes the Commission "to conduct on-site observations in a state, with the consent or at the invitation of the government in question". Under these provisions, and building on its pre-Convention practice, the Commission has performed some of its most important work[56].

Country studies and on-site observations tend, as a rule, to be undertaken by the Commission whenever it receives credible evidence that large scale violations of human rights are taking place in a given country. Although the Commission may not enter a country without its permission, it does not require the state's authorization to embark on the country study and may do so on its own motion[57]. After receiving a large number of petitions or complaints suggesting that large-scale violations of human rights are taking place in a certain country, the Commission might request information from the government in question and begin to gather additional information from other sources. Depending upon its preliminary findings, the Commission might next ask the government for permission to visit the country to observe conditions *in situ.* If the conditions appear to be very serious, the Commission is likely to ask permission to visit the country at an earlier stage of the proceedings.

In recent years it has been rare for OAS Member States to reject outright the Commission's request for permission to visit the country. What happens more often than not is that the government delays giving an affirmative response or postpones the visit of the Commission as long as it can. On the whole, however, the Commission has been successful in pressuring governments into agreeing to a visit and permitting it to enter and engage in unimpeded investigation[58].

At times the mere presence of the Commission in a country has produced an improvement of conditions there and even saved lives. The publi-

---

[56] See generally, Inter-American Commission on Human Rights, Ten Years of Activities 1971–1981, 251–311 (1982); *Vargas Carreño,* Las Observaciones *in loco* practicadas por la Comisión Interamericana de Derechos Humanos, in: Inter-American Commission on Human Rights, Human Rights in the Americas 290 (1984); *Norris,* Observations in Loco: Practice and Procedure of the Inter-American Commission on Human Rights, 15 Texas International L.J. 46 (1980).

[57] Commission Statute, Art. 18(c).

[58] See *Vargas Carreño, supra* note 56. See, e.g., Inter-American Commission on Human Rights, Report on the Situation of Human Rights in Argentina, OEA/Ser.L/V/II. 49 doc. 19, corr. 1 (1980); Inter-American Commission on Human Rights, Report on the Situation of Human Rights in Suriname, OEA/Ser.L/II. 61, doc. 6 rev. 1 (1983).

cation of an adverse Commission report and its submission to the OAS General Assembly for further action has frequently also produced beneficial results [59]. In fact, the Commission's most significant successes over the years are tied to its country reports and on-site observations, and to the publication of its findings. In the late 1970's and early 1980's, when many Latin American countries were governed by oppressive military regimes, the Commission found itself forced to publish a substantial number of such reports.

B. The Court

The Inter-American Court of Human Rights consists of seven judges nominated and elected by the States Parties to the Convention [60]. Unlike the Commission, which has its seat at the headquarters of the OAS in Washington, D.C., the Court's seat is at San José, Costa Rica, the country where the Convention was drafted. The Court came into being with the entry into force of the Convention in 1978. It was not formally constituted, however, until 1979, when the judges were elected. Its Statute, approved by the OAS General Assembly in 1979, entered into force in 1980 [61]. The Commission, which was established in 1960, has been in existence almost two decades longer than the Court.

The Court has contentious and advisory jurisdiction. In exercising its contentious jurisdiction, the Court acts exclusively as a Convention organ in that its jurisdiction is open only to the States Parties to the Convention. No such limitations are imposed on its advisory jurisdiction [62], which may be invoked by all OAS Member States and by all OAS organs. The Court's advisory jurisdiction applies, furthermore, not only to the interpretation of the Convention but also to other human rights treaties applicable in the Americas.

1. Contentious Jurisdiction

The contentious jurisdiction of the Court is defined in Art. 62 of the Convention, which reads as follows:

> "1. A State Party may, upon depositing its instrument of ratification or adherence to this Convention, or at any subsequent time, declare that it recognizes as binding, *ipso facto,* and not requiring special agreement, the jurisdiction of the Court on all matters relating to the interpretation or application of this Convention.

---

[59] This was true in Argentina, for example.
[60] See generally, *Buergenthal, supra* note 4.
[61] The Statute of the Court is reproduced in Handbook, *supra* note 8.
[62] See generally, *Buergenthal, supra* note 5.

2. Such declaration may be made unconditionally, on the condition of reciprocity, for a specified period, or for specific cases. It shall be presented to the Secretary General of the Organization, who shall transmit copies thereof to the other member states of the Organization and to the Secretary of the Court.
3. The jurisdiction of the Court shall comprise all cases concerning the interpretation and application of the provisions of this Convention that are submitted to it, provided that States Parties to the case recognize or have recognized such jurisdiction, whether by special declaration pursuant to the preceding paragraphs, or by a special agreement."

Art. 62 indicates that a state is not deemed to have accepted the contentious jurisdiction of the Court merely by ratifying the Convention. The Court acquires the requisite jurisdiction over a State Party only when it has either filed the declarations referred to in paras. 1 and 2 of Art. 62 or concluded the special agreement mentioned in para. 3. The Court's jurisdiction has to date been accepted by Argentina, Colombia, Costa Rica, Ecuador, Honduras, Peru, Uruguay, and Venezuela.

Art. 61 (1) of the Convention specifies that "only the States Parties and the Commission shall have the right to submit a case to the Court". Individuals who have filed a complaint with the Commission cannot consequently bring that case to the Court; it may be referred to it only by the Commission or a state. Art. 61 (2) prescribes, moreover that before the case may be filed with the Court, the relevant Commission proceedings applicable to it must be "completed"[63].

The judgment rendered by the Court in any dispute submitted to it is "final and not subject to appeal"[64]. Moreover, the "States Parties to the Convention undertake to comply with the judgment of the Court in any case to which they are parties"[65]. Two provisions of the Convention apply to the types of judgments the Court may render. There is, first, Art. 63 (1) which reads as follows:

"If the Court finds that there has been a violation of a right or freedom protected by this Convention, the Court shall rule that the injured party be ensured the enjoyment of his right or freedom that was violated. It shall also rule, if appropriate, that the consequences of the measure or situation that constituted the breach of such right or freedom be remedied and that fair compensation be paid to the injured party."

---

[63] For a case dealing with this subject, see Government of Costa Rica (In the Matter of *Viviana Gallardo, et al.*), Decision of Nov. 13, 1981, Inter-American Court of Human Rights, No. G.101/81 (1981), reprinted in: *T. Buergenthal & R. Norris,* Human Rights: The Inter-American System, vol. 3, Booklet 25, at 7 (1983) and 20 International Legal Materials 1424 (1981).

[64] Convention, Art. 67.

[65] Convention, Art. 68 (1).

The other provision is Art. 68 (2) which deals with money damages. It provides that the "part of a judgment that stipulates compensatory damages may be executed in the country concerned in accordance with domestic procedure governing the execution of judgments against the state".

The Court has the power also to grant temporary injunctions. This authority is spelled out in Art. 63 (2) of the Convention, which reads as follows:

> "In cases of extreme gravity and urgency, and when necessary to avoid irreparable damage to persons, the Court shall adopt such provisional measures as it deems pertinent in matters it has under consideration. With respect to a case not yet submitted to the Court, it may act at the request of the Commission."

This extraordinary remedy, which has thus far not been utilized, is available in two distinct circumstances: in cases pending before the Court and in complaints being dealt with by the Commission that have not yet been referred to the Court for adjudication. Of course, the requested relief may only be granted after the Court has determined, if only in a preliminary manner, that it has jurisdiction over the parties.

Although the Court lacks the power to enforce its judgments or preliminary rulings, one provision of the Convention bears on this subject. It reads as follows:

> "To each regular session of the General Assembly of the Organization of American States the Court shall submit, for the Assembly's consideration, a report on its work during the previous year. It shall specify, in particular, the cases in which a state has not complied with its judgments, making any pertinent recommendations"[66].

This provision enables the Court to inform the OAS General Assembly of situations involving non-compliance with its decisions, and it permits the Assembly to discuss the matter and to adopt whatever political measures it deems appropriate.

In the first six years of its existence, the Court has dealt with only one contentious case[67]. The Commission has thus far not referred a single contentious case to the Court. This situation has not helped the development of an effective inter-American system for the protection of human rights.

---

[66] Convention, Art. 65.

[67] Government of Costa Rica, *supra* note 63.

2. *Advisory Jurisdiction*

The jurisdiction of the Inter-American Court of Human Rights to render advisory opinions is more extensive than that of any other international tribunal in existence today [68]. It is spelled out in Art. 64 of the Convention, which reads as follows:

> "1. The member states of the Organization may consult the Court regarding the interpretation of this Convention or of other treaties concerning the protection of human rights in the American states. Within their spheres of competence, the organs listed in Chapter X of the Charter of the Organization of American States, as amended by the Protocol of Buenos Aires, may in like manner consult the Court.
> 2. The Court, at the request of a member state of the Organization, may provide that state with opinions regarding the compatibility of any of its domestic laws with the aforesaid international instruments."

An analysis of Art. 64 indicates, first, that standing to request an advisory opinion from the Court is not limited to the States Parties to the Convention: any OAS Member State may seek it. Second, the advisory jurisdiction is not limited to interpretations of the Convention; it also extends to interpretations of any other treaty "concerning the protection of human rights in the American states". Third, all OAS organs, including the Inter-American Commission on Human Rights, have standing to request advisory opinions. Fourth, all Member States of the OAS may seek advisory opinions from the Court regarding the compatibility of their domestic laws with the Convention or any of the aforementioned human rights treaties.

The Court has to date rendered five advisory opinions. Four of these opinions were filed under Art. 64 (1) [69] and one under Art. 64(2) [70]. In these

[68] On the advisory practice of the Court, see *Buergenthal, supra* note 5.

[69] "Other Treaties" subject to the Consultative Jurisdiction of the Court (Art. 64 American Convention on Human Rights), Advisory Opinion No. OC-1/82 of Sept. 24, 1982 [hereinafter cited as Advisory Opinion on "Other Treaties"], Inter-American Court of Human Rights, Ser. A: Judgments and Opinions, No. 1 (1982), reprinted in: *Buergenthal & Norris, supra* note 63, vol. 3, Booklet 25, at 21 (1983) and 22 International Legal Materials 51 (1983); The Effect of Reservations on the Entry into Force of the American Convention (Arts. 74 and 75), Advisory Opinion No. OC-2/82 of Sept. 24, 1982 [hereinafter cited as Advisory Opinion on Effect of Reservations], Inter-American Court of Human Rights, Ser. A: Judgments and Opinions, No. 2 (1982), reprinted in: *Buergenthal & Norris, supra* note 63, vol. 3, Booklet 25, at 39 (1983), 22 International Legal Materials 37 (1983); Advisory Opinion on the Death Penalty, *supra* note 55; Compulsory Membership in an Association Prescribed by Law for the Practice of Journalism (Arts. 13 and 29 of the American Convention on Human Rights), Advisory Opinion No. OC-5/85 of Nov. 13, 1985.

[70] Proposed Amendments to the Naturalization Provisions of the Political Constitution of Costa Rica, Advisory Opinion No. OC-4/84 of Jan. 69, 1984 [hereinafter cited as Advisory Opinion on Proposed Amendments], Inter-American Court of Human Rights, Ser. A: Judgments and Opinions, No. 4, 1984.

opinions, the Court has been able to clarify the meaning of these provisions. For example, it has held that OAS organs seeking an advisory opinion will satisfy the requirement that the request fall "within their spheres of competence", if they can demonstrate a "legitimate institutional interest" in the subject matter[71]. The Court has also ruled that the "other treaties concerning the protection of human rights in the American states", which the Court may be asked to interpret under Art. 64, are not necessarily only OAS or inter-American treaties, but any treaties bearing on the enjoyment or enforcement of human rights in a state belonging to the inter-American system[72]. U.N. human rights treaties might, therefore, qualify under certain circumstances. In interpreting Art. 64 (2), the Court has held that the reference to "domestic laws" in that provision will not necessarily always bar a state's request for an advisory opinion relating to proposed legislation as distinguished from laws already enacted[73].

In a very important advisory opinion concerning the application of the death penalty in Guatemala[74], the Court dealt with an issue of considerable importance to the functioning of the inter-American human rights system. In this case, the Commission requested an advisory opinion in the course of its investigation of charges that Guatemala was engaging in large-scale violations of human rights. The proceedings before the Commission appeared to be more in the nature of a country study than an individual petition case. Guatemala, which had ratified the Convention but not accepted the jurisdiction of the Court, took the position that the Court lacked jurisdiction to grant the Commission's advisory opinion request because it was a disguised contentious case that could not be heard without Guatemala's consent. The Court rejected Guatemala's motion and accepted the Commission's request on the ground that the request was designed to assist the Commission in the discharge of the functions the OAS Charter, the Convention and Commission's Statute assign to it[75]. This holding would appear to enable the Commission, by means of the advisory route, to obtain judicial interpretations of disputed provisions of the Convention or of other human rights treaties, thereby facilitating the resolution of disputes which could not be referred to the Court as contentious cases for lack of jurisdiction[76].

Advisory opinions are not, of course, binding in any formal sense. They do not, furthermore, make findings that State X or Z, for example, has violated the Convention. On the other hand, it is probably true that an advisory

---

[71] Advisory Opinion on Effect of Reservations, *supra* note 69, at para. 14.
[72] Advisory Opinion on "Other Treaties", *supra* note 69, at paras. 38 and 48.
[73] Advisory Opinion on Proposed Amendments, *supra* note 70, at para. 28.
[74] Advisory Opinion on the Death Penalty, *supra* note 55.
[75] *Ibid*, at paras. 37 and 38.
[76] The full scope of the Court's holding on this subject remains to be clarified. See *Buergenthal*, *supra* note 5, at 10–12.

opinion rendered by the Court has as much judicial legitimacy as a decision rendered in a contentious case. These considerations cannot but affect the legal and political strength of a government's position that is in conflict with a ruling of the Court in an advisory opinion. It is often also politically easier for a government to comply with an advisory opinion, which by its very nature does not stigmatize it as a violator of human rights, than it would be for the government to lose a contentious case, which is potentially always more embarrassing. The advisory route available in the inter-American system might, therefore, contribute more to its effectiveness than the contentious jurisdiction, although the mere existence of the latter strengthens the effectiveness of the former. At the same time, it cannot be denied that the system will in the long run lose its effectiveness unless the Court's contentious jurisdiction is also used on a regular basis.

IV. General conclusions

The weaknesses and strengths of the inter-American human rights system explain its failures and its successes. One of the principal weaknesses of the system is related to the fact that the OAS, as an organization, lacks an institution comparable to the Parliamentary Assembly of the Council of Europe in which national parliamentarians are represented and serve in their personal capacities and not as government delegates. The Inter-American Court and the Commission cannot, consequently, derive political support within the OAS from an institutional human rights lobby or, for that matter, any political institution whose members are not subject to government instructions. Given this institutional setting, what the Commission and Court can and cannot do frequently depends upon governments that are serious violators of human rights. Thus, for example, until relatively recently many of the most important countries of South and Central America were governed by military regimes. This fact explains why for decades the OAS and many of its influential members lacked the political will or interest in taking meaningful action relating to the observance of human rights. The achievements of the Commission in those years are a considerable tribute to some of its politically very astute members and to the valiant support of a small number of democratic nations. The growing number of democratic regimes that have come to power in the last few years and are committed to the active pursuit of human rights in the Americas is a force that is beginning to make its influence felt in the OAS.

That the inter-American human rights system did not originate with a specific human rights treaty has been both good and bad. Had the OAS waited for the entry into force of an American Convention on Human Rights before taking any action in the field, human rights would have been violated in the region with even greater impunity than they were violated in the 1960's and 1970's. Moreover, the OAS Charter-based system which emerged in that period was particularly well-suited for dealing with the large-scale violations of human rights then taking place. The system was legally ambiguous, giving the Commission considerable flexibility to adjust its activities to the needs of a particular situation. Although that system was at times quite effective in dealing with large-scale violations of human rights, it has never been very successful in coping with individual complaints.

The entry into force of the American Convention has permitted the existence side-by-side of the juridically more formal Convention system with that of the more flexible Charter-based system, giving the Commission and Court many more institutional tools for dealing with human rights violations than are available in other human rights systems. Thus, for example, the power of the Commission to undertake country studies and on-site investigations without having to wait for formal requests or individual petitions is particularly useful in a region with the problems for which the Americas are known. The procedures of the juridically formal European human rights system would be much too cumbersome to cope with the human rights emergencies that arise in Latin America, for example. It is clear at the same time, however, that thus far the individual petition machinery of the inter-American system has been a complete failure. Individual cases appear to get lost in a system that is geared to large-scale violations. In part that is due to the fact that the Commission treats individual petitions under the Convention in much the same way as those that come in under the Declaration. By blurring the juridical differences that exist between these two types of petitions, the Commission has failed to take advantage of the greater powers it has under the Convention to dispose of complaints. The petition system consequently still operates as it did before the Convention entered into force, which may explain, but certainly not excuse, the fact that no contentious case has as yet been referred to the Court by the Commission.

The Commission's failure to take full advantage of the Convention and the institutions it establishes must be balanced against its significant achievements in developing the enforcement mechanisms to deal with large-scale violations. It is clear, however, that the Convention system, because it is less susceptible to politization, can in the long run give greater legal and political legitimacy to OAS efforts to promote human rights in the Americas than mechanisms that come into play only when a government is committing massive violations of human rights, by which time it is often too late for many of the victims.

Completed fall 1985

La Charte Africaine en tant que mécanisme de protection des droits de l'Homme

ETIENNE-RICHARD MBAYA

Introduction

Dans le Préambule de la Charte de l'OUA, à l'intention des peuples africains, les hommes d'Etat africains y déclarent soutenir la lutte contre le «néo-colonialisme sous toutes ses formes», ils affirment être conscients «du fait que la liberté, l'égalité, la justice et la dignité sont des objectifs essentiels à la réalisation des aspirations légitimes des peuples africains», et ils se réfèrent expressément à «la Charte des Nations Unies et à la Déclaration Universelle des Droits de l'Homme» aux principes desquels ils réaffirment leur adhésion.

La Charte Africaine des Droits de l'Homme et des Peuples est donc pour l'instant l'instrument régional le plus récent relatif aux droits de l'Homme qui ait été adopté par une Organisation régionale.

Nous allons donc essayer d'évaluer son rôle et sa signification en examinant 3 questions majeures, à savoir:

- Est-ce que la Charte Africaine apporte de nouveaux aspects au concept des droits de l'Homme? Par conséquent, en quoi la Charte Africaine des Droits de l'Homme diffère-t-elle d'instruments relatifs aux droits de l'Homme déjà existants?
- La Charte Africaine des Droits de l'Homme sert-elle d'instrument pour le développement et, en ce cas, de quelle manière?
- Quelles sont les chances pour la Charte de servir d'instrument de protection des droits de l'Homme et des Peuples et d'empêcher que ces droits ne soient violés sur le continent africain?

A. De l'historique

L'Organisation des Nations Unies a été créée en 1945 par les Alliés vainqueurs de la seconde guerre mondiale. La Déclaration Universelle des Droits de l'Homme a été proclamée en 1948, mais dans le cadre de son programme, l'ONU a prévu des organisations régionales dont trois existent déjà: Le

Conseil de l'Europe, l'Organisation des Etats Américains et l'Organisation de l'Unité Africaine. Régionalement, le Conseil de l'Europe a élaboré la Convention Européenne des Droits de l'Homme et des Libertés Fondamentales (1950); L'Organisation des Etats américains, la Convention inter-américaine des Droits de l'Homme (1969); et l'Organisation de l'Unité Africaine, la Charte Africaine des Droits de l'Homme et des Peuples (1981) qui semble s'être inspirée des deux précédentes.

Au début des années 60 assez fécondes, où la majorité des pays africains accédèrent à l'indépendance nationale, les droits de l'Homme devinrent l'objet principal de la lutte des peuples africains.

En effet, dès 1961, des juristes africains réunis à Lagos, sous les auspices de la Commission Internationale de Juristes, ont proposé la rédaction d'une Charte Africaine des Droits de l'Homme, permettant de créer un tribunal auquel pourraient recourir des individus ou des groupes. Un appel similaire fut lancé de Dakar par des juristes d'Etats africains francophones, en 1967. A son tour, «l'African Bar Association» proposa plus tard une Commission des Droits de l'Homme. De même, le Nigéria proposa, à la 23e session de la Commission des Droits de l'Homme, que les Nations Unies établissent des commissions régionales là où il n'en existait pas encore.

Unanime à fustiger, à juste titre et avec force, l'Apartheid et la violation des Droits de l'Homme en Afrique du Sud, l'Afrique, excipant du droit positif international, a longtemps considéré les droits de l'Homme et les libertés démocratiques comme des domaines relevant de la compétence exclusive de droits chez son voisin, et il a fallu les scandales de certains régimes politiques africains, la désapprobation de l'opinion publique internationale . . . pour que l'Afrique se décidât à «dénationaliser» la question des violations des droits de l'Homme, pour la poser à l'échelle du continent.

L'évolution de la situation internationale était aussi favorable à l'idée d'une Charte Africaine des Droits de l'Homme. L'Acte Final d'Helsinki de 1975, signé par les Etats-Unis, le Canada et 33 pays européens, dont l'Union Soviétique, manifesta ce souci du respect des Droits de l'Homme. Bien que, sans succès, un effort fut également tenté pour inclure les droits de l'Homme dans le pacte renouvelé CEE-ACP, soit la Convention de Lomé; le décor était donc planté à l'intérieur et à l'extérieur pour le début de la Charte Africaine des Droits de l'Homme et des Peuples. Pourtant, il fallut encore 10 ans jusqu'à ce que le Sommet de l'OUA en 1979, à Monrovia, priât le Secrétaire Général d'organiser une Commission Régionale des Droits de l'Homme.

La rédaction finale de la Charte fut effectuée et ensuite adoptée à l'unanimité par le Sommet de l'OUA à Nairobi en juin 1981. Bien qu'adoptée, la Charte avant d'entrer en vigueur requiert la ratification d'une majorité absolue des Etats-membres de l'OUA, soit 26 [1].

---

[1] Cette condition est désormais remplie par la ratification de la Charte par le Niger le 15 juillet 1986. L'état de ratifications est le suivant: Bénin, Botswana, Burkina

B. Des structures de la Charte Africaine

La Charte Africaine, adoptée à Nairobi en 1981, contient 3 parties avec un Préambule en forme de résolution, présentant ainsi tout un programme politique:

- la 1ère partie concerne les droits et les devoirs;
- la 2ème partie institue l'organisation d'une Commission Africaine des Droits de l'Homme et des Peuples et définit le mandat de celle-ci ainsi que les principes d'application;
- la 3ème partie statue les dispositions générales après la mise en vigueur de la Charte.

I. Du Préambule

Le Préambule de la Charte Africaine souligne avec force une approche intégrationniste et «développementaliste» des droits de l'Homme: «Convaincus d'accorder désormais une attention particulière au droit au développement; que les droits civils et politiques sont indissociables des droits économiques, sociaux et culturels, tant dans leur conception que dans leur universalité, et que la satisfaction des droits économiques et culturels garantit la jouissance des droits civils et politiques». Elle innove même en mettant un accent particulier sur le droit au développement qui postule le droit à la paix et à la sécurité, tant sur le plan national que sur le plan international, ainsi que le droit à un environnement satisfaisant et global; en outre, le droit au développement impose aux Etats un devoir de solidarité à deux dimensions, africaine et internationale (art. 21, al. 4). Aussi peut-on déceler dans la Charte Africaine, un projet commun de société, du moins une esquisse de projet, pour toute l'Afrique, ce qui expliquerait la richesse comme les ambiguïtés, les silences ou lacunes et les limites du texte que nous allons cerner plus loin.

La Charte Africaine fait siens et réaffirme les principes et objectifs de la Charte Constitutive de l'OUA (du 23 mai 1963): «la liberté, l'égalité, la justice et la dignité sont des objectifs essentiels à la réalisation des aspirations légitimes des peuples africains»; «l'engagement qu'ils (les Etats-membres de l'OUA) ont solennellement pris . . . d'éliminer sous toutes ses formes, le colonialisme de l'Afrique, de coordonner et d'intensifier leur coopération et leurs efforts pour offrir de meilleures conditions d'existence aux peuples d'Afrique»; «favoriser la coopération internationale en tenant dûment compte

---

Faso, République centrafricaine, Comores, Congo, Egypte, Gabon, Gambie, Guinée, Guinée-Bissau, Guinée équatoriale, Libéria, Mali, Niger, Nigéria, Rwanda, République Arabe Saharaouie Démocratique, Sao Tomé-et-Principé, Sénégal, Sierra Leone, Somalie, Soudan, République-Unie de Tanzanie, Tchad, Togo, Tunisie, Uganda, Zambie, Zimbabwe. La Charte est entrée en vigueur le 21 octobre 1986.

de la Charte des Nations Unies et de la Déclaration Universelle Des Droits de l'Homme».

De même, elle réaffirme son «attachement aux libertés et aux Droits de l'Homme et des Peuples contenus dans les déclarations, conventions et autres instruments adoptés dans le cadre de l'Organisation de l'Unité Africaine, du Mouvement des Pays Non-Alignés et de l'Organisation des Nations Unies»; ce faisant, la Charte porte en elle un corps de droits dont le développement et la réalisation constitueront un véritable instrument de libération et d'épanouissement de l'Homme.

Il est remarquable que, d'emblée, à l'article premier, les hommes d'Etat africains, réitèrent leur reconnaissance des droits et devoirs énoncés et leur détermination à les promouvoir et à les protéger.

La plupart des dispositions contenues dans la Charte Africaine se trouvent donc déjà énoncées dans la Déclaration Universelle des Droits de l'Homme et d'autres instruments, tels que le Pacte International sur les Droits Civils et Politiques, le Pacte International sur les Droits Economiques, Sociaux et Culturels, de nombreux textes complémentaires comprenant diverses déclarations ainsi que les deux autres Chartes régionales dont l'une sur le plan européen et l'autre couvrant le continent américain.

La Charte fait bien de rappeler cependant l'universalité de l'être humain, en insistant sur le fait que les droits fondamentaux de ce dernier, sont fondés sur les attributs de la personne humaine.

Compte tenu donc de la liste des dispositions des droits de l'Homme traditionnels, la Charte Africaine suit le modèle des instruments relatifs aux droits de l'Homme établis antérieurement.

Aussi, quatre domaines de la Charte Africaine donnent une nouvelle signification aux aspects qui, jusqu'alors, manquaient à la conception «traditionnelle» des droits de l'Homme.

- L'importance accrue des Droits des Peuples en tant que droits collectifs par rapport aux droits individuels;
- Le droit à l'autodétermination et le droit au développement;
- Des devoirs des individus;
- L'Apartheid en tant que crime contre l'Humanité:

L'engagement des Etats-membres de l'OUA d'aider les pays africains encore sous régime colonial à réaliser leur indépendance fut une force majeure en vue d'établir l'OUA. Ce qui plus tard influença également la rédaction de la Charte dite de Bandjul. En 1981, c'est de la réalisation de l'indépendance de la Namibie que les signataires de la Charte avaient le plus grand souci; bienentendu, en relation avec la lutte pour le suffrage universel en Afrique du Sud.

Le Préambule de la Charte Africaine souligne clairement les préoccupations particulières des auteurs. On est donc en droit de dire que l'autodétermination et le droit au développement étaient considérés comme centraux à l'ensemble de la Charte.

II. Des catégories des droits et des devoirs garantis dans la Charte Africaine

Les documents de base pour les relations inter-africaines étaient les deux Chartes de l'ONU et de l'OUA. Dans son Préambule, en plus de quatre articles de substance, la Charte de l'ONU mentionne le respect des droits de l'Homme comme une base de relations internationales.

Dans son Préambule et dans ses vues, la Charte de l'OUA réaffirme les principes de la Charte des Nations Unies et de la Déclaration Universelle des Droits de l'Homme. Elle mentionne également le droit à l'autodétermination, l'éradication du colonialisme, le bien-être et la prospérité des peuples africains et un soutien matériel, moral et diplomatique aux mouvements de Libération[2].

Paradoxalement, l'assertion prohibitive selon laquelle l'OUA n'était pas «un tribunal habilité à juger des affaires intérieures d'un quelconque de ces Etats-membres», était typique de l'inhibition que les membres s'imposaient, non tant pour protéger leurs droits légitimes que pour écarter la préoccupation internationale devant de gros abus relatifs aux droits de l'Homme dans quelques Etats africains.

La dénomination «Droits de l'Homme et des Peuples» donnée à la Charte Africaine est une tentative de répondre à trois préoccupations. Elle tente, d'abord et avant tout, d'instaurer un compromis entre deux courants africains contradictoires qui opposent les progressistes et les modérés. Elle veut en même temps rapprocher les partisans de la théorie des droits individuels avec ceux de la théorie des droits collectifs dans la théorie générale des Droits de l'Homme. Elle fournit enfin quelques aspects de nouvelles dispositions introduites dans la Charte, qui concernent non seulement les droits civils et politiques que peuvent réclamer les individus, mais encore le droit à la souveraineté permanente sur les ressources naturelles et le droit à l'autodétermination qui ne peuvent se réaliser que collectivement sous leurs aspects sociaux, économiques et culturels.

S'inspirant de la Charte des Nations Unies, de la Déclaration Universelle et de la Charte de l'OUA et d'autres instruments internationaux, la Charte Africaine des Droits de l'Homme et des Peuples reconnaît franchement, au para. 7 de son Préambule, la conviction qu'il est «essentiel d'accorder désormais une attention particulière au droit au développement; que les droits civils et politiques sont indissociables des droits économiques, sociaux et culturels, tant dans leur conception que dans leur universalité, et que la satisfaction des droits économiques, sociaux et culturels garantit la jouissance des droits civils et politiques».

---

[2] *E. R. Mbaya,* La Charte Africaine: Vers une codification des droits de l'Homme en Afrique; Cours professé dans le cadre de la 16e Session d'Enseignement de l'Institut International des Droits de l'Homme, Strasbourg 1985.

La première série des droits et devoirs mentionnés dans la Charte indique l'engagement à un développement total – économique, social, culturel, moral, politique, etc. . . . – qui doit être fondé sur les droits de l'Homme.

Les droits garantis sont une combinaison de droits civils et politiques aussi bien que sociaux, économiques et culturels, dont la jouissance pourra être individuelle ou collective. Ces droits peuvent être exercés sans aucune distinction, quant à la race, au groupe ethnique, à la couleur, au sexe, à la langue, à la religion, à l'opinion publique, politique ou autre, à l'origine nationale et sociale, à la fortune, la naissance ou quelque autre situation sociale.

La deuxième série des droits est composée des droits de groupe (collectifs) prévus aux arts. 18 à 26: l'art. 18 reconnaît la famille comme l'unité naturelle, base de la société; les droits des femmes et des enfants sont protégés; les personnes âgées ou handicapées ont droit à des mesures spéciales assorties à leurs besoins physiques ou moraux; l'égalité de tous les peuples dans la jouissance du même respect et des mêmes droits s'exprime dans l'art. 19 avec la disposition additionnelle stipulant que rien ne pourra justifier la domination d'un peuple par l'autre.

a) Des droits civils et politiques

La Charte Africaine garantit sans restriction les droits civils et politiques traditionnels suivants: les droits à l'égalité, à un jugement équitable et à la dignité personnelle. Les éléments d'un jugement équitable sont détaillés à l'art. 7: droit à la défense, à un avocat de son choix, à l'appel, au jugement dans un délai raisonnable par un tribunal impartial et à la présomption d'innocence. D'autres droits: le droit à la vie, à la liberté d'association, d'assemblée et de mouvement sont soumis à restriction. Ces droits peuvent être limités ou soumis à dérogation par la loi.

Comme dans la Convention Européenne et dans quelques constitutions nationales, l'art. 13 garantit le droit de participer au Gouvernement, soit directement, soit par des représentants librement choisis, et protège l'accès à la propriété publique et aux services publics, sur une base de non-discrimination. L'indépendance du pouvoir judiciaire est également protégée.

b) Des droits économiques, sociaux et culturels

La deuxième catégorie de droits est formée des droits collectifs prévus aux arts. 18 à 26. En outre, la Charte protège le droit à la propriété mais prévoit «des restrictions dans l'intérêt d'un besoin public ou dans l'intérêt général de la communauté», en accord avec les dispositions de lois appropriées. Il n'y a pas de mention d'indemnité, soit «prompte, effective et adéquate» au sens occidental traditionnel ou «appropriée» ou raisonnable au sens de l'ONU. La Charte garantit également le droit au travail «dans des conditions équitables et satisfaisantes» à «un salaire égal pour un travail égal[3]».

Ces dispositions plutôt onéreuses servent à rappeler aux Etats-membres qu'ils doivent étendre les bienfaits de leurs ressources à la généralité de leurs citoyens plutôt qu'à une minorité, comme cela semble maintenant être le cas dans beaucoup d'Etats.

c) Du droit au développement

Une des revendications les plus importantes de la Charte est celle du Droit au Développement. Cependant, les gouvernements africains, on le sait, rencontrent de sérieux obstacles dans leurs tentatives pour venir à bout du sous-développement[4]. Ces obstacles sont de deux ordres: exogènes et endogènes. Le Nouvel Ordre Economique International constitue l'obstacle le plus fondamental au développement, créé par «le monde extérieur» (comme l'appelle la Banque Mondiale). Les efforts entrepris pour changer cette situation grâce au dialogue Nord-Sud, processus de longue durée engagé dans le cadre de l'instauration d'un Nouvel Ordre Economique International sont jusqu'à présent restés infructueux[5]. Il existe, d'autre part, de nombreux obstacles endogènes assez complexes. Par exemple, ce sont dans les milieux ruraux où vivent 80 à 90% des populations africaines que se rencontrent les problèmes de développement de l'Afrique les plus difficiles à résoudre.

La problématique du développement et de la coopération internationale occupe une place de choix dans l'esprit de la Charte Africaine des Droits de l'Homme et des Peuples.

«Le développement peut se comprendre comme un processus dynamique impliquant une plus complète réalisation du potentiel de chaque individu, communauté et nation, en vue d'accomplir ses possibilités sociales, économiques et culturelles»[6].

«La stratégie de développement effectif au niveau, soit national, soit international, doit être basée sur le respect des droits humains et impliquer des mesures destinées à promouvoir la réalisation de ces droits. Elle doit être efficace pour favoriser le développement de la manière la plus significative»[7].

Le rapport du Secrétaire général des Nations Unies sur le droit au développement mentionne brièvement 7 points comme devant nécessairement être inclus dans le processus du développement:

---

[3] Charte Africaine, art. 15.

[4] *M. Bennouna,* Droit international du développement (1983).

[5] *M. Bettati,* Le nouvel ordre économique international (1983) (Que sais-je?, No 2088).

[6] Report of the Secretary-General of the UN to the Commission on Human Rights, "The International Dimensions of the Right to Development as a Human Right", UN Doc. E/CN.4./1334, Jan. 1979.

[7] *Ibid.* p. 10.

1. La réalisation des possibilités de la personne humaine en harmonie avec la Communauté devrait être estimée comme la valeur centrale du développement;
2. La personne humaine devrait être considérée comme le sujet et non l'objet du processus de développement;
3. Le développement exige la satisfaction des besoins élémentaires aussi bien matériels que non matériels;
4. Le respect des Droits de l'Homme doit être fondamentalement reconnu dans le processus de développement;
5. La personne humaine doit pouvoir participer pleinement à la formation de sa propre réalité;
6. Le respect des principes d'égalité et de non-discrimination est essentiel;
7. Le processus doit comporter obligatoirement l'atteinte d'un certain degré d'autonomie individuelle et collective[8].

Les caractéristiques ci-dessus soulignent le fait que le développement est étroitement lié aux droits de l'Homme et qu'en l'absence de libertés élémentaires individuelles, un véritable développement ne peut s'épanouir. Un autre obstacle majeur sur la voie du développement est l'interdépendance de l'économie mondiale qui laisse peu de place au développement indépendant des pays du Tiers-Monde.

Le concept principal dans la stratégie du Nouvel Ordre Mondial est justement le développement, qui a cependant divers rapports et connotations surtout sous son aspect juridique[9].

Le droit au développement a été reconnu récemment à l'échelon international, même s'il n'a pas encore atteint l'unanimité, quant à sa définition. Il fait entrevoir que tous les droits sont étroitement liés à celui de l'existence, accompagnés d'un niveau de vie progressivement amélioré et donc, du développement. Il mentionne les arts. 55 et 56 de la Charte des Nations Unies et les arts. 22 à 27 de la Déclaration Universelle des Droits de l'Homme, ainsi que les statuts des organisations spécialisées accordant de l'importance à la collaboration et à la solidarité internationales[10].

L'inclusion du droit à l'autodétermination et l'engagement d'assistance dans la lutte contre l'Apartheid ont été les 2 points sur lesquels il y eut un accord unanime entre les Etats-membres de l'OUA. Ces deux aspects de la Charte représentent les préoccupations africaines pressantes des années 1980.

---

[8] *Ibid.* p. 13.

[9] *E. R. Mbaya,* Human Rights in North-South Relations, in: Law and State, A biannual Collection of Recent German Contributions to these Fields, Vol. 30, edited in Conjunction with Numerous Members of German Universities and Research Institutions by the Institute for Scientific Co-operation (1984).

[10] *K. M'Baye,* Discours à l'Institut International des Droits de l'Homme, Strasbourg (1972).

Parallèlement à ces dispositions de la Charte, l'Assemblée et d'autres réunions de l'ONU ont voté un grand nombre de résolutions condamnant l'Apartheid. Toutefois, nous le savons, ni cette rhétorique, ni la création d'un Centre contre l'Apartheid, ni les groupes anti-Apartheid surgis dans le monde entier n'ont encore eu un impact concret sur la pratique de l'Apartheid en Afrique du Sud. Tout au moins, l'ONU a-t-elle déclaré l'Apartheid comme «un crime contre l'Humanité». Cet engagement explicite de combattre le colonialisme et l'Apartheid a différencié la Charte Africaine des Conventions européenne et américaine des Droits de l'Homme.

Parmi d'autres droits des Peuples reconnus dans la Charte, notamment le droit de poursuivre leur développement économique et social, les Etats-parties à la Charte peuvent disposer librement de leur fortune et de leurs ressources nationales pour renforcer l'unité et la solidarité africaines.

Cette perspective ne relève pas de l'utopie car les Africains commencent à délaisser le développement par l'industrie lourde au profit d'une satisfaction plus directe de la population et surtout de la paysannerie. Car la priorité donnée à l'industrie lourde n'aboutit pas à la dynamisation d'un ensemble de secteurs liés à cette industrie, mais bien au contraire à la dépendance face aux «transnationales» (usines clés en mains – produits manufacturés ...).

Il est intéressant d'observer que les économies africaines secrètent spontanément des réponses à la crise, qui vont dans des directions autres que celles dictées par le capitalisme (culture vivrière, artisanat, petite industrie). Il y a donc spontanément création et développement d'un secteur de production intégré, extérieur à la logique capitaliste, mais dépassant la simple logique traditionnelle et assurant l'essentiel de la production des forces de travail des paysans, artisans et ouvriers (à besoins locaux = produits locaux). La production sociale de telles unités est malgré tout supérieure à celle de la grande industrie, parce qu'elle économise les coûts de collecte et de transport des matières premières d'un côté et de l'autre, les coûts de transports et de distribution des produits (économie auto-centrée et co-développement).

L'affirmation du droit des Peuples à disposer de leurs ressources naturelles doit normalement permettre aux pays du Tiers-Monde de retrouver une égalité sur la scène internationale, et, partant, un accomplissement de leur souveraineté. C'est ce à quoi tendent les pays du Tiers-Monde depuis des années, à travers les instances internationales: Assemblée Générale de l'ONU, Conseil Economique et Social, CNUCED et Organisations régionales.

L'ensemble des textes émanant de ces organisations, et dont la Charte des droits et des devoirs économiques des Etats constitue le couronnement, établit les lignes directrices d'un véritable droit au développement. Mais ce droit ne saurait s'accomplir que par l'instauration d'un Nouvel Ordre Economique Mondial [11].

---

[11] Assemblée Générale de l'ONU, déclaration concernant l'instauration d'un Nouvel Ordre Economique International, résolution 3201 (S-VI) du 1er mai 1974.

Le droit au développement implique pour son accomplissement, deux types de mesures. D'une part, dans les rapports bilatéraux, pays développés – pays en voie de développement, il fait appel à des mesures dérogatoires au droit international. D'autre part, il nécessite une action collective à l'échelle de la planète tendant à restructurer l'Ordre Economique Mondial [12].

d) Des droits des Peuples

Les droits de l'Homme ne sont pas en Afrique un article d'importation.

C'est forts des traditions africaines et enrichis du corps de droit anglo-saxon et du droit continental européen, héritage de la colonisation, que les auteurs de la Charte Africaine ont privilégié, en les soulignant, les droits Civils et Politiques en tant que droits individuels: droit à la vie (art. 4) et au respect de la personne humaine: «La personne humaine est inviolable. Tout être humain a droit au respect de sa vie et à l'intégrité physique et morale de sa personne. Nul ne peut être privé arbitrairement de ce droit». L'accent mis sur ces droits par rapport à d'autres (contenus dans les déclarations et conventions internationales) s'explique par le souci des auteurs de la Charte de lutter contre certaines pratiques malheureuses devenues un moyen de gouvernement en Afrique: internements administratifs de durée indéterminée, sans motif; condamnations, même à mort, sans que le prévenu ait été entendu ou ait bénéficié de l'assistance d'un défenseur; la torture et les exécutions sommaires fréquentes dans les prisons, les camps militaires ou les commissariats de police . . .

La Charte Africaine reconnaît et garantit en outre des droits économiques, sociaux et culturels. Si le droit de former des syndicats peut être compris dans le droit d'association, on peut regretter qu'aucune mention n'ait été faite du droit de grève; droit de propriété, qui doit s'analyser comme propriété collective aussi bien que privée [13].

L'originalité de la Charte Africaine est d'avoir lié les droits de l'Homme aux droits des Peuples [14]. L'innovation consiste en la prise en charge d'un trait essentiel des sociétés africaines: la solidarité du groupe, la symbiose entre l'individu et la société; de la communauté; de la base (famille, ethnie, village) à la Société globale, de type étatique. La proclamation des droits des Peuples traduit surtout la volonté, du moins les aspirations ou tendances actuelles de certains Etats africains de privilégier le «Peuple», disons l'Etat par

---

[12] *M. Virally,* Le principe de réciprocité dans le droit international contemporain, Recueil des Cours 122 (1967-III), p. 3 ss.

[13] Déclaration Universelle des Droits de l'Homme: art. 17: «1. Toute personne aussi bien seule qu'en collectivité a droit à la propriété. 2. Nul ne peut être arbitrairement privé de propriété.»

[14] *F. Rigaux,* Le droit, la libération des peuples et l'édification d'un nouvel ordre mondial, La Pensée, mai–juin 1982, p. 69 s.

rapport à l'individu, sinon dans la pratique du moins dans un discours politique de nature populiste. Pour *M. B. Ngom,* «le Droit des Peuples évoque plutôt une notion qui appartient au droit international. On en use pour parler d'entités ethniques ou culturelles qui, à un moment de leur histoire, cherchent à se dégager d'une domination étrangère. Ces droits préexistent à une organisation souveraine. Il s'agit plutôt d'un droit à l'indépendance. La seule justification de la présence de la notion des «Droits des Peuples» dans la Charte devrait être logiquement liée à l'existence des derniers bastions coloniaux [15]. Mais les violations des droits des peuples continuent après la colonisation [16]. En effet, l'expérience montre que si l'indépendance nationale est une phase nécessaire pour le respect des droits des Peuples et des droits de l'Homme, elle n'en est pas une condition suffisante. La dépendance économique et le maintien des liaisons étroites qu'elle permet avec le capital international conduit à la continuation, sous d'autres formes, de la violation des droits des Peuples. Cette violation des droits des Peuples, en tant que conséquence de la dépendance économique, est menée à la fois par le capital international, qui en est le principal bénéficiaire, et par les aristocraties ou les bourgeoisies privées ou étatiques des pays sous-développés [17].

Plus timide que la Charte d'Alger (1976) [18], la Charte Africaine n'a pas osé consacrer clairement les droits des minorités, ni surtout poser le principe que les atteintes à ces droits constituent des crimes internationaux, justifiant le recours à la force, bref, la résistance à l'oppression, considérée comme le plus sacré des droits par la Déclaration de 1789 ... L'ambiguïté est volontairement entretenue, car pour bien des auteurs de la Charte, le mot Peuple désigne aussi l'ethnie ou la nationalité; c'est pourquoi, bien que la Charte Africaine n'ait «pas osé consacrer clairement les droits des minorités ...», elle en dit assez cependant pour que, dans la pratique, il soit possible aux peuples opprimés de saisir la Commission chargée de faire respecter les droits des peuples, y compris ceux qui sont parties intégrantes des Etats-membres de l'OUA [19].

Sous réserve de l'approfondissement et de l'affinement théorique du mot *Peuple,* et de la pratique (qui sera en grande partie fonction du doigté et du dynamisme de la Commission de Sauvegarde), relevons les droits que la Charte Africaine proclame comme droits des Peuples. La Charte énumère et privilégie comme droits des Peuples, les droits suivants: égalité des peuples

---

[15] *B. Ngom,* La Charte Africaine des Droits de l'Homme et des Peuples, in: Fenet, Droits de l'Homme, Droits des Peuples (1982).

[16] *E. Jouve,* Le droit des Peuples (1986), p. 112.

[17] *M. Benchikh,* Droit international du sous-développement (1983), p. 95 ss.

[18] Déclaration Universelle des Droits des Peuples, Alger, 4. 7. 1976 (1977).

[19] *M. A. Glélé,* La Charte Africaine des Droits de l'Homme et des Peuples: ses virtualités et ses limites, Revue de Droit Africain, No 1, 1985, pp. 13–39. Voir aussi: *A. Cassese/E. Jouve* (dir.): Pour un droit des peuples (1978); *A. Uribe,* Légitimer le droit des peuples, Le Monde diplomatique, septembre 1976.

(art. 19); droit à l'existence (art. 20); «tout peuple a droit à l'existence»; droit du Peuple à la libre disposition de ses richesses et ressources naturelles (art. 21), droit qui doit s'exercer dans l'intérêt exclusif des populations.

Par ailleurs, la Charte proclame le droit collectif de tous les peuples d'Afrique (art. 21 al. 4) au développement économique, social et culturel.

Ainsi, les droits des Peuples se situent dans la perspective du droit international et des relations internationales qui les fondent et qui doivent contribuer, dans l'intérêt de tous, à rendre l'interdépendance des Etats et des Peuples, dynamique, et la solidarité agissante. Il est heureux que la Charte Africaine prône l'avènement de l'ère des peuples, contre l'Etat Leviathan, et prêche la solidarité entre les Etats et les Peuples du monde.

La principale originalité de la Charte Africaine aura été d'introduire la notion de droits des Peuples; en dépit de ces ambiguïtés soulignées, ce concept peut conduire à l'instauration, au plan intérieur, de véritables régimes démocratiques et, dans la vie internationale, à une société internationale plus juste et plus fraternelle.

e) Des devoirs

La Charte Africaine établit une corrélation entre droits et devoirs, car les auteurs de la Charte Africaine ont voulu éviter l'individualisme forcené, l'irresponsabilité et l'égoïsme qui menacent les sociétés africaines contemporaines. C'est cet accent particulier, cette volonté de majorer, de souligner les devoirs, en se fondant sur les traditions africaines, qui constitue l'originalité du chapitre II (arts. 27 à 30) de la Charte.

Les devoirs de l'individu: le citoyen n'a pas que des créances sur la collectivité nationale ou l'Etat, il a également à son endroit des obligations [20].

Somme toute, ces devoirs édictés par la Charte ne sont pas excessifs, ils font partie de l'univers culturel de tout homme: en Afrique, ils sont encore pleinement vécus et assumés; on voudrait les voir se perpétuer, et ne pas disparaître avec une certaine forme de «développement ou modernisation». Si la Charte consacre son chapitre II aux Devoirs, elle n'y traite que des Devoirs de l'individu; ceux de l'Etat n'apparaissent pas, dans l'ordonnancement juridique, en contrepoids, par symétrie. Ils ont été énoncés dans le chapitre I «des Droits de l'Homme et des Peuples» comme corollaires des droits reconnus et garantis.

Ainsi, droits et devoirs s'équilibrent et s'intègrent harmonieusement, tant en ce qui concerne l'individu que dans les rapports de ce dernier avec la Communauté nationale de l'Etat [21].

---

[20] *M. A. Glélé,* La loi fondamentale, in: Encyclopédie Juridique de l'Afrique.

[21] *A. Verdoodt,* Naissance et signification de la Déclaration Universelle des Droits de l'Homme (1964). – Il convient également de mentionner la grande Encyclique du Pape Jean XXIII «Pacem in Terris» qui est tout entière bâtie sur la dichotomie «Droits–Devoirs» de l'homme. De même, *H. Gros Espiell* parle aussi des de-

L'accent mis par le constituant africain sur les devoirs de l'homme face à ses droits s'explique probablement à la fois par la conception même de l'individu dans la société africaine et par la prise de conscience de l'état de sous-développement dans lequel se trouvent les pays africains.

Lorsque l'on recherche quels sont les devoirs pris en considération par les constituants africains, le devoir de travailler, le devoir de contribuer aux charges publiques en s'acquittant des impôts et des autres contributions sociales, le devoir de participer à la défense de la patrie et le devoir d'obéir à la loi sont le plus souvent cités [22].

En introduisant ainsi les devoirs individuels dans un instrument international (art. 29), la Charte Africaine crée une innovation. Jusqu'ici, on énumérait habituellement des droits qui, par implication, imposaient des devoirs sur les Etats. D'autre part, la Charte reconnaît les devoirs de l'individu vis-à-vis de la famille, de la société, de l'Etat et de la Communauté internationale africaine. Les devoirs vis-à-vis de la famille incluent le respect, l'aide aux parents et la préservation d'un développement harmonieux; les devoirs envers l'Etat comprennent la protection et le renforcement de la solidarité sociale et nationale, la contribution à la défense nationale et le paiement des impôts.

III. De la Commission

La Charte établit une Commission de 11 membres ne comprenant pas plus d'un citoyen du même Etat. Les membres sont normalement élus pour une durée de 6 ans.

Dans l'esprit même de la Charte Africaine des Droits de l'Homme et des Peuples, la Commission est appelée à remplir quatre fonctions:

- la fonction de promotion des droits de l'Homme;
- la fonction de protection des droits de l'Homme par communications des Etats et par d'autres communications dont individuelles;
- la fonction d'interprétation de la Charte;
- et toute autre fonction.

Nous l'avons dit, la Charte Africaine des droits de l'Homme et des Peuples a été précédée par la Convention Européenne des Droits de l'Homme de 1950 et la Convention Américaine des Droits de l'Homme de 1969. Malgré certaines similitudes, elle a certains traits distinctifs qui reflètent le caractère spécial des systèmes juridiques africains.

---

voirs des individus dans «Le système interaméricain comme régime régional de protection internationale des droits de l'homme», Recueil des Cours 145 (1975-II), p. 1 ss.

[22] *K. Vasak,* Les Droits de l'Homme et l'Afrique, Revue belge de droit international 1967, p. 459 ss. Voir aussi *J. Ziegler,* Sociologie de la nouvelle Afrique (1964), pp. 23, 27.

Tandis que les Cours établies par les Conventions américaine et européenne peuvent examiner les cas présentés d'abord aux Commissions, il n'y a pas de «deuxième voie» pour rendre justice selon la Charte Africaine. Quant à l'OUA, elle ne peut pas, selon la Charte, rétablir la justice.

A la différence des Conventions européenne et américaine, de beaucoup antérieures, la Charte Africaine insiste sur le droit au développement.

Finalement, la Charte Africaine réaffirme la confiance dans le droit international général, relatif aux droits de l'Homme et des Peuples, basé sur les instruments de l'ONU et de l'Afrique. Comme moyen subsidiaire de déterminer les principes du droit, elle se réfère à d'autres Conventions internationales générales ou spéciales, établissant des règles connues et reconnues expressément par les Etats-membres de l'Organisation de l'Unité Africaine, par les coutumes africaines compatibles avec les normes internationales touchant les droits de l'Homme et des Peuples, les coutumes généralement acceptées comme lois, les principes généraux de droits reconnus par les Etats africains aussi bien que les précédents et la doctrine légaux.

Ainsi, la Charte Africaine souscrit à la théorie de consentement relative à l'effet contraignant du droit international, refusant la validité des normes auxquelles les parties n'ont pas consenti et à la rédaction desquelles les parties n'ont pas contribué. Ceci représente une vue conservatrice et pleine de bon sens, dans un monde d'inégalité politique, économique et militaire et d'intérêts disparates, mais ayant besoin de normes acceptables en vue de relations mutuellement bénéfiques.

Ainsi, le mécanisme suivant les prescriptions du début doit assurer des fonctions de promotion et de protection. Ces fonctions comprennent ce qui suit:

1. Rassemblement, formulation et collaboration.

a) Rassembler des documents, entreprendre des études et recherches sur les problèmes africains du domaine des Droits de l'Homme et des Peuples; organiser des Séminaires, des symposiums et des conférences, répandre l'information, encourager les institutions nationales et locales consacrées aux Droits de l'Homme et des Peuples; et, le cas échéant, donner son opinion ou formuler des recommandations aux gouvernements;
b) Formuler les principes et règles pour résoudre les problèmes légaux relatifs aux Droits de l'Homme et des Peuples et aux Libertés Fondamentales susceptibles de fournir une base de législation aux gouvernements africains;
c) Collaborer aux efforts d'autres institutions africaines et internationales en vue de la promotion et de la protection des Droits de l'Homme et des Peuples.

2. Assurer la protection des Droits de l'Homme et des Peuples selon les conditions prévues dans la Charte.

3. Interpréter toutes les dispositions de la présente Charte sur demande d'un Etat-partie, d'une institution de l'OUA ou d'une organisation africaine reconnue par l'OUA.
4. Accomplir toute autre tâche qui pourrait lui être confiée par l'Assemblée des Chefs d'Etat et de Gouvernement.

La tâche de la Commission comprend encore des enquêtes, l'examen de communications reçues des Etats (sous certaines conditions; aussi d'individus) et l'accomplissement d'études approfondies et l'envoi de rapports et recommandations confidentiels à l'Assemblée des Chefs d'Etat et de Gouvernement.

La Commission peut faire usage de toute méthode appropriée de recherches, elle peut interroger le Secrétaire Général de l'OUA ou toute autre personne capable de la renseigner.

a) Communications en provenance d'Etats

Un Etat peut signaler à d'autres Etats des violations des dispositions de la Charte; copies de telles communications doivent être envoyées au Président de la Commission et au Secrétaire Général de l'OUA. Un Etat concerné peut également signaler les violations de la Charte directement à la Commission après avoir dûment averti l'Etat adverse et le Secrétaire Général de l'OUA.

La Charte reconnaît expressément la règle du remède local: elle ne peut traiter un problème qui lui est soumis qu'après s'être assurée que tous les remèdes locaux, s'ils existent, sont épuisés, à moins que le processus d'utilisation de ces remèdes ne soit trop prolongé. De plus, la Commission a l'obligation de soumettre, à chaque session ordinaire de l'Assemblée des Chefs d'Etat et de Gouvernement, un rapport sur ses activités.

b) Communications d'organisations non-étatiques

La Commission peut recevoir des communications provenant d'organisations non-gouvernementales et d'individus. En cas d'urgence, la Commission se rapportera au Président de l'Assemblée qui pourra lui-même demander cette étude approfondie.

A la différence des cas signalés par des Etats, les membres de la Commission doivent décider à la majorité simple qu'il est opportun de prendre en considération ces cas individuels. La Commission ne considère pas les cas déterminés par des Etats selon la Charte de l'ONU, la Charte de l'OUA ou la Charte des Droits de l'Homme et des Peuples; et un point peut intéresser particulièrement les individus se plaignant de violation des Droits de l'Homme dans leur propre Etat; avant toute considération de substance, toute communication sera signalée à l'Etat en cause par le Président de la Commission.

c) Etudes approfondies et caractères confidentiels des mesures prises par la Commission

Les violations massives des droits proclamés par la Charte peuvent amener la Commission à procéder à une étude approfondie du problème et à un rapport accompagné de l'énumération de faits et de recommandations.

En somme, le mécanisme de mise en vigueur prévu dans la Charte, mécanisme qui est représenté par une commission obligée de travailler en étroite collaboration avec des gouvernements à toutes les étapes de son travail, soulève beaucoup de questions. Par exemple, dans quelle mesure l'indépendance et l'impartialité des membres sont-elles à l'abri des pressions gouvernementales? L'obligation de signaler les plaintes individuelles à l'Etat accusé ne nuit-elle pas aux droits individuels? Et, enfin, quelle peut être son efficacité dans un système qui encourage le règlement des conflits mais manque du pouvoir de les régler?

Pour l'avenir, il est même souhaitable de créer une Cour africaine des Droits de l'Homme, qui doit se pencher sur le «crime contre l'Humanité» (autrement dit l'Apartheid) et contre la violation des Droits de l'Homme.

Tout d'abord, la Commission n'aura qu'un rôle de conseiller et d'informateur sur la propagation du principe des Droits de l'Homme (art. 45).

Cette limitation ne doit pas être comprise comme une demi-mesure politique: elle traduit un réalisme sobre.

D'une part, la protection juridique ne peut être effective que sur la base d'un niveau de formation suffisant, en particulier dans la perspective d'une conscience en faveur des Droits de l'Homme; vu de la sorte, le travail d'explication devient primordial. En effet, lorsque le droit s'éloigne des réalités sociales et méconnaît les données concrètes, il s'expose à être transgressé, il devient une contrainte inutile. On dira d'une convention, d'une disposition conventionnelle qu'elle accède à l'effectivité quand il apparaît que sa pleine réalisation impose la recherche des fins supérieures, des potentialités que les parties, sans les avoir énoncées, doivent nécessairement avoir envisagées.

Aussi les procédures juridiques posent *a posteriori* de nombreux problèmes aux nouveaux Etats africains, surtout en raison de frais, mais aussi parce que le parti ne peut parler à son gré devant le Tribunal et parce que la transformation de son cas en un cas justiciable lui est largement incompréhensible, étant donné que le langage juridique ne relève pas, la plupart du temps, de sa langue maternelle.

IV. Compatibilité de la protection des Droits de l'Homme avec les normes internationales

Il faut reconnaître que, surtout grâce à la préoccupation excessive de la Charte de l'ONU pour les notions de collaboration internationale, de souveraineté des Etats et de non-interférences dans les affaires intérieures des

Etats, l'action de l'ONU dans l'établissement des processus nécessaires pour garantir la protection des Droits de l'Homme a été plutôt prudente et lente[23]. La Conférence des Droits de l'Homme en 1968, à Téhéran, commentant l'attitude de l'ONU en matière de processus de mise en œuvre, a déclaré: «Bien que l'ONU ait accompli un notable progrès dans la définition de normes pour la jouissance et la protection des Droits et des Libertés Fondamentales de l'Homme, il reste beaucoup à faire pour l'actualisation de ces droits et libertés.» Toutefois, puisqu'on reconnaît de plus en plus que des droits sans protection effective peuvent être à peine considérés comme des droits, l'ONU elle-même semble disposée à renforcer des processus plus effectifs de mise en œuvre.

Ce qui ressort de la considération des processus de mise en œuvre de l'ONU, c'est leur similarité avec ceux de la Charte Africaine et leur inefficacité. Puisque les Gouvernements eux-mêmes sont parfois les pires violateurs des Droits des Peuples, leur système régional qui manque de mécanismes de contrôle – sous prétexte de protection de confidentialité – les invite simplement à ignorer les cas de violations.

Concernant les nombreux problèmes complexes de développement qui s'imposent aux nations africaines, on voit clairement que tout mécanisme de mise en œuvre compatible avec les normes internationales, mais étranger aux normes africaines, a de très faibles chances de survie. Il fallait établir une Convention africaine des Droits de l'Homme qui ne serait pas une simple photo-copie des Conventions internationales existantes mais serait adaptable, praticable, exprimant les problèmes particuliers de l'Afrique, dont le principal est celui du sous-développement économique.

Il n'est pas douteux que, si l'on veut traiter des problèmes africains, les solutions africaines sont préférables aux concepts étrangers mal compris et inadaptables, développés dans un environnement tout à fait différent. Nous pouvons ainsi citer le Président Kaunda, intervenant comme médiateur dans le conflit frontalier entre le Kenya et la Somalie: «. . . les Africains étaient capables de résoudre leurs propres problèmes sans le concours d'institutions influencées par ces mêmes puissances qui étaient à condamner pour l'inextricable situation de l'Afrique de nos jours»[24]. L'argument de la solution africaine peut ne pas créer beaucoup de difficultés si l'on reconnaît clairement ses limites, mais il peut en causer lorsqu'on l'étend trop loin et qu'on s'en serve comme écran opposé à l'observation par les Etats de normes en matière de Droits de l'Homme, reconnues internationalement. L'expérience a montré que, sans un système plus efficace de s'assurer l'accord des Etats, ceux-ci recouraient toujours à leur souveraineté et se vantaient de posséder

---

[23] *Th. Buergenthal/R. Norris/D. Shelton,* Protecting Human Rights in the Americas. Selected Problems (1982).

[24] Keesings Contemporary Archives 1967–1968, p. 22 386. Voir aussi: *B. Boutros-Ghali,* Le mouvement afro-asiatique (1969) (avec la collaboration de S. Dreyfus).

une information vitale relative à la sécurité nationale, information non-accessible aux citoyens ordinaires.

Apparemment, dans l'intention de réaliser un mécanisme adapté aux besoins de l'Afrique, la Charte insiste sur des recherches de négociations, le recours à la médiation et à la conciliation, réputées en accord avec les traditions et la civilisation africaines. Les traditions africaines peuvent abhorrer la confrontation inhérente aux procédures judiciaires, mais dans cette quête moderne du moyen le plus efficace d'assurer un développement basé sur les droits de l'Homme, les Etats africains doivent prendre en considération la philosophie du Roi Sobhuza: «rejeter celles des traditions africaines devenues vétustes, de même que les concepts étrangers sans lien avec le territoire, mais combiner ce qu'il y a de meilleur dans les deux systèmes pour satisfaire aux besoins de l'Afrique» [25].

La complexité du problème de développement africain défie évidemment tous les efforts d'une Commission unique en vue de solutions. Il est clair, qu'au contraire, plusieurs instruments de mise en œuvre sont nécessaires. Dans des circonstances où la Charte elle-même reconnaît le besoin d'études approfondies relatives aux causes et conséquences de déprivations des Droits de l'Homme, aucun de ces instruments ne peut être estimé superflu.

Aussi la Charte Africaine se caractérise-t-elle par une juxtaposition courageuse de maîtrise politique du présent mais, en même temps, de lacunes de codification. Les lacunes de codification de la Charte Africaine ne se trouvent pas seulement dans la langue indifférenciée, mais aussi dans la langue politique utilisée par ses auteurs. Il n'est pas encore trop tard pour combler ces lacunes; cela contribuerait à renforcer la qualité de tout le document. D'un autre côté, il ne correspond pas à l'essence d'une Charte régionale des Droits de l'Homme de répéter ou de réaffirmer ce qui est déjà connu: c'est justement le fait bien compris que la Charte est incomplète, en corrélation avec la référence contenue dans le Préambule qui pourrait garantir sur le plan des codifications internationales des droits de l'Homme, que la Charte de l'OUA ne veut pas être un succédané, mais une tentative trouvant ses racines dans la volonté politique spécifique de l'Afrique, de traiter ses propres problèmes de manière exemplaire.

La notion de droits, décrite dans la Charte Africaine, sera très probablement déformée par quelques régimes du Continent, si un passé récent permet de pronostiquer l'avenir. De tels gouvernements insisteront sur les devoirs des individus envers leurs Etats, mais piétineront leurs droits et leurs espoirs légitimes. Il y a eu quelques gouvernements qui ne sont pas persuadés que le bien de leurs sujets était leur principale responsabilité. Dans des si-

---

[25] *M. A. Odesanya*, Reflections on the Pacific Settlement of Inter-State Disputes in Africa, in: Papers of the Third Annual Conference of the Nigerian Society of International Law, March 1971, p. 48. Voir aussi: *E. Berg*, Non-alignement et nouvel ordre économique mondial (1980).

tuations de ce genre, le clivage entre gouvernants et gouvernés était critique. Toutefois, il est sain de recommander les devoirs en même temps que les droits pour obtenir un juste équilibre.

Les Droits de l'Homme dépassent maintenant la responsabilité exclusive d'Etats distincts. La Charte de l'ONU a mis en route clairement le processus de leur internationalisation. De nouvelles étapes eurent lieu dans la Déclaration Universelle des Droits de l'Homme, les Conventions sur les Droits de l'Homme et d'autres instruments.

La Charte de l'OUA y faisait référence; mais il était encore possible pour quelques régimes d'affirmer qu'ils appartenaient exclusivement à leurs lois intérieures. La Charte Africaine a éliminé tous ces doutes qui pouvaient persister relativement aux statuts des Droits de l'Homme et, désormais, les Etats africains ne peuvent s'engager en dehors du droit coutumier international qui, sans nul doute, inclut le respect de ces droits.

L'adoption de la Charte devrait donc être considérée comme un jalon dans le développement des Droits de l'Homme sur le Continent et il reste maintenant aux individus, groupes et institutions concernés à continuer la lutte pour la réhabilitation de la personnalité humaine après les dégradations du commerce des esclaves, du fascisme et du colonialisme[26].

Conclusion

Le programme de la Charte Africaine est ainsi tout à fait impressionnant. Mais les juristes africains sont inquiets au sujet de la possibilité d'application des droits qu'elle protège. Tant que la Charte ne prévoira pas de mécanisme pour rendre ces devoirs obligatoires, il y a risque qu'ils soient utilisés pour limiter les droits protégés. Une autre cause d'inquiétude concernant la mise en œuvre est que la Charte ne crée pas une Cour des Droits de l'Homme. Contrairement aux mécanismes européen et inter-américain de contrôle, la Charte Africaine crée une Commission pour examiner les plaintes. Si cette Commission conclut qu'une plainte révèle une série de violations, elle réfère le cas à l'Assemblée des Chefs d'Etat et de Gouvernement de l'OUA qui prend la décision finale. Quelques juristes africains ont suggéré que le mécanisme prévu dans le traité africain soit en accord avec la préférence traditionnelle africaine pour le consensus et la médiation en tant qu'opposés à la procédure judiciaire. On est donc en droit de craindre que l'Assemblée des Dirigeants de l'OUA discute probablement avec un défenseur pour lui recommander de céder même si on pense que cette attitude a plus de chance de

[26] *E. R. Mbaya,* La Charte Africaine des Droits de l'Homme et des Peuples: Mythes et Réalités (1984).

réussir qu'un jugement de tribunal. On craint donc que ce mécanisme n'amène à étouffer certaines affaires.

De plus, les publications critiquant la politique du gouvernement sont interdites dans beaucoup d'Etats africains et il y a peu de chance que cela change, bien que la Charte garantisse la liberté d'expression.

Beaucoup de juristes craignent que la situation récessive de l'Afrique en matière d'économie et de sécurité ne mine les efforts de protection des Droits de l'Homme comme la récession en Occident et la baisse des prix mondiaux des matières premières africaines exportées, ont dévasté les économies des Etats africains. D'où un accroissement de l'instabilité politique. Accroissement aussi des efforts de l'Afrique du Sud pour déstabiliser les Etats voisins. Dans tout le Continent, les gouvernements craignent de ne pas pouvoir faire face; ainsi la répression s'est accrue. A long terme, la protection des Droits de l'Homme en Afrique va dépendre de l'évolution politique et économique; mais la Charte Africaine des Droits de l'Homme et des Peuples représente un grand pas en avant. Pour être efficace et utilisable en ce qui les concerne, le meilleur ensemble de procédés internationaux capable de développer des nations de traditions diverses (historiques, culturelles, socio-économiques et politiques), doit être un système compatible avec les références internationales de la protection des Droits de l'Homme, mais en même temps, assez adaptable pour s'accomoder aux besoins et problèmes africains, capable aussi d'améliorer rapidement la situation des individus et des groupes[27].

La Charte se veut être le reflet des valeurs de la région africaine qui l'a vue naître. C'est ainsi qu'elle met en exergue certaines valeurs de la civilisation africaine telle la «famille», défenderesse des valeurs de la Communauté, telle la «solidarité», pierre angulaire des relations sociales en terre d'Afrique. Il faut citer en plus les spécificités de la société et du droit africain que la Charte a tenté d'intégrer: le rôle effacé du temps, la corrélation vivante entre droits et devoirs, la préférence accordée à la conciliation comme mode de règlement des différends. Et aussi et surtout, la place importante accordée au Droit des Peuples à l'autodétermination et à ceux dits de la «troisième génération» (droit à la paix, droit au développement, droit à un environnement satisfaisant . . .).

Compte tenu de ses virtualités et limites que nous avons essayé d'analyser ci-dessus, la Charte Africaine se présente comme une reconnaissance et une consécration continentale des Droits de l'Homme et des Peuples en Afrique et, plus qu'un espoir, un véritable moyen, une arme à perfectionner, à affiner de manière à en faire un outil de libération, de dignité, de liberté et d'épanouissement.

---

[27] *J. Quigley,* OAU Boots Human Rights, in: Africa News, 22 August 1983.

La Charte Africaine des droits de l'Homme et des Peuples est une tentative courageuse d'assumer le présent, une tentative à laquelle nous souhaitons le succès, malgré les possibilités d'améliorer, surtout sa capacité à se faire valoir, face aux affaires politiques courantes.

Pour comprendre cette Charte en tant que système africain de protection des Droits de l'Homme, il est nécessaire de lier son étude à celle des mouvances politiques qui ont donné naissance à l'OUA en 1963 et, plus tard, à l'adoption de la Charte Africaine, en 1981. La conclusion découlant de ces études nous enseigne que les événements de ce genre, malgré leur caractère de manifestation de volontés concordantes, restent souvent le résultat d'un conflit de volontés.

Approaches to Human Rights in Asia

HIROKO YAMANE

Introduction: specificity of the behaviour of the Asian States in the concerted efforts of the international community with regard to human rights

In comparison to the massive and varied human problems facing Asia, the efforts which have been made in the name of human rights in this continent appear ridiculously insignificant and disproportionately small. This is perhaps because many of the revolutions and social reforms carried out in Asia for human dignity and social betterment have been under the banner of other concepts, and not in the name of human rights.

How to make a boundary between what the human rights struggle is and what it is not, is in fact very difficult, and we should not stigmatize a continent which does not often use the concept of human rights. Between the largest interpretation of human rights which includes almost all human and social problems such as development, peace and cultural identity, and the classicial liberal interpretation which particularly emphasizes civil and political rights, there is a wide spectrum of thinking and approaches with radically different aspirations and interests involved. If we are to enumerate all the problems and approaches to human rights in the Asian context, including the fights for human rights carried out under other names, it would be almost impossible to exhaust them and to assess their significance.

Given the complexity of the Asian region, and faced with the increasingly varied approaches to human rights concomitant to the participation of the non-Western and/or Third World in the international community, why is it significant to discuss the "approaches to human rights in Asia"? Is there any "specificity" of the approaches to human rights characteristic of Asia?

A valid answer to this question seems to be provided when particular orientations of the Asian countries with regard to human rights are discerned comparatively and within the framework of the universal perspective. If these orientations exist for particular reasons, and if these same orientations imply "alternative" approaches to human rights in Asia as compared to other regions, then it would be a starting point for making a realistic assessment of the situation, and reflexion on the ways and means of furthering respect for human rights.

In the first part of the paper, we shall review briefly the ways in which Asian countries participate in the concerted efforts of the international community to promote and protect human rights. The second part will describe what seems to be specifically characteristic of the approaches to human rights in Asia. The third part will draw up some suggestions as to the possible directions to which human rights protection, research and education could be oriented in Asia, based on the conclusions drawn from the first two parts of the paper.

I. Pattern of participation of the Asian countries in the concerted effort of the international community for the protection of human rights

(1) The ratification of international instruments

Asian governments tend to show a degree of reluctance to engage actively in human rights issues, especially at the international level. Although the record of ratification of international instruments is not the best indicator of a country's concern for international promotion and protection of human rights, it does provide some guide.

Only Afghanistan, India, Japan, Mongolia, Sri Lanka, and Vietnam have ratified both the International Covenant on Civil and Political Rights and the International Covenant on Economic, Social and Cultural Rights. The Philippines has ratified only the latter. In 1981, the People's Democratic Republic of Korea ratified the International Covenant on Civil and Political Rights. No Asian country has ratified the optional protocol as of 1 January 1985.

Another indication is provided by the extent to which countries of the Asian region have ratified international labour conventions as adopted by the ILO. A survey undertaken by the ILO in 1980 indicated that, on the whole "the ratification pace for Asia remains slower, and the regional average . . . is lower than corresponding figures for other regions"[1]. This position is also reflected in the number of Asian ratifications of certain of the Conventions which are categorized by the ILO as relating to basic human rights. Thus for example, the most widely accepted ILO standards among those concerning basic human rights are the two Conventions relating to forced labour: the Forced Labour Convention, 1930 (No. 29) and the Abolition of Forced Labour Convention, 1957 (No. 105). As regards the first of these, the rate of

[1] Application of ILO standards, Report of the Director-General, Report 1 (Part 2) to the ILO Ninth Regional Conference, Manila, 1980 (Geneva, ILO, 1980).

ratification by Asian countries is comparable to that of the general ILO membership, while the rate is noticeably lower (by some 25%) for the second convention. Similarly, while the Right to Organize and Collective Bargaining Convention, 1949 (No. 98) has been ratified by a majority of Asian countries, the Freedom of Association and Protection of the Right to Organize Convention, 1948 (No. 87) has been ratified by only one third of the Asian countries.

(2) Types of Asian cases brought to the attention of the international organs for the protection of human rights: their non-representativity

Important documents produced by different international organs for examining the cases of human rights violations (for example, reports of the Commission of Human Rights, reports submitted by states parties under Art. 40 of the International Covenant on Civil and Political Rights, to the Human Rights Committee, reports of the ILO Governing Committee on the Freedom of Association, reports of the Unesco Committee of Conventions and Recommendations) illustrate unevenly the type of human rights violations which have allegedly occurred in the Asian region.

For example, the Reports of the Committee on Freedom of Association published by the ILO during 1980–83 illustrate alleged violations of trade union freedom in the very broadest sense of the word as it is understood by the Committee on Freedom of Association of the Governing Body of the ILO[2]. As everybody will recall, this procedure can be used by trade union organizations, whether international or national, against any Member State of the ILO regardless of whether or not they have ratified Conventions no. 87 and no. 98.

During the period of four years, 19 complaints were lodged against 8 Asian countries and, more specifically, 2 against Bangladesh, 9 against India, 2 against Malaysia, 1 against Pakistan, 1 against Philippines, 2 against Sri Lanka and 1 against Thailand[3].

The reply to this question probably resides in the degree of knowledge of this useful and efficient procedure by the Asian trade union organizations and in the degree of interest attached to Asian problems by international trade union organizations.

The examination of these complaints leads us to make the following remarks which should be conducive to some constructive proposals concerning the protection of human rights in Asia.

---

[2] Official Bulletin Vol. LXIII, 1980; Vol. LXIV, 1981; Vol. LXV, 1982; Vol. LXVI, 1983; ILO Reports of the Committee on Freedom of Association (from 207th to 233rd session).

[3] 226th session, paras. 181–191.

(i) It is encouraging that the majority of the complaints have been lodged by the Asian trade union organizations themselves (with the exception of the cases concerning Thailand and the Philippines), and not by other international watchdog organizations.
(ii) On the other hand, one must be aware that the substantive points raised in these cases are not to be considered as specifically Asian, as they are similar to problems which unfortunately often occur in the third world countries.
(iii) The complaints reveal the very restrictive trends followed by the Asian countries in the implementation of trade union freedom. This trend is clear in the interpretation of the scope of the activities allowed to the trade union, especially the definition of the right to strike. For example, in India, this right is not considered as a fundamental right, perhaps for technical constitutional reasons. These countries also give very wide interpretation to the "essential services" whose trade union activities are drastically limited. In these "essential services" there is a phenomena that we may call militarization of some professional activities as the freedom of the employees is much limited. Last but not least, the emergency repression legislation (national security act, etc.) limits, if not suppresses, trade union activities.
(iv) The case concerning Thailand[4] merits attention. Whereas most cases brought to the committee for examination concern the alleged violation of trade union principles committed directly by the State, the Thai case in question, the origin of which is a murder of trade union leaders by the order of a private firm, concerns the duty of the State to *make the trade union principles respected.*
(v) It is also encouraging to note the growing role of the judicial procedures for the settlement of the trade union disputes. At the same time, however, these procedures take a lengthy period of time before the resolution of conflicts is achieved.

With regard to the Unesco Committee on Conventions and Recommendations which examines the complaints concerning the alleged violations of human rights which fall within Unesco's field of competence, only 7 complaints against Asian states were brought into consideration among approximately 100 cases since the establishment of the new procedure 104 EX/3.3 in 1978. Most of these 7 complaints were lodged not by the alleged victims themselves but by non-Asians and concern mainly the freedom of expression of university teachers and authors of books.

These normative procedures perhaps benefit only a very tiny fraction of the population suffering from all kinds of human rights violations and touch only a limited type of human rights violation which might not be represen-

---

[4] Case no. 1110, 226th session.

tative of the problems in the region. However, these human rights practices at the international level do contribute to creating a "conscious society" – conscious at least of the loss of prestige vis-à-vis the international community in the case of violations. In this sense, human rights are becoming slowly but progressively one of the "measures of civilisation" in Asia, as in other regions.

(3) Participation of non-governmental organizations in the international efforts for the protection and promotion of human rights

Other initiatives for co-operation for the protection and promotion of human rights in Asia have come rather from private organizations of lawyers, university professors, and human rights militants, as well as religious groups [5]. One such example of the role of a non-governmental initiative in establishing regional co-operation for the protection and promotion of human rights was the action by the Asia and Pacific branch of Amnesty International [6]. Another example is the Permanent Standing Committee on Human Rights created in August 1979 within Lawasia.

The classical approach to human rights is reflected in the activities of Lawasia. Lawasia, an organization of lawyers from sixteen nations of Asia and the Western Pacific region, authorized, at its conference in September 1979, the creation of a Human Rights Standing Committee. At its first meeting in Hong Kong in March 1980, the Committee decided that it would receive and investigate complaints of human rights violations forwarded by lawyers, bar associations and "other responsible voices of opinion" within the region. The Committee will examine facts, seek comments from the parties concerned and "present a report referring to both comments, together with its own conclusions".

An important statement of principles regarding the implementation of human rights in the Lawasia region was also adopted. Recognizing the different levels of economic development existing within the region, as well as differences of culture, religion, historical progress and educational standards, and taking full account of the existence from time to time of emergencies threatening the life of the nation, the committee established a list of rights which all countries within the region should respect at the present time. The list includes the right to life, the right of accused persons to a fair and public

---

[5] These movements are mostly Christian (Churches' Commission on International Affairs, World Council of Churches, World Student Christian Federation, Christian Conference on Asia (Asia Pacific) and Centre for the Progress of Peoples) but recently Islam reformists became actively concerned by human rights (for example, Muslim youth movement ABIM, in Malaysia).

[6] Report of the First Pacific Regional Conference of Amnesty International, ICM, September 1976, NS 132/76.

trial and to counsel of his choice, equality before the law, freedom from torture and degrading treatment, the right of detainees to prompt review by an independent and impartial tribunal and the right of every person to legal assistance.

This "minimum standard" approach to human rights has recently been criticized by other lawyers and university law professors in South and South-East Asia.

The attempt to adapt human rights defense to the Asian reality of massive misery and impoverishment created a collective concern of South and South-East Asian lawyers for the quest for alternative approaches to the ways and means of protecting and promoting human rights in Asia. At the Seminar organized by the International Commission of Jurists in Penang, Malaysia, in December 1981, a consensus was created among the participating lawyers of South-East Asia that the role of the lawyer should not be limited to regulating litigations, but should be more preventive and revolutionary in the sense that, by helping the poor organize themselves, the lawyer could contribute to the structural change of society [7]. Following the initiative taken by twelve lawyers [8], the Regional Council on Human Rights in Asia was founded on 18 February 1982 in the Philippines.

Underlying the new trends in the thinking and action concerning human rights, described above, is the will to reformulate human rights in a way that will enable them to become the motivating force of the impoverished masses of Asia, instead of remaining a culture of Western-educated lawyers. They try also to de-ideologize human rights by separating human rights rhetoric from international politics of alliances and foreign aid.

What has emerged from this criticism of human rights as tools perpetuating classes and foreign domination is a concept of self-reliance, *i.e.* to develop the ability to determine what one wants and how to get it. This amounts to the revendication of an "alternative model of development" where people participate not only in the process of development policy formulation, but also in the implementation of the policy by demanding the government's obligation to show, at each stage of its realisation, coherence of the policy, and responsiveness to the needs of the people.

In organizing the Regional Council on Human Rights in Asia on 18 February 1982, they agreed that one objective would be:

> "To adopt a regional declaration of human rights that reflects the culture, values and aspirations of the peoples of the region, to disseminate the declaration as widely as possible within the region, and to seek the support of the peoples of the region for the declaration".

---

[7] International Commission of Jurists, "Rural Development and Human Rights in South-East Asia" (Geneva, 1982).

[8] From Indonesia, Malaysia, Philippines and Thailand.

The members of the Council went over the final draft paragraph by paragraph, line by line and made many changes. On 9 December 1983, they unanimously approved the Declaration of the Basic Duties of ASEAN Peoples and Governments. They then proceeded as a body to the ASEAN Secretariat in Jakarta, to whom they submitted the Declaration for transmittal to, and adoption by, the governments of the region.

The most striking aspect of this Declaration is that it adopts the formula of "limiting" the power of the government and not of increasing the right of the individual. According to the drafters of the Declaration, this is due to the following reasons:

First, because they expected ASEAN governments to react to a declaration of human rights like bulls to a red rag. Second, because the international bill of rights adequately covers individual rights, and what needs to be stressed in third world countries, specially in Asia, are the duties of governments to their people.

Likewise, Art. V, Social Justice, and specially the requirement that governments take positive steps to equalize social services and the quality of life in rural and urban areas, and between and within geographical regions of each country, reflects the type of human rights problems which characterizes the region.

II. Some specific aspects of the approaches to human rights in Asia

(1) Fading away of the Western paradigm: 1950–1980

While the Asian States were busy consolidating national unity and pushing economic growth, certain lawyers, professors, and journalists in Asia were seriously involved in the international, intellectual discussion on human rights, organized mostly by international organizations[9]. These discussions constituted a meeting ground for Western lawyers and diplomats and well-educated and mostly Western trained scholars from Asia. Taking the Western institutions for the protection of human rights as a model, these discussions were characterized by two contradictory trends which they believed to be reconciliable with time: optimism concerning the importation of West-

[9] For example, Seminar on The Rule of Law in a Free Society organized by the International Commission of Jurists, New Delhi, 1959; Seminar on Human Rights in Developing Countries organized by the United Nations in Kabul in 1964; South East Asian and Pacific Conference of Jurists organized by the International Commission of Jurists "The Dynamic Aspects of the Rule of Law in the Modern Age", Bangkok, 1965; Round Table on Human Rights and Philosophical Traditions, organized by Unesco, Oxford, 1965; Seminar on Right to Freedom of Movement organized by the International Commission of Jurists, Bangalore, 1968.

ern models on the one hand, and awareness of the socio-economic, political and cultural obstacles of the traditional societies in Asia on the other hand. Establishing an Asian regional convention on human rights, as that in Western Europe, was under active consideration as though this was a most natural and logical form of protection of human rights at the regional level.

This hope of the intellectuals, however, somewhat lacked consideration for *realpolitik* in the region, as well as the practical implications of applying such an intergovernmental institution to the socio-economic conditions in Asia. Responding to the questionnaire sent by the Human Rights Commission, the Government of Japan cast doubts about the concrete aspect of realizing an Asian Commission for Human Rights, nonetheless accepting the idea of such an institution. According to their reply [10], such an attempt would be desirable only when the initiatives come from "Asian countries" themselves and not from the non-Asian big powers, and on the condition that the diversity of socio-economic and cultural conditions in the region is realistically taken into account.

The same project – the establishment of an Asian Commission for Human Rights – was discussed with equal enthusiasm at the 6th Lawasia Conference, as well as the UN Regional Seminar on the National, Local and Regional Arrangements for the Protection of Human Rights, held in Colombo, in June 1982.

It should be recognized, however, that the importance of the discussion on this subject has lost its weight in the light of the growth of other approaches to human rights protection in the Asian region in the seventies.

(2) Emerging approaches to human rights protection in Asia

The following approaches to human rights protection are gradually replacing the obviously imported models of human rights protection:

a) Concentration on concrete problems

It is undeniable that various forms of international co-operation are needed for the protection of human rights. Such international co-operation is particularly effective for the purpose of investigation and information gathering. However, these international activities could fall into their self-created trap, if they do not really contribute to the solution of human rights problems, thus creating a credibility gap between nice ideals and harsh reality.

There is an increasing tendency in most countries of Asia to deal with specific, concrete problems, rather than to indulge in the realm of generalities

---

[10] Human Rights Commission at 35th session, item 5, 24 January 1969. Document E/CN4/975/add. 1.

and ideals. In fact, massive poverty of the peoples of Asia, ethnic divisiveness and the poorly integrated social strata of Asian societies, together with recurring external aggression and internal subversion cannot be effectively dealt with by sporadic discussions nor by normative instruments of a general nature: these situations require everyday vigilance by those who are concerned, and specific remedies.

It is natural, then, that academic and activist organizations which deal with specific and concrete human rights problems have multiplied recently in Asia. A good example of such institutions is the organizations for legal aid for the rural and urban poor, the landless, the workers, oppressed women, and minority groups. The institutes for legal aid which started in Jakarta, Manila and in many cities of India are spreading to almost all the countries of South and South-East Asia and the Republic of Korea.

Other types of concrete problems dealt with by activist organizations include: child labour, communal violence, and pollution including the problems of nuclear fallout, etc.

(b) Reliance on internal remedies

Foreign domination of all kinds – military, economic and ideological – in the Asian region also gradually led to a distrust of international or regional institutions which have always been dominated by foreign powers. The will not to be the victim of ideological and military domination by the big powers or of economic domination by neighbouring countries gave rise to an attitude conducive to relying on national institutions for the protection of human rights or other solutions within the national framework.

This "nationalistic" tendency is illustrated by Japan's civil liberties bureau which shows a certain efficiency in solving those subtle human rights problems that are characteristic of particular types of human relations in Japan.

The recently established South-East Asian Council for Human Rights (a private organization located in Manila) is particularly interested in increasing the capacity for protecting common types of human rights problems in this sub-region, eliminating by implication, paternalistic influence and vested interests of the dominant powers in the region.

(c) Reliance on horizontal solidarity

The great risks involved in confronting government directly with its military-police coercive power led the human rights militants to create horizontal solidarity between the leaderships, often under the subtle guise of religious organizations, consumer protection, or civil protection from pollution, and those social categories which particularly suffer from human rights violations.

Thus, human rights protection in Asia often takes the form of civic or community defense without necessarily creating direct and permanent confrontation with government and without necessarily referring to human rights.

(d) Positive assessment of collective rights, especially of common property, of means of production and livelihood (water, land, forest resources)

The strictly individualistic character of the legal system which was introduced during the colonial period is under scrutiny, due to its shortcomings in solving the problems of massive poverty and of the access to the essentials: food, water, land and forest resources. Protracted legal court cases which concern individualistic problems led some lawyers to initiate proceedings which lead to out-of-court settlements. Problems of massive poverty often depend on agrarian or other structural reforms for their solution. A new legal approach to this problem, consisting of conscientizing the community concerned and developing plans to help the local community to stand up for their own rights, has been developed in South and South-East Asia. In order to cope with the paralyzing aspect of an often individualistic outlook of law, defence of specific collective rights over water, land and other means of production has been carried out, under the slogan "people's rights" or "people's law".

III. Suggestions for further study

The preceding overview of the particular situation challenging those concerned by the protection of human rights in Asia suggests that the following field of investigation could be explored with a view to improving the method of protection.

(1) Emergency legislation

In the examination of the complaints concerning the trade union rights (Part I (2)) brought to the ILO, it was indicated that emergency legislation is applied very broadly, without much distinction as to the conditions of its implementation, nor of the objects and degree to which it could be applied.

Granted that emergency legislation is sometimes a matter of necessity, there is room for improvement in its definition and conditions of application, in order to avoid abuse and mismanagement.

Emergency legislation should be more refined, for example, by distinguishing the degrees of its urgency (the state of emergency, state of siege, etc.), and clearly defined as to the scope of its application (zones, cases). Its application should be controlled judicially through the institutionalized mechanisms of checks and balances.

(2) Protection of non-nationals

The Asian region being a continent of stateless persons, refugees and migrants, research on nationality problems will be particularly important in the region. Human rights of non-nationals, stateless persons, refugees, foreigners) should be examined comparatively and protected accordingly.

(3) Implementation of humanitarian law for enhancing the respect for human rights

Related also to the abundance of movements, divisions and armed conflicts in Asia, it might be useful to exploit humanitarian law more effectively and especially the Geneva Convention of 1949 and its additional protocols. Attention should be drawn to certain provisions in situations of armed conflict that are not of an international character. For example, Art. 3 of the Geneva Convention of 12 August 1949 stipulates:

> "In the case of armed conflict not of an international character occurring in the territory of one of the High Contracting Parties, each Party to the conflict shall be bound to apply, as a minimum, the following provisions:
> (I) Persons taking no active part in the hostilities, including members of armed forces who have laid down their arms and those placed *hors de combat* by sickness, wounds, detention, or any other cause, shall in all circumstances be treated humanely, without any adverse distinction founded on race, colour, religion or faith, sex, birth or wealth, or any other similar criteria.
> To this end, the following acts are and shall remain prohibited at any time and in any place whatsoever with respect to the above-mentioned persons:
> (a) violence to life and person, in particular murder of all kinds, mutilation, cruel treatment and torture;
> (b) taking of hostages;
> (c) outrages upon personal dignity, in particular humiliating and degrading treatment;
> (d) the passing of sentences and the carrying out of executions without previous judgment pronounced by a regularly constituted court, affording all the judicial guarantees which are recognized as indispensable by civilized peoples".

It is known that the foregoing principles have been developed in Protocol II (1977) to the Geneva Conventions. Given the fact that almost all the

Asian countries ratified these Conventions of 1949, whereas only Afghanistan, Bangladesh, China, Laos, Republic of Korea und Vietnam ratified the 1977 Protocol to these Conventions and very few have done so in relation to the international instruments concerning human rights, should not the ways and means of implementing this humanitarian law approach be further explored, as a way of enhancing the respect for human rights?

(4) Personalisation of protection

The existence of a large number of poorly integrated ethnic groups, and the existence of rigid social hierarchies, determining social functions and roles of the individual, has many implications in the implementation of human rights. Human rights and, in particular, authority structures (family, religion, economic structure and political power) should be examined, with a view to identifying what social and cultural factors are important in determining the context of human rights in Asia. This type of research will lead to a reflexion on the diversity of possible solutions to human rights problems in the mostly ancient, traditional societies of Asia.

It seems important that the protection of the rights of specifically defined social categories (tribal groups, women, refugees) should be improved.

However, what is fundamentally lacking in Asia is the consciousness of being a "man" equal to other men, which is essential in resisting arbitrary disciplinary action by the administrative authorities. Awakening the individual's conscience to the need to defend fundamental rights would be the first step towards organizing movements for influencing governments effectively and for liberating people from the social disciplines imposed by the powers that be. The kind of individual who will be fostered by this evolution will be the only reference point for the human rights struggle and will make it possible to arrive at a genuine agreement among the different movements concerned with human rights.

Conclusion

The history of ideas and religions has shown that, beneath the thin layer of words, symbols and rituals which constitute, superficially, the ideas or religions, there are social practices which determine the ways in which the ideas and religions function in society.

Thus, the conquest of the world by ideas and religions depended, among other things, on the *rapports de force* which existed when different sets of ideas encountered. Whatever the complexity of the social forces which favoured or did not favour the acceptance of certain ideas or religions, there were always reasons why certain succeeded in certain social contexts.

From the above description of the development of the protection of human rights in Asia, it is clear that it is not the *rhetoric* of human rights which the peoples of Asia need and appreciate. It is the development of human rights *techniques* which would help defend their rights and solve their problems efficiently. Whether the defense of their rights is done in the name of human rights or under other names is less important than the real question of how the peoples of Asia would increase their capacity to defend themselves from oppression of all kinds.

Protection of Fundamental Human Rights within the Legal Order of the European Communities

JOSEPH H. H. WEILER

Introduction

Analysis of legal protection of fundamental human rights within the context of the European Communities does not lend itself easily to the specific model developed for dealing with States or even the Council of Europe system. The reasons are obvious enough [1].

In the first place, as is well known, the Treaties do not contain a Bill of Rights, a fact which has conditioned in a very specific way developments in this field. Secondly, despite the fact that the Community has seen a massive expansion of its fields of competences into areas well beyond the original common market conception, Community law and policy have not created major problems of protection of fundamental human rights. To be sure, the well known cases concerning human rights are a reminder that any legislative and administrative exercise of power can give rise to difficult problems concerning individual rights; moreover, we may safely assume that the cases which have reached the European Court do not represent the total number of potential or actual violations by the Community of individual rights. But none the less it is also a relatively safe assumption that in terms of actual *violation,* the Community does not create a major concern. (This of course does not necessarily mean that there might not be good reasons, despite a sound level of protection, to promote for example a more structured system of protection such as a Community Bill of Rights).

At the core of the Human Rights "issue" in the European Community is a basic tension – perhaps even a paradox. To understand this tension is to understand much of the underlying dynamics of legal and political developments in this field.

---

[1] There is an immense literature on this subject. For the most recent overall review see *Dauses,* La protection des droits fondamentaux dans l'ordre juridique communautaire, 20 Rev. Trim. Dr. Eur. 16 (1984).

On the one hand, Human Rights, and the machinery for their protection represent an *integrational* value and instrument. Basic freedoms enshrined and protected by law are among the elements which give society and its members a sense of identity. The very nebulous, yet existent feeling of belonging, say, to what may be called Western Democracies may be traced in part to this protection. And in non-unitary systems such as federations, "federal human rights" have played a strong integrational role.

On the other hand, protection of Human Rights is typically designed to protect the individual against public authority; against even majority rule. In the context of the European Community then, the protection afforded the individual will be *against* the Community and its policies. Clearly there is no problem when the protection prevents bad faith *abuse* of power. But to be meaningful, protection will have to extend on occasion even against policies adopted in good faith to further the goals of European Integration.

The Court, and other bodies dealing with Human Rights in the context of European Integration, might well find themselves in difficult policy dilemmas in trying to reconcile these conflicting purposes of a higher law of Human Rights in the EEC.

The Human Rights "saga" of the European Community is well known and does not need an elaborate reiteration. Briefly stated, in the absence of a written Bill of Rights, the European Court of Justice, in an exercise of bold judicial activism created a higher law superstructure of fundamental human rights, to be culled from different sources and against which the acts of the Community organs could be reviewed in the normal course of judicial review provided by the Treaty. In the course of this paper I shall outline briefly the salient points of this development. More interesting in my view will be to examine not simply the broad phenomenon but also in a detailed fashion the actual practice by the Court, in a specific case, of the method it has developed. Of particular interest is in fact the "comparative method" which is at the basis of the Court's jurisprudence. This paper will pay attention then both to some of the synthetic/systemic issues raised in this field as well as to the more detailed clinical practice.

I propose to deal first with some historical jurisprudential dimensions concerning the background to the development of a judge made bill of rights. Some of the historical material remains relevant today as well. I shall then examine closely one paradigmatic case of the European Court of Justice. In a third brief section I shall say a few words on the relationship of the EEC to the ECHR system. In a fourth section I shall speculate about some future developments in this area.

A. The Historical Dimension

Why does the Community not have a written Bill of Rights? Some Speculations

As mentioned above, neither the Treaty of Paris nor the Treaty of Rome contains a specific list or Bill of enumerated fundamental human rights to check the Community organs and provide criteria for judicial review. By speculating on the reasons for this omission we might identify some problems for future development.

Traditionally, resistance to enumerated Constitutional bills of rights is tied to a principled resistance to judicial review as such[2]. This does not, however, explain the lacunae in the Community. In both Treaties we find well-developed systems of judicial review particularly as regards the activities of Community organs[3]. In the absence of an authentic "legislative history" of the Treaties[4] we must try to explain this omission by reference to the political climate prevailing at the time of their conclusion and to the original conception of the Community by its fathers. Inevitably, this analysis is speculative.

As regards the Coal and Steel Community, several inter-related factors may afford a plausible explanation for the lack of a Bill of Rights. Despite the overt political origin of the venture, evident both in the Schuman declaration and the Preamble to the Treaty of Paris, the Coal and Steel Community was perceived as confined within limited economic parameters. The High Authority was given law-making powers, but the subjects of this law were conceived as primarily large industrial undertakings and the Member States themselves. The traditional concept of human rights, in particular, seemed in the immediate post War period to have little bearing on the prospective activities of the Coal and Steel Community. One must not forget that in that epoch the notion of "fundamental" social and economic rights were far less developed and in any event seemed less pressing and relevant in the wake of World War II and the tasks of reconstruction. Thus, there was probably no overt intention to exclude guarantees from the individual. Indeed, it was in that very epoch that the European Convention on Human Rights was adopted, in an exemplary, perhaps unique, manifestation of national and governmental self-restraint. *Probably the very same sentiments which explain the voluntary association within the ECSC explain the subscription to the ECHR.* The two ventures, however, must have seemed distinct rather than co-extensive.

---

[2] Cf. *J. Jaconnelli,* Enacting a Bill of Rights (1980).

[3] See Arts. 169, 170, 171, 173, 175, 176, 177, 184, 215 EEC.

[4] The *travaux* of the Treaties establishing the European Community were not published. This is an interesting indication of the constitutional rather than international nature of the Treaties.

Speculation becomes more complicated in relation to the EEC. The Community, after all, is active in broad fields, albeit economic, where the need for explicit protection of fundamental rights might have been foreseen. The Treaty of Rome, which contains chapters on social policy, movement of migrants, rights of establishment and the like could hardly have been regarded as immune to violation of fundamental human rights – even the traditional ones. Thus, the possible political reasons for the omission of a Bill of Rights, excluding the unlikely explanation of mere forgetfulness, must be more subtle.

I would first return to the actual provisions for judicial review in the Treaty. It is somewhat surprising that the Treaty, influenced in its judicial and legal provisions by French law, embraces such a developed system of judicial review of legislation; such a system was long alien, even anathema, to the French tradition[5]. A closer look at these provisions reveals that their purpose was not so much to subject the Community organs to a higher law, but rather to guarantee that the Community and its organs would not overstep their jurisdictional limits. The language of these articles, principally Art. 173, which bases review on the grounds of "infringement of this Treaty", "misuse of power" and "lack of competence" seems to confirm this interpretation. Judicial review in the Community was thus more akin to the Canadian model of federalism in which the preservation of the distinction between central and constituent-unit areas of competence was the hall mark of the system. The judicial review provisions of the Treaty were intended in large measure to protect against encroachments by the Community of the rights of the Member State, rather than the rights of individuals.

If that was the spirit of the original system of judicial review it is little wonder that a Bill of Rights would not have seemed particularly necessary[6].

There might however be yet another explanation for the omission of a Bill of Rights which may be of relevance even today. It may be that in the political climate prevailing in 1957 at least some of the Member States were fearful of any expansion in the powers to be granted to the Community's central organs. In ratifying the Treaty of Rome, the Member States, no longer as idealistic as in the immediate post-war era, were committing themselves to an unprecedented experiment in contemporary international history. A Bill of Rights would have offered a means of curtailing even further the liberty of Community organs. Paradoxical as it may sound, the Member States might have feared that the very listing of rights that *must not be* encroached upon

---

[5] Cf. *Cappelletti,* The Mighty Problem of Judicial Review and the Contribution of Comparative Analysis, Legal Issues of European Integration 1 (1979).

[6] Canadian judicial review under the BNA was largely based on a similar conception. The limited measure of judicial review for infringement of fundamental rights in Canada usually turned on the jurisdictional propriety of the alleged violation rather than its substantive correctness. See *J. D. Whyte & W. R. Lederman,* Canadian Constitutional Law (1977).

might have become an invitation to extend enumerated powers and competences to the limits of those rights. We should not forget that in the proposals for the European Political Community of 1953, human rights were to have pride of place. The issue must have been discussed at least in the context of the Treaty of Rome and for some reason discarded. The argument that a question of competences was one basis for rejecting a bill of rights is not as fanciful as it may at first seem. We find a clear analogue in the legislative history, and the interpretation thereof, of the Bill of Rights in the American Constitution. In trying to interpret the reason for enacting the delphic Ninth Amendment (The enumeration in the Constitution of certain rights shall not be construed to deny or disparage others retained by the people) several Supreme Court Justices[7] have noted the Founding Fathers' fear that, in the words of *Ely*, "... the inclusion of a Bill of Rights in the Constitution would be taken to imply that federal power was not in fact limited to [those powers granted by the Constitution], that instead it extended all the way up to the edge of the rights stated in [the newly introduced Bill of Rights][8]". Thus, the very listing of limitations on the authority of the central power may undermine the principle of enumeration by implying that the state (or, in our case, the EEC) has inherent power to the extent of those limitations.

We might find an even more deep-rooted explanation of the omission – one that touches the very architecture of the Community legal order. Today we are habituated to thinking of the Community as the fully fledged constitutional order which it has become. In 1957, neither the doctrine of direct effect nor the doctrine of supremacy had emerged. If they were nascent in the Treaty, as the Court later claimed, they were certainly very well hidden, and introduction of these concepts involved a series of daring acts of judicial activism. The simple fact remains that in 1957 the protection of the individual from the Community measures allegedly violative of his or her fundamental rights would have seemed to rest with the national orders. Violations by the Community would have been judged within the national legal orders according to the yardstick provided by each Member State's system, both under national constitutional law and the ECHR. A Community measure coming into conflict with such national guarantees would be subordinated to them. An individual could simply refuse to comply with an allegedly violative Community measure and have as a valid defence the infringement by that measure of standards accepted in his or her national order. Or, at worst, the Member State concerned could enact a national statute abrogating the offensive Community measure.

---

[7] E. g. Justice Black and Madison himself. See *J. Ely*, Democracy and Distrust at 34 n. 83 (1980).

[8] *Ibid.* at 34. This of course is not the total explanation for the enactment of the Amendment.

Finally, there is the simple but plausible explanation that in the post-war period socio-economic diversity had developed to such an extent that reaching a consensus on a common bill of socio-economic rights already seemed impossible. Perhaps it was better to leave such an emotive issue outside the Treaty rather than risk national parliamentary opposition at the ratification stage.

All theses factors retain their relevance today, at least in the context of discussion of any radical tampering with the current situation, and may be worth further discussion in conference.

Protection of Human Rights: The Judicial Evolution

Be these historical speculations as they may, we may turn now to a recapitulation of the actual evolution of legal protection of fundamental human rights in the Community order, an evolution in which the European Court has been the major protagonist.

The landmarks of this judicial itinerary are among the most famous in the contemporary history of European legal integration. In *Stork*[9] and *Geitling*[10] decided in 1958 and 1959, the judges (but not, interestingly, the prophetic Advocate General Lagrange)[11] rejected an invitation to review and censure a Community ECSC measure allegedly violating a basic right recognized in one or another of the Member States. Several reasons may explain the Court's reticence at that time. The material context of these cases – and, inevitably the outlook of the Court – was within the range of the ECSC. To break into the emotive language of human rights and higher law might have seemed somewhat incongruous. But the issue is not merely semantical. The Treaty of Paris was much less of a *Traité Cadre* than the Treaty of Rome: The scope for teleological interpretation would appear to be more limited at least within the bounds of judicial propriety.

The reasons for this judicial reticence go even deeper. The fusion of the Community and national legal orders was limited and fragile. At that time the ECSC was perceived by the Court as an autonomous entity. The Court's task was to protect the separation of the ECSC and the Member States and to defend the High Authority's independence *vis-a-vis* national governments. Later, in the EEC, the main threat to the independence of the Commission (the successor of the High Authority) clearly seemed to come from its sister Community organ, the Council of Ministers. In *Stork* the major threat as perceived by the Court was in forcing the High Authority to look over its shoulders at each step to ensure that it was not infringing on constitutional guarantees of the member States. The Court, in the oft-quoted passage from

[9] Case 1/58 [1959] ECR 17.
[10] Joined Cases 36, 37, 38 & 40/59 [1960] ECR 423.
[11] *Ibid.* at 450.

Stork[12], clearly affirms these notions of separation and autonomy:

> "[T]he Court is only required to ensure that in the interpretation and application of the Treaty ... the law is observed ... Consequently, the High Authority is not empowered to examine a ground of complaint which maintains that when it adopted its decision, it infringed principles of German Constitutional Law".

It should not be forgotten that in the absence of a clearly established doctrine of supremacy, there would be little to stop the review of Community actions under national constitutional law from expanding to *any* national norm. (In fact, in the *Stork* decision one finds the first indication of the subsequent supremacy decisions.) Finally, this judicial reticence reflected not only the Court's perception of the Community order. It also reflected the Court's self-perception. Other cases from the same period[13] suggest that the Court saw itself much as a traditional international tribunal. The Court's self-limiting – not to say self-deprecating – characterization of itself in *Stork* thus typifies, in the area of human rights, the international phase in Community development.

Ten years later we find the same Court[14] speaking a different language. Faced with a similar dilemma of an individual challenge to Community Law on the grounds of violation of fundamental rights the Court retracted its earlier reasoning and held that protection of fundamental human rights did form part of those legal interests which the Court could and would protect. Moreover, the Court held that the extent of these rights was to be ascertained by a comparative distillation of the very constitutional legal orders of the Member States, including international treaties (notably the ECHR) which hitherto had been considered irrelevant. The result was to be a homogeneous Community body of law[15].

The specifics of the Court's comparative distillation method are unclear. To date, the Court has identified several sources for the elaboration of its own norms. Some rights are directly traceable to the Treaty itself[16], some derive from the constitutional traditions of the Member States[17], and some

---

[12] At 26.

[13] E.g. Case 9/56 *Meroni* [1957–1958] ECR 149 and Case 8/55 *Fedechar* [1954–1955] ECR 299.

[14] Naturally the composition of both the Court and the Legal Service of the Commission will have changed somewhat in the intervening period. One cannot altogether forget this personal element. Cf. *Stein*, 75 AJIL 1 (1981).

[15] The court casts its net wide by specifying that Treaties might include ones in the elaboration of which the Member States participated even if they were not subsequently ratified. This, it is widely believed, was a result of the very late French final acceptance of the ECHR.

[16] E.g. some forms of non-discrimination. See Arts. 7 and 119 EEC.

[17] See discussion *infra*.

from the international treaties in which Member States have collaborated or to which they are signatories: principally the European Convention on Human Rights[18]. The inclusion of the ECHR is significant since it gives the Court a concrete source – akin to the American Bill of Rights – on which to build its own normative basis. And yet this abundance of sources serves to complicate rather than facilitate the actual process of distillation. Later I shall return to some of the problems inherent in this process.

Whence the authority of the Court to subject the Community's legislative activity to review on the basis of an unwritten higher law? Was this process legitimate or a judicial indulgence in unwarranted activism?

For opponents of judicial activism, this situation conjures up the classic risk of a *gouvernement des juges.* In the community context, however, this classical conflict is largely fallacious. Judicial activism is often characterized as subverting the principle of majoritarian decision-making. In the Community context however, the legislative process is hardly majoritarian. The legislative process of the Community influenced only slightly by the European Parliament, controlled increasingly by civil servants in the form of the COREPER and dominated by an executive only notionally controllable by the national chambers, is a far cry from a representative democratic process. If the new jurisprudence of the Court represents a *gouvernement des juges* it is designed to control a *gouvernement des fonctionnaires.* We have here one explanation of the transformation of the Court's attitude since the days of *Stork.* The absence of a written Bill of Rights coupled with a decline in the accountability of the Community and the emergence of a "democratic deficit" can on this construction both explain the motive of the Court and deflect the classic objection to this type of judicial activism in the Community situation.

As to the legal basis for the Court's evolution, the concept of "general principles of law" in a *Traité Cadre* is probably wide enough to lend itself to such an interpretation. There can be an attempt to find a textual basis for the Court's jurisprudence in either Art. 173 EEC or in Art. 164 EEC[19]. But inevitably although the Court is charged with reviewing the legality of legislation with a reference to any rule of law relating to the application of the Treaty (173) or, more significantly in 164 that in the application of the Treaty the "law is observed" (which might suggest a higher law), both routes beg to some extent the question. The Court has been content to leave the precise legal basis vague and it is more honest to recognize the new jurisprudence for

[18] On the position of the Convention and its application as EEC law, see *Mendelson,* The Impact of European Community Law on the Implementation of the European Convention on Human Rights, 3 Yearbook of European Law 99 (1983).

[19] Art. 173 EEC mentions the infringement of any rule of law relating to the application of the Treaty as a criterion of judicial review. Art. 164 EEC states: "The Court of Justice shall ensure that in the interpretation and application of this Treaty the law is observed".

what it is: A certain judicial leap rooted more in the political philosophy of the Community and its Member States than in strict legal grounds. (The notion that the Community could not have received *competences* from its Member States to act in a manner inconsistent with their own constitutions is seductive, but must be rejected both in international legal terms and, as the Court will painfully point out, as too strict a basis for its jurisdiction).

The ambit of operation of the EEC is perceptibly wider than that of the ECSC. The language of human rights, in a functional situation such as *Stauder*[20] does not seem so incongruous. The text of the Treaty of Rome itself is conducive to the type of judicial comparative technique evoked as a solution to the source of human rights. Art. 215 EEC, to give the clearest example, explicitly refers to the comparative method and to the national legal orders as a source of law. Legally, then, there would seem to be a sound ground on which to found the Courts caselaw.

But the justification of judicial extension as an attempt to close the democratic deficit constitutes only part – perhaps not even a major part – of the explanation for the Court's change of heart and may even be a rationalization. The prime motivation for judicial extension was not, I believe, simply a benevolent interest in human rights nor even in the democratic structure of the Community. At the source of the mutation one finds the same protective sentiment which induced the Court to *reject* the fundamental right initiative ten years earlier. The difference is that in the new constitutional configuration of the Community – a configuration to the evolution of which the Court itself had contributed – the expedient reply to the question of extending the scope of the Court's review was affirmative rather than negative. For, as we know, in the intervening years, the Court had instilled the central concept of supremacy in the normative structure of the Community. In its own self-perception another profound metamorphosis had taken place. No longer did the Court see itself as an international tribunal determined to preserve the *autonomy* of the system it oversaw, but rather a constitutional Court of a supranational order determined to preserve the integrity and unity of the system it had evolved. The "surface language" of the Court in *Stauder* and its progeny is the language of human rights. The "deep structure" is all about supremacy. The Court anticipated the threat to the doctrine of supremacy and the integrity of the Community system, later realized by the German and Italian Constitutional Courts, posed by national jurisdiction over alleged human-rights violations by the Community. *Stauder, Nold* and *Internationale Handelgesellschaft* become thus in the political circumstances of the late 60's and early 70's an inevitable sequel to *Van Gend en Loos, Costa* v. *ENEL* and their progeny: An attempt to protect the concept of supremacy threatened because of the apparent (largely theoretical) inadequate protection of fundamental human rights in the original Treaty system.

[20] Case 29/69 [1969] ECR 419.

In this light the Court's reiterated statements in favour of human rights must be evaluated with caution. If the Court's act of judicial protection is not motivated principally by solicitude for human rights, it may result as regards some Member States in a removal of guarantees at the national level. To allay fears of abuse, the Court will have to demonstrate that it is willing to use the new power to annul measures backed by the concerted will of the Council of Ministers. To be sure, it has done so on many occasions on lesser criteria than violation of human rights. And the Council of the 80's is not the fragile High Authority of the 60's. But here lies, I submit the unresolved issue of the legitimacy of this particular instance of judicial activism. If it is true that the Court developed its human-rights doctrine to protect the integrity of the Community legal order rather than the individual, will it, in a case pitching on the one hand human rights and on the other hand an *important* Community policy, be ready to prefer the individual to the Community? One may wonder first whether justice may be seen to be done – in the type of conflict stipulated above – when the adjudicator is so committed as to suggest a judgment *in re sua.* Second one may wonder, and there are indications in the Court's jurisprudence that this question is not entirely theoretical[21], whether justice will in fact be done.

One cannot conclude this brief historical section without a final illustration of the interaction between the various Community political actors, among which we must clearly, for present purposes, include the Court. In 1979, the Commission proposed the accession of the Community to the ECHR. Various interpretations, which need not concern us here have been put on this suggestion and its merits. It would appear that the recommendation is for the time being unlikely to be implemented. One effect of the proposal would be to impose the European Court of Human Rights above the European Court of Justice in matters concerning the adjudication of allegedly violative Community measures. The Court, by its very position, had no way of commenting fully and openly on this suggestion. But in its judicial activity since publication of the Memorandum of the Commission it has striven, as I shall show below, to show its superiority as an adjudicator *vis-a-vis* the Court in Strasbourg. Thus, although there was no explicit criticism of the Court in the Memorandum of the Commission, it will indeed have had a positive effect it induces the Court to put more substance into the framework it has created.

---

[21] There is sometimes the feeling that the Court is more lenient with Community organs than with the Member States. Cf. *Schermers,* in: T. Sandalow & E. Stein, Courts and Free Markets (1983). For a full discussion with reference to cases see *Weiler,* Eurocracy and Distrust, 61 Washington L. R. 1103 (1986) esp. note 48.

B. Judicial Adjudication of Fundamental Human Rights in the Community Legal Order: The Case of Hauer

I do not propose to engage in a detailed case-by-case analysis of the human rights jurisprudence of the European Court but instead to examine one paradigmatic instance of that jurisprudence with a view to highlighting both the technique and the problems inherent in the Community jurisdiction.

Hauer v. *Land Rheinland-Pfalz* [Case 44/79 (1979) ECR 3727] although not the latest in judicial pronouncements affords indications of all the major themes and can thus serve as a useful case-study. In particular, this case deals with a subject matter – property rights – which is part of the living matrix of Community activity and may be considered more typical than say the odd case on religious freedom [22] or the like. The case came to the European Court by way of a request for a preliminary ruling by the Verwaltungsgericht Neustadt an der Weinstrasse. For our purposes only some of the facts are relevant. The plaintiff, Hauer, was contesting within the German system of administrative law, a decision by the German authorities to deny her authorization to plant vines on a plot of land which she owned in the region of Bad Durkheim. This denial was based, *inter alia* on a Council Regulation (1162/76) which prohibited for a period of three years all new planting of vines.

Hauer's claim was based in part on the contention that the regulation could not apply to cases such as her own since her application was lodged before promulgation of the regulation. I shall not deal with this aspect of the case.

In the second place she claimed that the regulation amounted to a violation of her fundamental rights to property and to her right freely to pursue a trade or profession. She further contended that these rights were guaranteed by Arts. 12 and 14 of the Grundgesetz of the Federal Republic. This last point is of significance since, as is well known, the Federal Constitutional Court of the Federal Republic had held that secondary Community legislation in violation of fundamental rights protected by the Grundgesetz may not apply within the German legal order.

Potentially thus the case raised issues going not merely to the human rights question but to the integrational underpinning of the Community order which, as we have seen, constituted the principal, even if not exclusive, rationale for judicial activity in this field.

---

[22] See e.g. Case 130/75 *Prais* [1976] ECR 1589. And see generally, *Mendelson,* The European Court of Justice and Human Rights, 1 Yearbook of European Law 125 (1981).

C. The Principles and Method of the Court

The treatment of the question by the European Court is truly classical and worth following step by step.

Step 1 (Recital 14 of the Judgment):

> "As the Court declared in its judgment of 17 December, 1970, *Internationale Handelsgesellschaft* [1970] ECR 1125, the question of a possible infringement of fundamental rights by a measure of the Community institutions can only be judged in the light of Community law itself. The introduction of special criteria for assessment stemming from the legislation or constitutional law of a particular Member State would, by damaging the substantive unity and efficacy of Community law, lead inevitably to the destruction of the unity of the Common Market and the jeopardizing of the Cohesion of the Community".

Comment: In this curt opening statement are already encapsulated some basic themes. It is interesting to note that the first point taken up by the Court is not the fundamental rights issue as such (which only comes up in the next recital of the judgement) but the constitutional-integrational issue. The Court affirms the autonomy and supremacy of the Community legal order ("... can only be judged in the light of Community law itself") and then gives the rationale: the danger of damaging a) the substantive unity of Community law; b) the efficacy of Community law; c) the unity of the Common Market; d) the cohesion of the Community.

The idea of uniformity of Community law runs deep in the jurisprudence of the Court. Any differentiation which corresponds to national boundaries is always regarded as anathema. In the notion of substantive unity one might also find a commitment to equality before the law. The unity of the Common Market is a more functional and specific concern: The Court cannot, in its view, allow different economic operators, by virtue of their location in this or that Member State, to benefit or suffer from a differentiated regime affecting their activities as governed by Community law. This would run counter to the notion of creating one marketplace. The reference to the efficacy of Community law is also easy enough to grasp. Bowing to the specificities of this or that national legal order will destroy the cardinal principle of supremacy. Finally, in the notion of cohesion of the Community the Court may simply be summing up all earlier considerations or alluding to a wider, meta-legal notion: the sense of one community which can only be instilled as a *social reality* in a system which applies equally across the board.

These principles are not, however, without their difficulties, albeit on a theoretical rather than practical level.

a) Although the Court boldly refers to the *Internationale Handelsgesellschaft* saga, it must be remembered that it was in that context that the German Federal Constitutional Court launched its challenge to the Community order. To be sure, in a subsequent decision the harshness of the challenge was attenuated, but, strictly speaking, the German position has not changed. What is often called the problem of maximal and minimal standards (to which I shall return) namely the possibility of the Community standard "falling short" of the German one poses itself here in a manner which would not arise in the context of cases coming for most other jurisdictions. The Court, in theory was taking a risk (in my view justified) with the very notion of Community cohesion. Since, if Hauer, unsatisfied with the Court's decision were to appeal further (within the German system) to the Federal Constitutional Court, the scene would be open to a veritable constitutional crisis if the latter court were to give a wider interpretation to the aforementioned rights. It is partly at least as a result of this danger that the European Court, in the latter parts of the Hauer judgment will try, unlike many other human rights cases, to demonstrate the thoroughness and method of its treatment, as if to give an object lesson in human rights jurisprudence.

b) The question of uniformity and unity gives rise to a series of more delicate problems. Firstly there is the question of jurisprudential consistency by the European Court itself. In a line of cases concerning Member State procedural law, the European Court has allowed the application of such procedures in the vindication of *European Community rights,* even if the result is that individuals contesting national measures as violative of the same Community law, may end up with totally different results depending on the specific national procedural law in which the case takes place. The results might be affected by different national rules on time-limitations for bringing an action (ranging in the different Member States from one month to thirty years), on quantum of damages, and on eligibility for recovering taxes unjustly imposed[23]. It is true that the origin of this differentiation is rooted in national *procedural* law whereas in *Hauer* and other human rights cases the Court alludes to *substantive* unity. This distinction is not altogether convincing. Rights have a meaning only in terms of the remedy available for their vindication. The substantive unity of the right if accompanied by disunity of the remedy becomes a hollow concept. I would certainly not wish to suggest here that the Court was wrong in allowing the prevalence of national procedural law. However, the list of evils it lists in *Hauer* which could result from the adoption of "... special criteria for assessment stemming from the legislation or constitutional law of a particular Member State" loses much of its force when confronted with this other line of cases. (Procedural law is after all also based on national legislation.) The Community seems to have survived despite this differentiation.

---

[23] See e.g. Case 33/76 *Rewe* [1976] ECR 1980 and its progeny. For an extensive discussion, see *Weiler,* Il sistema comunitario europeo (1984) Part III.

A second issue related to unity and uniformity may be articulated as follows: Assume that the standard of judicial review adopted by the Court in "... the light of Community law itself" differs from the normal standard in the specific jurisdiction. Assume further that it is a "higher standard" (though on this issue of High and Low standards I shall offer a critique below) so that the type of danger possibly arising in the German (and Italian) context does not pose itself. It remains the case that two different standards will have been introduced into the *national* legal system depending on whether a specific violation emanates from the Community authorities or from Member State authorities operating within their own sphere of competences. To the extent that we regard Community law as "the law of the land" this disunity might be considered no less troubling.

Step 2 (Recital 15 of Judgment):

> "The Court also emphasized in the judgment cited, and later in the judgment of 14 May 1974, *Nold* [1974] ECR 491, that fundamental rights form an integral part of the general principles of the law, the observance of which it ensures; that in safeguarding those rights, the Court is bound to draw inspiration from constitutional traditions common to the Member States, so that measures which are incompatible with the fundamental rights recognized by the constitutions of those States are unacceptable in the Community; and that, similarly, international treaties for the protection of human rights on which the Member States have collaborated or of which they are signatories, can supply guidelines which should be followed within the framework of Community law".

Comment: Here the Court states both its principled commitment to the protection of human rights and, in abstract terms, the method by which it will operate in culling the rights in the absence of a written code.

First, in the notion of "general principles of law" which may be found in the Treaty itself, the Court provides the formal legal justification for this exercise. Courts cannot, with no such formal basis, interfere with the actions of legislatures.

More interestingly is the outline of method. The theoretical difficulties of the Court's task are quite evident in its statement.

a) There is a manifest melange of imperative and facultative language:

1. "The Court is *bound* [imperative] to draw *inspiration* [facultative] from constitutional traditions ...".

The force of the binding nature loses somewhat if it is simply inspiration which is sought. We understand, however, the Court's reluctance to draw more than "inspiration"; to go further than that would contradict indirectly its earlier statement that it will not "[introduce] special criteria for assessment stemming from the legislation or constitutional law of a particular

Member State". Moreover, the constitutional traditions of the Member States are the obvious place to seek this inspiration. Not simply because it will be there that one may be able to find a *European* content to human rights; but, from a more juridical point of view, since the legislator of the Community is a body consisting of the Governments of the Member States, each one of which committed from the municipal point of view to a respect for national standards (where those exist), the Court finds another legal underpinning for its exercise. Finally, from a juridico-political point of view the Court in this statement poses itself as a guardian against abuse of the Community system by the executives of the Member States. It will not allow them to do on the European level, free of the shackles of a controlling parliamentary chamber, that which they could not do (in terms of violation of fundamental rights) in the national context.

2. The tension between imperative and facultative language is accentuated in the next statement. If it is only *inspiration* that the Court is committed to, how can it then state:

> "... so that measures which are incompatible with the fundamental rights recognized by the constitutions of those States are unacceptable in the Community?".

The Court seems to backtracking into an imperative obligation to judge each Community measure in the light of fundamental rights recognized by the national constitutions and to strike down measures which are incompatible with any of them. Would this not be, *de facto,* introduction of the previously rejected "special criteria"? One is almost pushed to the conclusion that in *substance* the Court will strive to ensure that no Community measure in fact violates a constitutional guarantee in any of the Member States. (Though, this, as I shall explain below, might, at least in theory not always be possible). Its real concern is *jurisdictional:* It, the Court of Justice, should be trusted with this charge and the national legal order (and national courts) must accept its interpretation of these standards (which in any event are mostly broadly stated principles open to interpretative differentiation).

3. The same tensions emerge with reference to the other source of inspiration – international treaties and principally the European Convention for the Protection of Human Rights and Fundamental Freedoms. Here the Court alludes to *"guidelines"* offered by these instruments which *"should"* be followed. It is unlikely that the Court will, in *substance* ever allow a Community measure to violate a provision of the ECHR, but *jurisdictionally* it insists on interpreting the instruments itself.

b) The second difficulty with the statement of method stems from the word "common":

> "The Court is bound to draw inspiration from constitutional traditions *common* to the Member States ..." (emphasis added)

Once more, on a theoretical level, the problems are readily apparent. What about those standards which are not "common"? This may be illustrated better by reference to the issue of so-called "standards" which has been so prominent in the literature discussing protection of fundamental human rights in the Community. Traditionally, as we saw above, the problem is posed thus: what should happen if, in its distillation of the national and international traditions, the Court should arrive at a standard which is "lower" than that prevailing in one of the Member States. It would seem that the problem is solved if the Community and its Court would strive to pitch its standard at the highest level (within the abovementioned margin of interpretation) thereby avoiding a conflict with national systems with high standards.

However, this contradistinction of "high" and "low" standards is in my view erroneous. Almost invariably human rights issues posit a conflict between communal (state/local region/organization of states) and individual interest which must be balanced. Human right jurisprudence typically differs in the articulation of various balancing tests. The *Hauer* case offers a useful example: the right to free use of property is always balanced by societal concerns about the use of such property. In some cases the societal interest can be so overriding as to demand the actual confiscation of the property (with varying degrees of compensation and subject to principled decisions – proportionality etc.) as in the case of cumpulsory purchase for major social construction work. The collective "good" of a community is acknowledged not simply as a legitimate curb on individual rights but as a manifestation of a value which has comparable weight. In the final analysis taxation is also a manifestation of this principle[24].

In some societies, depending on the political and social culture the tendency would be to favour the assertion of the individual right to property by restricting the ability to interfere with that right. In other societies there might be a tendency to favour the vindication of the societal interest by rendering restrictive use of property easier.

The dilemma of non-"common" traditions cannot therefore be simply solved by an indication that the Community and the Court should aim for the "highest" standard. It is true that in most constitutional documents the *individual* right to property would be the value asserted, with the tendency perhaps to aim at a transnational protection corresponding to the "highest" level of individual protection of property rights. But such a "high" *individual* protection signifies of course a limitation on the possibility to assert the *societal* interest in property control. This "high" individual protection might therefore be problematic to a state which strikes a different balance which favours the collective right. A so-called "low" level of individual protection might signify a considered value choice between collectivity and individuality

[24] See *Bellini,* La tutela dei diritti fondamentali nell'ordinamento comunitario secondo la sentenza Hauer, 64 Riv. dir. int. 318 (1981).

with a corresponding stake in such a balance and an explicit or implicit rejection of the *values* underlying a different choice.

No clearer is this dilemma in the context of, say, the abortion issue (which of course does not touch the EEC and its Court). Is there any sense in speaking of a "low" or "high" standard as between those systems which favour in their balancing exercise the rights of the woman to autonomy, and privacy or those which favour the rights of the foetus to life?

At a theoretical level then, we see that the formula of the Court throws up a variety of inconsistencies and problems, the solution to which is not readily apparent. The life of law, however, as the saying goes, is not logic but experience, and it is to the practical solution in the *Hauer* case which we may now turn.

Step 3 (Recitals 17–19)

The Court distinguishes between the right to property and the freedom to pursue a trade; it deals first, and extensively, with the first of the two.

a) The Court first repeats its basic philosophy and methodology in this specific context:

> "The right to property is guaranteed in the Community legal order in accordance with the ideas common to the constitutions of the Member States, which are also reflected in the first Protocol to the [ECHR]".

Interestingly, the Court deals first with the protection afforded through the ECHR. After citing Art. 1 of the Protocol (Every ... person is entitled to the peaceful enjoyment of his possessions. No one shall be deprived of his possessions except in the public interest and subject to the conditions provided for by law and by the general principles of international law. The preceding provisions shall not, however, in any way impair the right of a State to enforce such laws as it deems necessary to control the use of property in accordance with the general interest or to secure the payment taxes or other contributions or penalties), the Court simply notes that the Council Regulation would come within the right of the State "to enforce such laws as it deems necessary to control the use of property in accordance with the general interest".

Two *comments* might be in order. First, it is clear that for the purposes of its decision the Court regards itself subject to the requirements of the Protocol despite the fact that the Community as such is not a signatory. Secondly, it is in my view evident that the Court regards the Convention and its Protocols as mere starting points, as the first and not most difficult steeplechase which the Community regulation has to pass. The provisions in the Convention, in the eyes of the Court do not

> "enable a sufficiently precise answer to be given to the question submitted by the Verwaltungsgericht (Recital 19)".

Much has been written and discussed as regards the relationship between the Community legal order and the ECHR. The indication in the *Hauer* case is that the European Court of Justice regards itself as able to give a protection which in substance is superior to that afforded by the Convention.

Step 4: The Comparative Method – phase one (Recitals 20–22)

In Recital 20 the Court establishes the basis for its comparative analysis.

> "[I]n order to be able to answer [the question], it is necessary to consider also the indications provided by the constitutional rules and practices of the nine [as they then were] Member States".

Comment: The reference to all Member States and to their constitutional *practices* suggests that the Court will have regard also to the British position where no written constitution exists and also to those constitutions which might not deal directly with the problem in a codified way. In practice the Court gives only three textual examples (from the German, Italian and Irish constitutions) but then goes on to declare that

> "In all the Member States, numerous legislative measures have given concrete expression to [the] social function of the right to property"

[namely]

> "that those rules and practices permit the legislature to control the use of private property in accordance with the general interest.
> [I]n all the Member States there is legislation on agriculture and forestry, the water supply, the protection of the environment and town and country planning, which imposes restrictions, sometimes appreciable, on the use of real property. More particularly, all the wine-producing countries of the Community have restrictive legislation, albeit of differing severity, concerning the planting of vines [etc.] . . . [which is not] considered to be incompatible in principle with the regard due to the right to property".

The conclusion of the Court, indeed the purpose of this first phase of comparative analysis is to affirm that the *type* of legislation embodied in the regulation is known and acceptable in all Member States.

Step 5: The Comparative Method – phase 2 (Recital 23)

The Court does not stop its judicial review at this point. Without stating this explicitly, it culls two further principles from the constitutional practices of the Member States: a measure of this kind. The Measure must

> "correspond to objectives of general interest pursued by the Community"

and, in a cumulative test (though the Court uses the word "or") the measure must not

> "constitute a disproportionate and intolerable interference with the rights of the owner, impinging upon the very substance of the right to property".

Comment: These two tests of substantive and procedural policy *bona fide* and proportionality are of course known in virtually all systems of administrative and legislative review. (In the common law system proportionality will often be referred to in terms of the "reasonableness" of the measure.)

Step 6: Judicial Review (Recitals 24–30)

It is not necessary to go into the detailed assessment by the Court of the aims of the agricultural policy at the basis of the contested regulation nor at its assessment of the reasonableness of the measure itself save to make some general comments on the method as a whole.

First it is clear that in assessing what is the "general interest" which the measure must serve the Court makes reference to the *Community* general interest and *not to an aggregate or cumulative Member State interest.* In adducing the general interest the Court looks at the preamble of the regulation and at the general objectives of the Common Agricultural Policy as enunciated in the Treaty.

Proportionality is also discussed in terms of the Community policy. The Court makes reference to the temporary nature of the regulation and the conjunctural situation of the Community as a whole suffering from a surplus in the vine sector. In the light of its analysis of these factors the Court concludes:

> "[T]he measure criticized does not entail any undue limitation upon the exercise of the right to property. Indeed, the cultivation of new vineyards in a situation of continuous over-production would not have any effect, from the economic point of view, apart from increasing the volume of the surpluses; further, such an extension at that stage would entail the risk of making more difficult the implementation of a structural policy at the Community level in the event of such a policy resting on the application of criteria more stringent than the current provisions of national legislation concerning the selection of land accepted for wine-growing.
> [T]he restriction ... is justified by the objectives of general interest pursued by the Community and does not infringe the substance of the right to property in the form in which it is recognized and protected in the Community legal order".

A similar albeit more brief analysis is utilized to dispose of the challenge based on the right to pursue a trade.

D. Conclusions: The Functional and Principled Division of Tasks between Community and Member State Orders

We are now in a position to offer a brief conclusion on the resolution of the theoretical problems raised by the earlier abstract analysis of the judicial method adopted by the Court.

In the filling the gap created by the absence of a bill of rights in the Treaties the Court will indeed turn to the constitutional traditions of the Member States and to the international sources alluded to above. However, what it is interested in is not an investigation of what precise answer this or that national court will give to the precise question posed (as is the case in, say, some cases of private international law adjudication and establishment of foreign law). It simply wishes to establish the over all principles and the direction that constitutional review will take in these other jurisdictions. We also know from other contexts that the Court will be quite content in the case of conflicting traditions to adopt the one most suited, in its view, to the Community situation.

Implicit in its actual process of judicial review, as distinct from its principled statements, is the knowledge that one is not dealing here with absolute values and with "high" and "low" standards but with some sort of balancing test. One does not have to be a legal realist to accept that it is quite possible, and this does not seem to worry the court unduly, that another tribunal, seised with the same issues, may reach a different outcome. The *jurisdictional* issue becomes all important: The Court of Justice implicitly asserts that it is the only Court that can exercise the balancing test since it alone has the expertise, data and knowledge to adjudicate the double test of policy *bona fide* and proportionality in the Community context.

The two-phased procedure of establishing first constitutional principle derived from the comparative analysis and then its application which is a strict *Community* affair is the correct statement of the method adopted by the European Court of Justice. The fundamental human rights recognized by the constitutions of the Member States which the Court undertakes not to violate are principles, general rules and direction. They are not predictions of adjudicatory outcomes in each Member State or in the transnational legal order such as the ECHR. It is worth mentioning already here what will always remain one difficulty with this method namely the inherent element of uncertainty of a system which does not have a written catalogue. However, since the individual (or, rather, his or her legal advisors) may turn to an entire array of municipal and international texts as a basis for protection, the absence of a *Community* catalogue may in fact be a blessing in disguise.

One final point should be made regarding the possibility of review of the Court's decision by a "higher" tribunal such as the European Court of Human Rights. We already noted that the European Court of Justice took a rather dismissive view to the utility in this case of the Convention. It is also true that it establishes rather convincingly that it would be difficult for any *national* constitutional tribunal to evaluate better the specific regulation in the Community context. This however does *not,* in my view, exclude the possibility of further review by an even higher body. The European Court of Human Rights does after all review the constitutional adjudication of national constitutional courts which are very well suited to understand their own national context as much as the European Court is suited to understand the Community context.

One of the basic ideas of transnational adjudication of human rights is its exercise by a tribunal which is veritably removed from the system in which the challenge is made. In principle this review of the adjudication of the European Court by a higher tribunal is feasible. In practice, with the lesson offered in *Hauer* it is doubtful if the European Court of Human Rights would find much to criticise in the approach of the European Court of Justice.

E. Protection of Fundamental Rights in the Community Regime and its Relation to the European Convention on Human Rights

An immense literature has emerged dealing with this issue. It was spawned first by the principled allusion of the European Court of Justice to the Convention among the sources which it would use in its jurisprudence and then its actual use. Interest reached a peak in the wake of a Commission Memorandum in 1978 advocating the adhesion of the Community to the ECHR.

I *do not* propose to give a systematic account of this relationship. Where necessary I have already made specific points elsewhere in this report. The relationship is tantalizing for the legal theorist grappling with two different and developing transnational orders. In practice the problems which are raised are more illusory than real.

There is of course a two way relationship between the two systems. Community law will have developed by the influence of the Convention. Equally, each time the Court of Justice applies – and interprets – a provision of the Convention, we have an element in the development of that regime.

Much has been written on the legal basis for the application of the Convention by the Court as a source for its jurisprudence. Indeed, the Commission and some of the Advocates General of the Court regard the Convention in its substantive provisions as binding on the Community organs; the joint declaration of the three political institutions did not go so far[25]. For some the theory of substitution (which explains Community competences in the

[25] OJ 1977 C 103/1.

context of the GATT) provides a basis [26]. It is difficult to accept this given the very late ratification by France and the differentiated regime of reservations and adhesions to Protocols practiced by the Member States. Another basis could be the duty enshrined in Art. 234 EEC that prior international duties and rights of the Member States should remain unaffected. A patently false theory is one which suggests that the Member States could not have given the Community competences to violate the Convention to which they were bound [27].

The issue today is largely moot. The Court has indicated its intention to look to the Convention whenever an issue of human rights comes up before it. The legal basis is not critical or at least no more urgent than finding a legal basis to the entire exercise of introducing this new layer of judicial review. And although in the *Panasonic* case (Case 136/79 [1980] ECR 2033) the Court dropped in its reference to the Convention the word "guidelines" and assimilated it to the Constitutional traditions of the Member States, not much turns on this semanticism. In its search for criteria it was only natural that the Court would have turned to the one text on which all Member States had agreed.

The procedural issues are equally intriguing in theory. Strictly speaking the Community as such is not a member to the Convention. This would mean that an application to Strasbourg against an act of a Community organ (assuming exhaustion of local remedies within the *Community* legal order) must fail as the applicants in the *CFDT* case ([1979] 2 CMLR 229) found out. Now that France has both ratified the Convention and accepted the right of individual petition, the view has been put forward that the Member States might be liable jointly, under the regime of the Convention, for violations by the Community. I cannot accept this view which depends too much on an international law vision of the Community and which disregards its internal procedures and the so-called constitutionalisation of the Treaties [28].

This would mean that as a result of the creation of the Communities and the transfer of competences to it by the Member States, there is a procedural gap in the protection of the individual before the Strasbourg organs. Likewise, though of lesser import is the fact that a Member State might in theory have to defend itself before the Commission or Court of Human Rights for

[26] See extensive discussion by *Mendelson, op. cit.* (note 22) at pp. 156–160.

[27] It is a well-known principle of international law that a State cannot, except in manifest cases, plead constitutional incompatibility as a ground for nonrespect of its international obligations. It could be argued that violation of human rights would be contrary to the notion of *jus cogens* under international law and found jurisdiction in that manner.

[28] In particular this view would disregard the separate international personality of the Community and its ability to take decision by majority against the will of a Member State.

actions incumbent upon it by virtue of Community membership. I think one would have to wait for an actual breach by the Community which did not get cleansed by the European Court of Justice before one could regard these issues as necessitating more radical action.

This being so one may also take position on the largely forgotten proposal of Community adhesion to the Convention. From the substantive point of view it does not seem as if adhesion is a real necessity. The main advantage which would accrue to the Community would be the enhancement of its international personality and stature – a further step to the "federal-state" image. And indeed, it is probably for this reason that the Member States of the Community have shown little enthusiasm for the suggestion, in other ways innocuous.

F. The Possibility of Incorporation

I would like to conclude this report by consideration of one highly speculative issue concerning the possible future of human rights jurisdiction in the Community legal order, namely the application of Community human rights standards to practices of the Member States rather than to that of the organs of the Community itself.

The term incorporation is borrowed from the constitutional and juridical history of American federalism. The first ten amendments to the United States Constitution[29] are traditionally referred to as the Bill of Rights. For a long period the provisions of the Bill were construed as a limit on the federal government without direct application to the individual states, each of which had its own constitution embodying some form of individual protection[30]. By contrast, the celebrated Fourteenth Amendment[31] which was introduced in the wake of the Civil War, was directed specifically to the states. Section One, which is of the greatest significance, proscribes the states from abridging the privileges or immunities of citizens of the United States, prohibits deprivation of life, liberty or property without due process of law and forbids a denial to any person within the state of the equal protection of the laws. It is not surprising that the broad, principled language of this section has made it a fountain of constitutional dispute and adjudication.

Beginning, it is generally held in 1925[32], the Supreme Court has "incorporated" the substantive rights and limitations enumerated in the federal

---

[29] U.S. Const. arts. I–X.

[30] See generally, *Karst* and *Jacobs,* The "Federal" Legal Order: The USA and Europe Compared – A Juridical Perspective in 1 Integration Through Law 165 (Bk. 1, 1986).

[31] U.S. Const. amend. XIV.

[32] See *Gitlow* v. *New York,* 268 U.S. 652 (1925).

Bill of Rights and applicable on their face to the federal government alone into the Fourteenth Amendment which is applicable to the individual states. The rights and limitations incorporated became thereby applicable to the legislative and administrative practices of state authorities. The effect has been to curb legislative and administrative practice hitherto limited only by *state* constitutional and adjudicatory norms, if they contradicted *central* constitutional and adjudicatory norms. It is important, for comparative reasons, to note that incorporation of federal rights, at least theoretically, establishes a "lowest common denominator"; it does not, where the nature of the right in question permits (as explained above), prevent the adoption of a additional layers of protection for the individual by the states [33]. The process has had opponents from several quarters judicial, political and academic. Among its supporters, even within the Supreme Court, there has been a measure of diversity as regards the interpretative analysis adopted to explain the process. Likewise, there have been debates about the utility and merits of incorporation in terms of the level of protection afforded to the individual [34].

Incorporation of human-rights law within the Community system appears at first sight improbable. We noted that the Treaty contains no explicit Bill of Rights, so that Community incorporation would entail not one but two acts of aggressive judicial activism. First, the creation of judge-made "constitutional" law for the Community and then its application to acts of the Member States.

In the process of incorporation we should be able to identify two anchors: One to define and elaborate the law of human rights at the central level, the second to project that law into state jurisdiction. In the American system these two anchors rest securely within the constitutional framework: the Bill of Rights and the Fourteenth Amendment, respectively. This explicit support favours incorporation. Not only does the Supreme Court have unassailable authority to engage in a human rights jurisprudence, but the fully-fledged federal court system with its autonomous criminal and civil jurisdictions provides a fertile ground in which human rights norms may be "tested" before their projection into the State systems [35].

In the Community system the first anchor is far less secure. The difficulties inherent in trying to develop a higher law of human rights by comparative distillation were discussed in detail above. The Court's motivation for activism in the field of human rights was the twin threat to the unifor-

[33] Cf. *Ely, supra* note 7, at 24.

[34] A decision by the central court will obviate the necessity of fighting for the right in every single constituent unit. Naturally, this could also be a disadvantage if the right is not recognised, even though non-recognition by the central court would not theoretically bar a state court for giving relief.

[35] The absence of a *separate* system of Community courts in the Member States is of course a major distinguishing mark from the US system.

mity and supremacy of Community law posed by the Member States' jurisdiction over alleged Community violations.

The resistance of the Member States and national supreme courts to this instance of extension was based on the fear that the nascent Community law would fall below the level of protection guaranteed by national law. Essentially, the Member State courts feared that the new higher law would offer insufficient protection. The Court could not solve this problem simply by applying the "highest" national standard. First, the higher standard is sometimes difficult to identify. Second, conflicting national rules would make a uniform Community law impossible. Third, this approach would, in effect, allow the Member States to dictate Community law, upsetting the principle of supremacy.

By contrast, resistance to incorporation is likely to spring from the opposite fear. The application of a Community criterion of individual protection to state practice – which would be the essence of incorporation – is not likely to be problematic where the Member State's protection would be of a similar character[36]. Incorporation is likely to have its greatest effect and provoke the greatest resistance in situations where the individual does not receive within the national system the protection afforded by Community standards. The resistance here would not come from Courts as much as it would from political organs.

It may be useful at this point to look at one decided case which has come close to adopting this notion of incorporation. This case illustrates the limitation of potential European incorporation and the crucial distinction between it and its counterpart in fully-fledged federal systems.

Roland Rutili[37], an Italian national, was barred by the French authorities on account of his trade-union activity, from residing in four 'departements' one of which was his previous habitual residence. He appealed against this prohibition claiming *inter alia* that it was at variance with the guarantees afforded him under the free movement of workers regime of the Community. There was no dispute that his status was such as to afford him that protection. The French authorities relied naturally enough on the reservation elaborated in the Treaty[38] and in "secondary legislation"[39] that allows exception to the positive rules of the regime when justified on grounds of public policy (*ordre public*). A reference was made to the European Court.

One issue which the European Court had to answer concerned the conditions under which a limitation on the free-movement regime would be justified on grounds of public policy. This necessarily involved a definition of the breadth of the concept of public policy.

---

[36] The reasoning of the national court might be different but it would be sufficient if the outcome was largely similar.

[37] Case 36/77 [1975] ECR 1219.

[38] Art. 48 (3) EEC.

[39] Reg. 1612/68 and Dir. 68/360.

Although the Court first confirmed that the Member States were "... *in principle,* free to determine the requirement of public policy in the light of their national needs"[40] this determination would be subject to Community control. Community control could of course derive from the substantive requirements of primary and secondary Community law. Thus, Directive 64/221 requires, *inter alia* consideration of the individual circumstances of the migrant. France would not be allowed to exclude or restrict movements of, say, non-French chess players merely because they were, as a class, unpopular in certain areas[41]. Likewise, the directive prohibits economic factors from consideration in the determination of public policy. Thus, high unemployment in a French 'departement' could not be invoked to justify the expulsion or restriction of unemployed Community migrant workers[42].

Apart from specific secondary Community law, the freedom of the Member States to determine the scope of public policy as a ground for restricting the freedoms of the Community migrant worker is limited by more general, but explicit, provisions in the Treaty. Most important is the principle of non-discrimination on grounds of nationality articulated in Art. 7 EEC. Thus, even if the definition of French public policy had not been at variance with specific provisions of Community law, some of which I outlined above, it could still fall foul of the Treaty regime if it involved a non-authorized discrimination between French nationals and Community migrants[43]. Up to this point the control of the national law and practice involves no more than a straight application of Community law.

But what would be the situation if the state concept of public policy did not violate explicit Community law? In other words, what if the national system permitted – in a *non-discriminatory* way – practices contrary to the standards of human rights accepted by the Court and applied to *Community actions*[44]? It would seem that under these conditions the Community could not afford legal protection. Or could it?

We may safely assume, following our earlier discussion, that if the *Community* secondary legislation determining the specific detailed Community concept of public policy came into conflict with fundamental human rights, these Community provisions would be reviewable by the European Court of

---

[40] Recital 26 (emphasis added).

[41] But see Case 41/47 *Van Duyn* [1974] ECR 1337.

[42] See generally, *D. Wyatt &A. Dashwood,* The Substantive Law of the EEC (1980) at 147.

[43] There are exceptions, e.g. in relation to public service. In fact, France did violate, even discriminate, on grounds of nationality as well as violating specific rules. See Recitals 42 and 31 of Judgment.

[44] This hypothesis is not entirely fanciful. The imagination and absence of sensitivity of public officials manages to surprise on occasion even the most hardened observers. In the U.K. until a public outcry put a stop to the practice, certain classes of female immigrants were subjected to virginity tests.

Justice. The Court would attempt to distill an applicable norm of higher law from the three sources they cite and review the allegedly offending Community legislation in accordance. But could this higher law also become a source for adjudicating a national concept which did not violate the specific provisions of Community law? This would be the effect of incorporation. In what for our purposes must be the key recital in its judgment[45], the Court seemed to be edging towards such a step.

Having earlier in the judgment asserted that the determination by Member States of public policy was subject to Community control, the Court then expanded on the explicit provisions of Community law on the subject, both general and specific, and in fact found the French practice in violation. Although in *obiter dictum,* the Court went on to suggest, in language virtually identical to that in the human rights cases, that the explicit rules of Community law limiting the power of the Member States to control aliens (by devices such as public policy) were not exhaustive. *They were a specific manifestation of the more general principle,* enshrined in Arts. 8, 9, 10 and 11 of the Convention for the Protection of Human Rights and Fundamental Freedoms[46] and in Art. 2 of Protocol no. 4 of the same Convention[47], which provide, in identical terms, that no restrictions for reasons of national security or public safety shall be placed on the rights secured by them other than such as are necessary for the protection of those rights "in a democratic society".

If the Community law is but a specific manifestation of a general principle it should follow that the general principle forms part of the Community regime which controls the practices of the Member States. It further follows, that a national practice which violated this general principle *without violating a specific rule of the Community regime,* would violate Community law and, by virtue of the principle of supremacy, be inapplicable. The Community higher law would have absorbed the corresponding lower national protection. Incorporation would occur.

This aspect of the decision is of course *obiter dictum* and has yet to be followed in a concrete situation. Although the point has since been argued in several cases[48], it has not been necessary for the Court to decide whether it would follow its statement in *Rutili*[49].

What would be the impact of this policy if it were followed? In *Rutili* the Court mentioned as its normative source the European Convention and its Fourth Protocol, emphasizing that all Member States were parties to it. This aspect apparently diminishes the potential importance of European in-

---

[45] *Rutili* at 1232.

[46] Signed in 1950.

[47] Concluded in 1963.

[48] See *Drzemczewsky,* The Domestic Application of the Human Rights Convention as European Community Law, 30 ICLQ 118 (1981).

[49] But cf. Case 118/75 *Watson and Bellman* [1976] ECR 1185.

corporation by comparison to the American doctrine. Certainly, the Court of Justice has less scope for an entirely independent jurisprudence. Nonetheless, the impact of incorporation would not be insignificant. In the first place, so far as the European Convention is concerned, although all Member States are signatories, the reservation regime varies from one to another. Likewise, the very Protocol cited by the Court has not been ratified by Italy and the Netherlands. Even more dramatic would be the consequence in Britain, Denmark and Ireland where the Convention does not normally form part of the law of the land. Here it would have to be enforced by the national courts if incorporated by the European Court in reviewing Member State practice, not simply a Community rule of law.

Secondly, mindful that in its jurisprudence the Court clearly designated the ECHR as a first hurdle which did not exhaust the sources of Community human rights law [50] one can imagine even farther-reaching implications. If in its comparative distillation the Court adopted a standard from the traditions in only some Member States, that standard would be transported into all other national legal orders. Moreover, incorporation would change not only substantive law, but procedural law as well. Decentralized judicial review of legislation exists in only a few of the Member States of the Community [51]. The process of incorporation coupled with the systems of compliance operative under Art. 177 EEC would introduce Community style decentralized review in the sphere of human rights to each of the ten partners.

In *Rutili,* however, we also find the jurisdictional limitation on potential Community incorporation which crucially differentiates it from the American version. We must turn here to the second anchor of the process – that which allows transnational rights to be projected into the state systems. In the U.S. any constitutionally protected fundamental right directed at the states applies to *any* state administrative and legislative practice regardless of the division of powers between the federal and state legislatures. Thus, the rights protected by the first Ten Amendments, once incorporated into the Fourteenth Amendment, are projected in an all-encompassing constitutional jurisdiction.

By contrast, in the Community even the widest potential incorporation is limited by the division of competences under the Treaty. The Court of Justice has been rigorous in respecting the jurisdictional divisions of power between the Community and its Member States. Even the "general prohibition" against discrimination on grounds of nationality was limited by the Court, faithful to the language of Art. 7, to "... *the field of application of the Treaty*" [52]. In *Rutili* this would mean that the protection afforded the Community worker could not be projected onto Community citizens not qualify-

---

[50] See discussion of *Hauer, supra.*
[51] See supplement to Bull EC 5/76 at p. 33–34.
[52] Recital 12 (emphasis added).

ing as "workers" in the Community sense of the word and certainly not to non-Community migrants. In one of the *Defrenne* cases[53] this limitation becomes even more striking. Although the Court, using its traditional formula for protection in the field of human rights, accepted a prohibition on sex discrimination as forming part of general principles of Community law derived *inter alia* from the *European Social Charter* and an *ILO* Convention[54], these principles could not, at the time of the decision, avail a woman plaintiff who had suffered discrimination as regards her pension rights. The second anchor, the means for projection, was at that time limited *rationae materiae,* to situations of *equal pay*[55]. The Advocate General in this case was most explicit, while accepting the protection in a particularly full-blooded version[56], to lay down the limits of Community judicial protection: ". . . in so far as the internal provisions [of the Member State] are not replaced by directly applicable Community provisions", the state level of protection must apply[57]. European incorporation would thus be limited in its scope to the substantive areas over which the Community has jurisdiction.

With the passage of time the effects of this limitation may be reduced. In the first place the Court has considerable discretion in determining the scope – *ratione materiae, personae* or *loci* – of Treaty provisions. In the second place, the Community legislator itself is continuously expanding the limits of Community competences. As the boundaries extend and the Community's jurisdiction itself become more comprehensive, the effects of potential Community incorporation might become more pronounced.

I should emphasise at this point that like the doctrine of supremacy, incorporation would have to be realized in a two-phase process: It must first be articulated by the Court and then, more crucially, be accepted by the national courts that would have to give it effect. I am sceptical about the prospects for the development of incorporation in the near future. The Court's pronouncements have been rather timid. More importantly, I see very little prospect of courts and governments in the Member States (especially those dualist states which have not for example "domesticated" the ECHR) accepting incorporation. Thus, I am far less optimistic than some writers who have foreseen the fairly imminent arrival of incorporation[58] although in the long run it might occur.

---

[53] Case 149/77 [1978] ECR 1365.

[54] See Recital 28.

[55] Recital 30.

[56] "I do not think that a lengthy consideration is necessary to show that the rule that there should be no discrimination is a general principle of the Community legal order . . .", *Defrenne* at 1304.

[57] Id. at 1385.

[58] Cf. *Drzemczewski, op. cit.* note 48 and for a more cautious statement *Cappelletti, op. cit.* note 5.

G. Conclusions

At this point instead of attempting any overall conclusions I propose simply to suggest some issues which may merit discussion in the light of the above description and analysis and which may especially profit from the *comparative* context of the conference.

a) To what extent is the absence of a written catalogue of Community fundamental human rights really an impediment to protection of the individual?

b) Is the very integrationist posture of the European Court of Justice a threat to its ability to adjudicate justly, or to seem to be doing so, in a context which posits the individual as against the Community?

c) In current proposals for institutional reform of the European Community such as the Draft Treaty establishing the European Union, there is a renewed call for a Union bill of rights. Has a bill of rights a political meaning (such as giving a sense of identity and identification with the system) which would merit a reopening of the debate about a written bill?

d) How real is the "gap" in protection afforded the individual given the nonadhesion of the Community to the ECHR?

e) Is the technique of national courts interpreting relatively open-ended Constitutional provisions so different from that of the European Court relying on its own sources of fundamental human rights?

The International Enforcement of Human Rights

General Report

RUDOLF BERNHARDT

Introductory Remarks

The original version of this report was submitted to the participants of the Heidelberg Colloquium in August 1985. That version is still the center-piece of the present printed version. However, during the discussion wishes were expressed that the general report should also include some additional remarks commenting on questions raised during the meeting. This report tries to meet some of these wishes, especially in part B. However, it has not been possible to summarize the discussion which was extremely useful and covered a great number of basic aspects of the international enforcement of human rights and which included, *inter alia,* valuable remarks on the Islamic conception of human rights made by Professor *Afchar.*

The general rapporteur has not refrained from expressing his personal views about some crucial problems, or from adding some considerations not discussed in the other papers.

A.

I. Human Rights in Present-Day International Law

Until the end of the Second World War, international law took greater notice of human rights only in special contexts: the protection of aliens and the protection of minorities by treaties. The relationship between the State and its own nationals remained in general an internal matter of each State.

This concept has changed profoundly in the last forty years. Human rights are not only politically a matter of international concern; their protection and enforcement is also guaranteed and regulated by norms of international law, and this on various levels.

Universally, the United Nations Charter invokes human rights as a basis of the new international community. Under the UN system, the Human Rights Declaration of 1948 and the 1966 UN Covenants are the most important corner-stones of post-war developments. These texts are discussed in the contributions of Professor *Henkin* and Professor *Tumanov.*

A great number of other international agreements on the universal level have been concluded, e.g. the Convention against racial discrimination of 1969 and the Anti-Apartheid Convention of 1973. In the broader context of the international protection of human rights, the work of other universal organizations, especially of the International Labour Organisation, should also be mentioned.

Under general international law, human rights texts are binding only if contained in international agreements, and only for those States which have formally accepted these agreements. Human rights proclamations contained in resolutions of organizations or conferences (UN Declaration of 1948, Helsinki Final Act of 1975) are not binding *per se.* But at least some central guarantees can now be considered as part of customary international law, e.g. the prohibition of torture.

The present report will concentrate on the UN covenants and their enforcement system. Non-binding texts and customary law do not contain institutionalized control mechanisms. Nevertheless, some problems – such as third-State "intervention" – can be similar for human rights agreements and customary law rules.

Besides the universal scene, regional human rights conventions are a very important factor in our field. The European Convention on Human Rights of 1950 (in force since 1953, with later additional protocols) is described in the report of Professor *Jacobs*. It is fair to say that the European control system is at present the most sophisticated and practically advanced system. The Inter-American Convention on Human Rights is described in the paper of Professor *Buergenthal;* the Convention came into force in 1978, and the Convention organs exist and seem to be making progress in the promotion of human rights in the Western hemisphere. Another important text, the African Charter of Human and Peoples' Rights, emphasizes, already in its title, that it is concerned not only with rights of the individual. The Charter, which came into force on 21 October 1986, is amply described in the report of Professor *Mbaya.* Developments in the human rights discussion in other regions – among the Arab States and in the Far East – will deserve closer scrutiny in the future; at present they have not attained major importance. This report will be based, as far as regional texts are concerned, on the three human rights conventions just mentioned. In addition, the written report submitted after the Colloquium by Mrs. *Yamane* and included in the present volume illustrates "Approaches to Human Rights in Asia".

As mentioned in several papers, it has become usual to speak of different kinds or generations of human rights. A traditional distinction exists between civil rights in the sense of individual freedoms from State interference on the one hand and social rights, *i.e.* rights to claim State welfare benefits, on the other. In recent years, a third generation of human rights has been proposed or promulgated; according to its proponents it should comprise the right to peace, the right of self-determination, the right to a clean environment, etc. It has rightly been stressed in the written "observations" of Professor *Partsch* that it is wrong by definition to speak of generations in this context since the first and second so-called generations are not and should not be substituted by any new generation – were it otherwise, it would no longer be meaningful to speak of human rights as basic rights of the individual human being. The only question is whether individual rights are or should be complemented by other rights or values.

The distinction between different categories of human rights is important in theory and practice for the implementing and enforcement machinery. Only the civil rights as freedoms from State interference are fully capable of being protected by international decision-making organs. Human rights commissions and courts can investigate and decide whether State organs have violated a human right in a given case and how far the individual concerned should receive compensation. Social rights, rights to receive some social benefits or support from State and society, can hardly be enforced by binding decisions in individual cases; they normally need policy decisions by legislative and executive organs. It is therefore correct that on the universal as well as on the regional level different conventions exist with different "enforcement" machineries for civil and social rights – e.g. for social rights the United Nations Covenant on Economic, Social and Cultural Rights and the European Social Charter. For the so-called third generation, no special enforcement procedures are available; only the normal measures and rules in and for inter-State relations exist. As far as such rights should exist, they cannot be discussed in this paper.

It is obvious that all the rights contained in international conventions are also found in the constitutional and legal norms of States. A full picture of the existing guarantees of human rights would have to include these national guarantees. But this has not been the task of the Colloquium. Any outside interference based solely on the allegation of the violation of internal law would constitute – at least if it reaches a certain intensity – intervention prohibited under general international law.

II. Enforcement of Human Rights

Enforcement is understood here in a very broad sense, comprising all measures intended and proper to induce respect for human rights. This broad definition needs some clarification and limitation. Forceful interference within a foreign territory in order to protect human rights – either of nationals of the intervening State or of other persons – cannot be discussed here. "Humanitarian Intervention" is still a much disputed notion, which is not and cannot be regulated in any human rights covenant; therefore, and for other reasons, it was excluded from this report and also in general from discussion during the Colloquium. Although according to the title of the Colloquium only *international* enforcement is addressed, national means to secure respect for internationally guaranteed human rights should be included. There can be no doubt that the State and its organs are primarily competent and responsible for the protection of human rights; this is shown *inter alia* by the usual requirement of exhaustion of local remedies before any international machinery can be set into motion.

If one tries to bring a certain order to the variety of possible enforcement measures, three categories could probably be distinguished: Enforcement by national means; enforcement by organs provided in the relevant human rights conventions; and enforcement by third-party activities trying to induce respect for human rights. These categories can be further subdivided in the following manner:

(1) Enforcement by National Means	(First category)
(2) Reporting Systems (3) Inter-State Complaints (4) Individual Petitions (5) Decisions by International Organs, especially by Human Rights Courts	as provided in international conventions (Second category)
(6) Activities of International Organizations (7) Activities of Third States (8) Activities of Non-Governmental Organizations and World Public Opinion	without a special treaty basis (Third category)

The present report – like most of the other reports – will concentrate on the second category of enforcement measures, but the other categories should not be completely neglected. The report will discuss the several points in the order just indicated.

(1) Enforcement by National Means

It is still nearly undisputed that treaties concluded under international law do not necessarily also form part of the internal legal order of States, but that States are free to decide themselves by what means treaties should be executed. According to prevailing opinion this holds true also for human rights agreements. As the report of Professor *Jacobs* indicates, there has been some dispute whether the European Convention on Human Rights obligates States to introduce the Convention into the internal legal order; the States and the Convention organs have until now not disputed the freedom of States to transform or not to transform the Convention itself into domestic law. According to this view, the Convention requires certain results – respect for the freedoms contained in the Convention –, but it does not prescribe the means for reaching these results.

Under the European system, one State (Austria) has given the Convention the rank of constitutional norms; in the majority of the State parties, the Convention forms part of the internal legal order; in certain States (United Kingdom, Ireland, the Scandinavian States), the Convention like other treaties remains an international norm without being part of internal State law. The first (Austrian) solution attributes to the Convention the highest rank. In the second category of States, Convention norms can theoretically be superseded by later-enacted laws, but in practice there is no real danger that this will happen. The third solution leaves the means for reaching the prescribed results to the internal legal order. There are good reasons for the (more political than legal) assumption that the incorporation of the Convention into the legal order of all participating States would improve the present situation and would help to set uniform European standards.

In the long range, it could also be advisable to find a common solution for the validity and enforceability of decisions of the Convention organs in the internal legal order of States parties. At present, no uniformity or clear solutions seem to be in sight.

As mentioned before, it is undoubtedly primarily at the national level that respect for human rights should be secured. The exhaustion of effective local remedies is and should be a precondition for any international enforcement.

(2) Reporting Systems

A considerable number of international texts impose upon States the obligation to report on the measures taken for securing respect of the obligations incurred and on the state of the relevant internal norms. Sometimes, the reports must be submitted to one of the normal organs of an organization (ECOSOC is the competent organ under the UN Covenant on Economic, Social and Cultural Rights); under other conventions special organs are created for scrutinizing State reports. In addition, the Committee established under the Convention against racial discrimination and the Human Rights Committee instituted under the UN Covenant on Civil and Political Rights play a prominent role. The independence of the Committee members is of general importance for the objective work of the institution. On the other hand, no binding decisions can be taken. Nevertheless, the activity of the two committees just mentioned may contribute to improving the human rights situation in a number of countries. The so-called General Comments of the UN Committee can be of value for future practice.

An over-all judgment on the effectiveness of the different reporting systems is hardly possible. As in many other fields of international law and relations, improvements and progress are not a matter of days; they need endurance and good will over a considerable length of time. It is to be hoped that reporting obligations will improve respect for human rights.

It should be remarked that reporting systems do not play an important role under the regional human rights texts discussed here. Only the Inter-American Commission has broad powers to receive and to discuss reports of the member States (cf. also the report for Africa). On the other hand, reporting obligations are well known in other conventions, e.g. the European Social Charter; this last example demonstrates that reporting obligations might be the only adequate solution for the enforcement of social rights.

(3) Inter-State Complaints

The UN Covenant on Civil and Political Rights (Art. 41), the Inter-American Convention on Human Rights (Art. 45) and the European Convention on Human Rights (Art. 24) all provide the possibility that one State party may bring a complaint against another State party before the respective Commission. Under the European Convention, no special declaration is necessary; the ratification of the Convention automatically creates the competence of the Commission to receive inter-State complaints. Under the UN system as well as under the American Convention, special declarations apart from the ratification of the conventions are necessary. Until now, 17 declarations have been made under Art. 41 of the UN Covenant. Neither under the Covenant nor under the American Convention have inter-State complaints until now played any role. The reasons are probably the same as those given below in connection with the European Convention.

As mentioned, under the European system inter-State complaints are possible without any further declarations of the member States. In the more than 30 years since the Convention's entry into force, the number of inter-State applications has remained minimal, compared with thousands of individual petitions. All in all, 18 inter-State applications have been submitted to the Human Rights Commission; these 18 applications in fact concerned only 6 complexes which can be summarized as follows:

Two Grek applications against the United Kingdom concerned Cyprus under British rule (1956/57).

One Austrian application against Italy was submitted in connection with certain events in South Tyrol (1960).

Several applications of Scandinavian States and the Netherlands against Greece concerned the military régime in the latter State (1967, 1970).

Two Irish applications were lodged against the United Kingdom in connection with events in Northern Ireland (1971/72).

Three applications were lodged by Cyprus against Turkey after the Turkish invasion of the island (1974/75, 1977).

Denmark, France, the Netherlands, Norway and Sweden lodged applications against Turkey (1982).

This account is interesting in several respects: out of the small number of cases, the majority concerns situations in which one State has complained of measures directed against persons with whom the complaining State felt a special relationship; only the 1967/1970 complaints against Greece and the last applications against Turkey have been lodged for general humanitarian reasons.

According to this record, the possibility of inter-State applications does not seem to be very helpful in the enforcement of human rights. States often hesitate to set enforcement machinery into motion "only" for the protection of foreign nationals against their own government. Political considerations, questions of expediency and even financial and bureaucratic obstacles may militate against taking up cases where no real national interests are involved. A State may even have good reasons for considering quiet diplomatic channels more suitable for the protection of human rights than the formal application to a human rights commission. This seems at least to be the reality of State practice.

(4) *Individual Petitions*

According to the existing human rights texts, as a rule the individual complaining of a violation of his rights still has no secured standing before international organs. In no case is it possible for an individual to apply directly to a human rights court. Even applications to an existing commission are normally subordinated to an express declaration of a State party that it accepts the competence of the commission to receive individual complaints. Only the Inter-American Convention – reversing the European system – declares that *ipso facto* and without any special declaration "Any person or group of persons or any non-governmental entity ... may lodge petitions with the Commission containing denunciations or complaints of violation of the Convention by a State party". The Inter-American system contains some other peculiarities: for instance the double role of the Commission as one of the organs of the Organisation of American States and as an organ under the human rights convention.

Under the UN Covenant, individual petitions are only admissable after a State has made a formal declaration under the optional protocol; until now, 34 States (less than 50% of the State parties) have made such declarations. Some practice exists already, but it can hardly be said that the right of individual petition has gained convincing support.

The African Convention seems to give the individual the right to submit "communications" directly to the Commission (Art. 55), but a number of conditions must be met and it is doubtful how far the Commission will really be able to provide help.

The European Convention (Art. 25) also requires special declarations from States to empower the Commission to receive individual petitions. At present, 18 out of 21 member States of the Council of Europe have made such declarations (Cyprus, Turkey and Malta are the remaining 3 States). In recent times about 500 individual petitions per year have been registered with the European Commission, and the system can be considered to work fairly well.

At this point, a few general considerations on the right of individual petitions in the international human rights system might be added, considerations which may not meet with universal approval. In the opinion of the general rapporteur, international human rights guarantees without the possibility of individual complaints to an impartial institution are insufficient and even contradictory. Human rights conventions are intended to protect the individual against State organs, and they reflect the truism that no State and no society is immune against the occurrence of human rights violations. If there does not exist a right of individual petition, the real goal of all human rights instruments, the effective protection of the individual's rights, cannot be reached. The argument that the individual is not a subject of the international legal order begs the question. Human rights guarantees in international law attribute to the individual a certain (albeit limited) legal personality, and the material guarantees should be complemented by procedural guarantees enabling the individual to defend and enforce his rights with the help of an impartial institution.

(5) Decisions by International Organs, especially by Human Rights Courts

At the outset of this section, it must be underlined that under a good number of human rights instruments no real decisions can be taken in cases in which State activities are challenged. Considerations of State sovereignty and other arguments against the interference of international institutions with internal matters of States have prohibited effective procedural guarantees. Under the UN Covenants and also under some regional instruments international organs can consider State reports and they can, under certain conditions, also receive petitions, but no final and binding decisions are possible. In these cases, the activities of human rights commissions and similar bodies can try to induce the State concerned to modify its practice or to correct wrong or harmful decisions, and reports of international bodies may arouse public opinion, but the systems lack any legal enforcement capability. In the view of the general rapporteur, this is not a good and satisfactory state of affairs, but it is still reality in present-day international law.

Under the European human rights system, the "normal" decision-making organ is not a legal, but a political institution, the Committee of Ministers. If a State has not accepted the jurisdiction of the European Court of Human Rights or if neither the Commission nor a State submits a case to the Court, the Committee of Ministers takes the final and legally binding decision. This system has often been criticized, and rightly so. A political organ, composed of members instructed by their governments and sitting *in camera,* decides the legal question whether a human rights provision has been violated. The system can only be accepted or tolerated if the Ministers as a rule approve the report of the impartial and independent Commission and if cases of greater importance are brought before the Court.

Another weakness of the existing human rights instruments lies in the fact that, even if a human rights court exists, the individual concerned has no right to submit his case to the court. Art. 44 of the European Convention provides: "Only the High Contracting Parties and the Commission shall have the right to bring a case before the Court". And Art. 61 (1) of the American Convention contains the same rule. The result of these provisions is that a judicial procedure takes place in which the individual concerned is the object and not a subject competent to set the machinery into motion. Under the European system, several changes in the Rules of Court have strengthened the position of the individual in so far as the person concerned can take an active part in the procedure – provided that the Commission or a State has submitted his case to the Court.

The similarities as well as the differences between the American and the European Human Rights Courts need no further explanation here, they are described in the reports of Professor *Buergenthal* and Professor *Jacobs*. The European Court, in existence since 1959, for many years had only a few cases to decide. The situation has changed: at present more than thirty cases are pending. The present workload of the Commission and of the Court necessitates new considerations relating to how the whole system can be improved and adapted to the new developments. The American Court is still a young institution, and no cases have yet been decided. The Court's exceptionally broad competence to deliver advisory opinions might gain further importance, some most interesting opinions having been pronounced in recent times.

Human rights courts do not have at their disposal either an international police force or any other organ empowered to take physical enforcement measures. As in many other international law fields, legal pronouncements are not accompanied by an effective enforcement machinery. Nevertheless, the American as well as the European Convention contain some relevant rules. Under Art. 65 of the American Convention, the Court submits annually a report on its work to the General Assembly of the Organization of American States, and "it shall specify, in particular, the cases in which a State has not complied with its judgment, making any pertinent recommendations". According to Art. 54 of the European Convention, "the judgment of the Court shall be transmitted to the Committee of Ministers which shall supervise its execution". Under the latter rule, in practice the State concerned has to report on the steps made in order to comply with the Court's judgment, and the reports are carefully considered by the members of the Committee or their deputies. On balance, the decisions of the European Court of Human Rights are regularly respected and executed by the State concerned; a good number of cases could even be found in which States have changed their law and/or their practice in order to comply with judgments which have been rendered against third States and are therefore not formally binding upon the former State.

An additional protection for the individual concerned might be the competence of a court to afford "just satisfaction"; this is provided in Art. 50 of the European Convention, and the Court has often made use of this provision. The American Convention contains the following, most interesting clause in Art. 68: "That part of a judgment that stipulates compensatory damages may be executed in the country concerned in accordance with domestic procedure governing the execution of judgments against the State". It remains to be seen whether this clause will become of some practical importance.

An evaluation of international human rights courts is dependent upon the personal views and experiences of the observer. On the universal level, a human rights court is hardly in sight; too divergent are the ideologies and policies behind the universal praise for the protection of human rights. On the regional level, it can be hoped that the American Court will gain further prestige and the opportunity to improve the respect for human rights. The experience of the European Court especially in the last decade shows that common regional standards in the human rights field can be developed by such a court, at least if the States and societies concerned share some basic values and convictions. In the practice of the European Court, serious violations of basic human rights are seldom at stake; more important seems to be the development of common standards on a relatively high level.

(6) Activities of International Organizations

As mentioned before, the promotion of human rights by international organizations is sometimes especially provided for in human rights instruments. But even without express statutory provisions, many international organizations discuss regularly human rights questions. A United Nations publication describes in nearly 400 pages the "United Nations Action in the Field of Human Rights". Some of the UN Specialized Agencies annually have human rights questions in different fields and connections on their agenda. The International Labour Organisation and UNESCO are prominent examples.

Discussions and resolutions of these organizations on human rights matters share the legal status of similar discussions and resolutions in other fields: as a rule, they are legally not binding. This can be otherwise if the relevant texts attribute binding force to an organ's decision, but this is still a rare exception which can hardly be found in human rights questions. One can imagine (cf. the discussion on apartheid) that grave violations of human rights might be considered under certain circumstances as a threat to the peace, and could lead to enforcement measures of the UN Security Council under Chapter VII of the Charter. But, in general, resolutions on human rights questions can only persuade or induce States to change their position, and they can try to mobilize world public opinion.

Regional organizations may also play an important role in improving respect for human rights. The Statute of the Council of Europe as well as the Statute of the Organization of American States give an important place to the protection of human rights. The Inter-American Commission of Human Rights, quite apart from its role according to the Human Rights Convention, is probably the most important regional organ for the furtherance of human rights. It is to be hoped that the African Commission on Human and Peoples' Rights, with its comprehensive mandate under Art. 45 of the African Charter, will some time in the future also play an important role in that continent.

(7) *Activities of Third States*

This general report should at least touch upon the question how far third States are competent, under international law, to raise human rights questions in connection with events in another State. This crucial and much discussed problem first needs some delimitation. We are not concerned here with the diplomatic protection of a State's own nationals nor are we concerned, as mentioned before, with so-called humanitarian intervention. It is also beyond doubt that the prohibition of the use of force (Art. 2(4), UN Charter) is valid also in connection with human rights questions. The only problem to be discussed here is whether one State can criticize events inside another State invoking the violation of internationally protected human rights. In this connection, it is sometimes said that such criticism constitutes unlawful interference within the domestic jurisdiction of the State concerned. Such a general statement is, according to the view of the general rapporteur, unfounded in international law. Already in 1923, the Permanent Court of International Justice declared that "the question whether a certain matter is or is not solely within the jurisdiction of a State is an essentially relative question; it depends upon the development of international relations". As far as the guarantee of human rights forms part of conventional or custumary international law in our time, these guarantees *per definitionem* no longer belong to the *domaine réservé* of States. It is another question whether certain procedures provided in human rights conventions exclude unilateral measures of third States. The answer depends, in my view, in the first place upon the interpretation of the relevant texts. In general, criticism of human rights violations brought forward with means compatible with international law seems to be in conformity with present-day international law.

(8) Activities of Non-Governmental Organizations and World Public Opinion

A few remarks are now devoted to the contribution of non-governmental organizations and world public opinion in improving respect of human rights. These remarks are not based on legal considerations, since international law neither supports nor prohibits non-governmental activities in this field. As far as the national law of certain States tries to restrict such activities, it must respect the territorial and personal limits of State jurisdiction. The general principles of international law involved here do not need further elaboration. Suffice it to say that any discussion on the enhancing of international human rights should not forget the role of non-governmental institutions.

Prominent among the non-governmental organizations concerned are Amnesty International and the International Commission of Jurists. By their activities and publications they try to improve the human rights situation in many parts of the world. The fact that many governments have criticized these activities, some of which may deserve criticism, does not detract from the merits of non-official defenders of human rights. It should also be mentioned that regional non-governmental cooperation in the human rights field seems to make progress in different parts of the world. It is, in the opinion of the general rapporteur, to be regretted that serious and honorable efforts by individuals and private institutions to further the respect of human rights are sometimes condemned by governments as being unlawful interferences with internal public order.

The press in general and the International Press Institute in particular are or can also be relevant factors in the improvement of international human rights.

III. Human Rights in the European Communities

This topic is amply discussed in the report of Professor *Weiler.* The special features and the development of the discussion in theory and practice, especially in the jurisprudence of the Court of Justice of the European Communities, need not be repeated here. Instead, some general considerations, connecting this topic with the broader subject of the Colloquium, might be appropriate.

The protection and guarantee of human rights started at the national level. From the *Magna Charta Libertatum* of 1215 to the Bills of Rights at the end of the 18th century and since then to a great number of constitutions and other legal enactments – it was always national law which tried to improve the respect for human rights. After the Second World War, it is still primarily the State and its government which both endanger and yet also guarantee basic human rights. But respect for basic human rights is no longer a question solely of national concern; international law and world public opinion now support the international protection and enforcement of human rights.

Compared with the effective use and the possible misuse of State power, the protection of the individual against activities of international organizations and their organs was until recently of no great interest. This has changed, although to a very limited extent, in view of the intensification of the work of international organizations and the progressive development of their structure and functions. One aspect – not further discussed in this report – is the considerable increase in the number of functionaries and employees of international organizations who need protection of their rights, now often provided by international administrative tribunals and boards. Another problem is posed whenever an organization has regulatory powers in relation to individuals in the member States of the organization concerned. This is the problem faced by the European Communities.

The European Communities – comprising the European Coal and Steel Community, the European Economic Community and Euratom – possess and make use of law-making powers, now for more than thirty years. When the relevant treaties were drafted, no human rights catalogue was envisaged or discussed; one reason seems to have been the assumption that the more technical and limited powers of the Communities make human rights violations improbable. This assumption appeared to be correct for a number of years. It is only since the end of the 1960s that the protection of the rights of individuals against acts of Community organs has become a problem of practical importance. Now, innumerable statements in legal literature and a good number of court decisions have discussed and still discuss the position of human rights in the European Communities. A broad consensus seems to exist that the Community organs are or should be bound to observe essential human rights, but the correct legal solution is doubtful. Undoubtedly, not all classic human rights need protection against Community activity, e.g. the prohibition of torture is hardly of relevance; other rights – e.g. the prohibition of retroactive legislation, and the protection of property – can be violated not only by the member States, but also by the Community organs.

Failing adequate express rules in the "constitution" – the basic treaties – of the European Communities, a good number of proposals have been made. They can be broadly divided into proposals *de lege ferenda* and solutions *de lege lata.*

De lege ferenda, two different routes are recommended: the elaboration of a special human rights catalogue of the European Communities on the one hand, and the adherence of the Communities to the European Convention on Human Rights on the other. Both solutions call for elaboration and ratification of new treaties or of amendments to the existing treaties, and they need much time. At present, it seems to be very doubtful whether either of these proposals will be accepted in the foreseeable future.

As to a solution *de lege lata,* a way has been paved by the Court of Justice of the European Communities in a number of decisions described in detail in Professor *Weiler*'s report. The jurisprudence – not always free from ambiguities – creates step by step a body of individual rights as part of the unwritten Community law by combining essential guarantees contained in the constitutions of member States with the rights in the European Convention of Human Rights. This solution undoubtedly has advantages as well as disadvantages: It improves the rights of the individual vis-à-vis the Community, but it entails many legal uncertainties until a problem is finally settled by decisions of the court in Luxembourg. Another problem is connected with the existence of several European institutions – Council of Europe / European Communities, Human Rights organs under the European Convention / Court of Justice of the European Communities – with different but overlapping competences in the human rights field. These and other problems have to be solved sometime in the future.

While effective judicial protection of international human rights remains generally inadequate, the law of the European Communities contains adequate procedural rights. Individuals as well as legal persons can either apply directly to the Court of Justice (Arts. 173 and 175, EEC Treaty), or they can submit claims to national courts which may ask the Court of Justice for a decision on the validity and interpretation of Community law (Art. 177).

B.

IV. Some Basic Problems and Additional Considerations

(1) Is it correct to concentrate on the rights of the individual against governmental interference – as has been done in this report and during the Colloquium in general – while neglecting social rights, the rights to work, etc. and also the rights to peace or to a clean environment? The answer to this question, raised during the Colloquium is both simple and difficult at the same time. The protection of the rights of the individual against State interference, the protection of the human being against State power, is still an important task of the international community; it undoubtedly deserves scholarly discussion; and in this field international law and an international machinery for the protection of human rights is especially advanced. For these reasons, during the Colloquium, it seemed and it still seems to be adequate to discuss primarily the human rights directed against governmental interference.

There is no doubt that "positive" social human rights, in the sense of claims to receive support, are in many parts of the world and in many societies of the same or even of greater importance for the individual than the rights protecting the person against State action. But, as has been mentioned before, social rights require different enforcement mechanisms, if there can be any enforcement at all. The international protection of social rights is based on different rules and requires different considerations which could not be included in the agenda of the Colloquium.

This is even more the case with the human rights of the so-called third generation. The discussion of these rights has, in the opinion of the author of this report, some deficiencies. It is obvious that peace, economic and social development, and the protection of the environment are of vital importance for mankind and for future generations. A good number of rules of international law exist for these fields, and more rules and more protection are necessary. But does it make sense to combine these problems with the discussion of human rights? Who is the subject and who is the adressee of a right to peace, a right to economic support across State boundaries, an international right to a clean environment? In any case, it seems to be justified not to include these topics in the discussion of the traditional human rights, although it cannot be denied that other rights and other obligations also need closer scrutiny and scholarly efforts.

(2) The question has been raised whether the rights of the individual are not over-emphasized while the obligations or duties are often neglected. Here again, differentiations and distinctions are necessary. In every State and society, the individual has to bear a great number of duties, e.g. to pay taxes, to render military service, etc. Human rights cannot hinder the State from claiming necessary contributions from its citizens. It is undoubtedly a central problem of the protection of human rights to strike a fair balance between individual freedoms and obligations towards the community. Human rights Conventions normally provide that limitations on human rights are permitted as far as they are provided by law and are necessary in a democratic society (e.g. Arts. 8–11 of the European Convention). It is up to the State organs and eventually to international human rights institutions to decide whether a "fair balance" between individual freedom and public necessity has been struck.

(3) What does "enforcement" of human rights mean? Some criticism has been voiced against the use of this notion in the international human rights context. The criticism is correct if enforcement is understood in the sense of physical force or other compelling coercion. But it is also legitimate to use the notion in a broader sense as explained in the first part of this report.

(4) What is the philosophy – if any – behind human rights and their international protection? The answer might be different for the universal covenants on the one hand and for the regional conventions on the other. On the universal level, common texts have been agreed upon in spite of the fact that human rights are explained and justified differently by Christians, Muslims, Marxists, etc. The only common "philosophy" seems to be that the individual needs protection and the international community should contribute to this protection. On the regional level, existing human rights conventions are not based on a specific religion or ideological understanding, but on a homogeneous democratic tradition and a common understanding of basic values (e.g. the rule of law) in the member States concerned. This common

basis is the prerequisit for the proper functioning of the human rights institutions in Western Europe.

Concluding Remarks

The great number of human rights texts at the international (universal and regional) as well as national levels could evoke the impression that the rights of the individual are well protected in our time. If reality would always and everywhere conform to the texts, the whole subject would not need much discussion. But it is safer to assume that the human rights texts reflect the need for better protection, and experience shows that the texts have had until now only a limited influence on reality. For this there are a good number of reasons, one of them being the central position of State sovereignty in international law and international relations.

State sovereignty and international protection of human rights coexist necessarily in a state of tension. States are still reluctant to entrust impartial institutions with the power to review acts allegedly in contravention of international obligations in the human rights field. The various international conventions discussed in the reports submitted to the Colloquium contain different supervisory and enforcement machineries. It is self-evident that none of these texts is without deficiencies; they all need improvements in order to better secure human rights in all parts of the world.

Many important human rights questions could not be adequately discussed in this general report or in the other reports. One of these questions concerns the multiplicity of texts and institutions and the ensuing overlapping of rules and competences. Another problem concerns the protection of human rights during war as well as internal strife; in this field; the Geneva Red Cross Conventions and the activities of the International Committee of the Red Cross play a significant role.

All in all, "international enforcement of human rights", the topic of this Colloquium, has on closer scrutiny not yet been really achieved, but remains a task for the future. Legal science can contribute, albeit to a limited extent, to achieving this goal.

List of Participants

Afchar, H., Professeur de droit, Paris, France

Bernhardt, R., Professor of Law, University of Heidelberg, Director, Max Planck Institute for Comparative Public Law and International Law, Judge, European Court of Human Rights, Heidelberg, Fed. Rep. of Germany

Buergenthal, Th., Professor of Law, Emory University Law School, President, Inter-American Court of Human Rights, Atlanta/Georgia, USA

Cappelletti, M., Professor of Law, Istituto Universitario Europeo, San Domenico di Fiesole (Firenze), Italy

Friedman, S., Dr., Secrétaire général, Association Internationale des Sciences Juridiques, Paris, France

Frowein, J. A., Professor of Law, University of Heidelberg, Director, Max Planck Institute for Comparative Public Law and International Law, Vice-President, European Commission of Human Rights, Heidelberg, Fed. Rep. of Germany

Garner, J. F., Professor, Nottingham, Great Britain

Henkin, L., Professor of Law, Columbia University in the City of New York, School of Law, New York, USA

Jacobs, F. G., Professor of European Law, King's College, London, Great Britain

Jolowicz, J. A., Professor of Comparative Law, Trinity College, Cambridge, Great Britain

Lorenz, W., Professor of Law, University of Munich, Vice-President, International Association of Legal Science, Institut für Internationales Recht der Universität München, München, Fed. Rep. of Germany

Malinverni, G., Professor of Law, University of Geneva, Faculty of Law, Geneva, Switzerland

Mbaya, E.-R., Professeur de droit, Université de Cologne, Seminar für Staatsphilosophie und Rechtspolitik, Köln, Rep. Fed. d'Allemagne

Mitrović, D., Professeur de droit, Belgrad, Yougoslavie

Özsunay, E., Professor of Comparative Law and Civil Law, Center for Comparative Legal Studies, University of Istanbul, Faculty of Law, Beyazit, Istanbul, Turkey

Partsch, K. J., Professor of Law, University of Bonn, Member of the UN Committee on the Elimination of Racial Discrimination, Ingelheim, Fed. Rep. of Germany

Reinikainen, V. O., Dr., Reinikainen Consultants, Geneva, Switzerland

Robert, J., Professeur de droit, Université de Paris, Antony, France

Schade, H. E., Research Assistant, Research Center for International Law, University of Cambridge, Cambridge, Great Britain

Tumanov, V. A., Professor of Law, Institute of State and Law of the USSR Academy of Sciences, Moscow, USSR

Tunc, A., Professeur de droit, Université de Paris I, Président, Association Internationale des Sciences Juridiques, Panthéon-Sorbonne, Centre d'Etudes juridiques comparatives, Paris, France

Weiler, J., Professor of Law, University of Michigan, Law School, Ann Arbor, Michigan, USA

Yahia-Cherif, S., Professeur, Conseiller, Avocat à la Cour, Alger, Algérie

Yamane, H., Division of Human Rights and Peace, UNESCO, Paris, France

Appendix

Texts of Selected Universal and Regional Human Rights Instruments

Universal Declaration of Human Rights [1]

PREAMBLE

Whereas recognition of the inherent dignity and of the equal and inalienable rights of all members of the human family is the foundation of freedom, justice and peace in the world,

Whereas disregard and contempt for human rights have resulted in barbarous acts which have outraged the conscience of mankind, and the advent of a world in which human beings shall enjoy freedom of speech and belief and freedom from fear and want has been proclaimed as the highest aspiration of the common people,

Whereas it is essential, if man is not to be compelled to have recourse, as a last resort, to rebellion against tyranny and oppression, that human rights should be protected by the rule of law,

Whereas it is essential to promote the development of friendly relations between nations,

Whereas the peoples of the United Nations have in the Charter reaffirmed their faith in fundamental human rights, in the dignity and worth of the human person and in the equal rights of men and women and have determined to promote social progress and better standards of life in larger freedom,

Whereas Member States have pledged themselves to achieve, in co-operation with the United Nations, the promotion of universal respect for and observance of human rights and fundamental freedoms,

Whereas a common understanding of these rights and freedoms is of the greatest importance for the full realization of this pledge,

Now, therefore, THE GENERAL ASSEMBLY *proclaims*

This Universal Declaration of Human Rights as a common standard of achievement for all peoples and all nations, to the end that every individual and every organ of society, keeping this Declaration constantly in mind, shall strive by teaching and education to promote respect for these rights and freedoms and by progressive measures, national and international, to secure their universal and effective recognition and observance, both among the peoples of Member States themselves and among the peoples of territories under their jurisdiction.

---

[1] Adopted on 10 December 1948.

Article 1

All human beings are born free and equal in dignity and rights. They are endowed with reason and conscience and should act towards one another in a spirit of brotherhood.

Article 2

Everyone is entitled to all the rights and freedoms set forth in this Declaration, without distinction of any kind, such as race, colour, sex, language, religion, political or other opinion, national or social origin, property, birth or other status.

Furthermore, no distinction shall be made on the basis of the political, jurisdictional or international status of the country or territory to which a person belongs, whether it be independent, trust, non-self-governing or under any other limitation of sovereignty.

Article 3

Everyone has the right to life, liberty and the security of person.

Article 4

No one shall be held in slavery or servitude; slavery and the slave trade shall be prohibited in all their forms.

Article 5

No one shall be subjected to torture or to cruel, inhuman or degrading treatment or punishment.

Article 6

Everyone has the right to recognition everywhere as a person before the law.

Article 7

All are equal before the law and are entitled without any discrimination to equal protection of the law. All are entitled to equal protection against any discrimination in violation of this Declaration and against any incitement to such discrimination.

Article 8

Everyone has the right to an effective remedy by the competent national tribunals for acts violating the fundamental rights granted him by the constitution or by law.

Article 9

No one shall be subjected to arbitrary arrest, detention or exile.

Article 10

Everyone is entitled in full equality to a fair and public hearing by an independent and impartial tribunal, in the determination of his rights and obligations and of any criminal charge against him.

Article 11

1. Everyone charged with a penal offence has the right to be presumed innocent until proved guilty according to law in a public trial at which he has had all the guarantees necessary for his defence.

2. No one shall be held guilty of any penal offence on account of any act or omission which did not constitute a penal offence, under national or international law, at the time when it was committed. Nor shall a heavier penalty be imposed than the one that was applicable at the time the penal offence was committed.

Article 12

No one shall be subjected to arbitrary interference with his privacy, family, home or correspondence, nor to attacks upon his honour and reputation. Everyone has the right to the protection of the law against such interference or attacks.

Article 13

1. Everyone has the right to freedom of movement and residence within the borders of each State.

2. Everyone has the right to leave any country, including his own, and to return to his country.

Article 14

1. Everyone has the right to seek and to enjoy in other countries asylum from persecution.

2. This right may not be invoked in the case of prosecutions genuinely arising from non-political crimes or from acts contrary to the purposes and principles of the United Nations.

Article 15

1. Everyone has the right to a nationality.

2. No one shall be arbitrarily deprived of his nationality nor denied the right to change his nationality.

Article 16

1. Men and women of full age, without any limitation due to race, nationality or religion, have the right to marry and to found a family. They are entitled to equal rights as to marriage, during marriage and at its dissolution.

2. Marriage shall be entered into only with the free and full consent of the intending spouses.

3. The family is the natural and fundamental group unit of society and is entitled to protection by society and the State.

Article 17

1. Everyone has the right to own property alone as well as in association with others.

2. No one shall be arbitrarily deprived of his property.

Article 18

Everyone has the right to freedom of thought, conscience and religion; this right includes freedom to change his religion or belief, and freedom, either alone or in community with others and in public or private, to manifest his religion or belief in teaching, practice, worship and observance.

Article 19

Everyone has the right to freedom of opinion and expression; this right includes freedom to hold opinions without interference and to seek, receive and impart information and ideas through any media and regardless of frontiers.

Article 20

1. Everyone has the right to freedom of peaceful assembly and association.

2. No one may be compelled to belong to an association.

Article 21

1. Everyone has the right to take part in the government of his country, directly or through freely chosen representatives.

2. Everyone has the right of equal access to public service in his country.

3. The will of the people shall be the basis of the authority of government; this will shall be expressed in periodic and genuine elections which shall be by universal and equal suffrage and shall be held by secret vote or by equivalent free voting procedures.

Article 22

Everyone, as a member of society, has the right to social security and is entitled to realization, through national effort and international co-operation and in accordance with the organization and resources of each State, of the economic, social and cultural rights indispensable for his dignity and the free development of his personality.

Article 23

1. Everyone has the right to work, to free choice of employment, to just and favourable conditions of work and to protection against unemployment.

2. Everyone, without any discrimination, has the right to equal pay for equal work.

3. Everyone who works has the right to just and favourable remuneration ensuring for himself and his family an existence worthy of human dignity, and supplemented, if necessary, by other means of social protection.

4. Everyone has the right to form and to join trade unions for the protection of his interests.

Article 24

Everyone has the right to rest and leisure, including reasonable limitation of working hours and periodic holidays with pay.

Article 25

1. Everyone has the right to a standard of living adequate for the health and well-being of himself and of his family, including food, clothing, housing and medical care and necessary social services, and the right to security in the event of unemployment, sickness, disability, widowhood, old age or other lack of livelihood in circumstances beyond his control.

2. Motherhood and childhood are entitled to special care and assistance. All children, whether born in or out of wedlock, shall enjoy the same social protection.

Article 26

1. Everyone has the right to education. Education shall be free, at least in the elementary and fundamental stages. Elementary education shall be compulsory. Technical and professional education shall be made generally available and higher education shall be equally accessible to all on the basis of merit.

2. Education shall be directed to the full development of the human personality and to the strengthening of respect for human rights and fundamental freedoms. It shall promote understanding, tolerance and friendship among all nations, racial or religious groups, and shall further the activities of the United Nations for the maintenance of peace.

3. Parents have a prior right to choose the kind of education that shall be given to their children.

Article 27

1. Everyone has the right freely to participate in the cultural life of the community, to enjoy the arts and to share in scientific advancement and its benefits.

2. Everyone has the right to the protection of the moral and material interests resulting from any scientific, literary or artisitic production of which he is the author.

Article 28

Everyone is entitled to a social and international order in which the rights and freedoms set forth in this Declaration can be fully realized.

Article 29

1. Everyone has duties to the community in which alone the free and full development of his personality is possible.

2. In the exercise of his rights and freedoms, everyone shall be subject only to such limitations as are determined by law solely for the purpose of securing due recognition and respect for the rights and freedoms of others and of meeting the just requirements of morality, public order and the general welfare in a democratic society.

3. These rights and freedoms may in no case be exercised contrary to the purposes and principles of the United Nations.

Article 30

Nothing in this Declaration may be interpreted as implying for any State, group or person any right to engage in any activity or to perform any act aimed at the destruction of any of the rights and freedoms set forth herein.

International Covenant on Economic, Social and Cultural Rights [1]

PREAMBLE

The States Parties to the Present Covenant,

Considering that, in accordance with the principles proclaimed in the Charter of the United Nations, recognition of the inherent dignity and of the equal and inalienable rights of all members of the human family is the foundation of freedom, justice and peace in the world,

Recognizing that these rights derive from the inherent dignity of the human person,

Recognizing that, in accordance with the Universal Declaration of Human Rights, the ideal of free human beings enjoying freedom from fear and want can only be achieved if conditions are created whereby everyone may enjoy his economic, social and cultural rights, as well as his civil and political rights,

Considering the obligation of States under the Charter of the United Nations to promote universal respect for, and observance of, human rights and freedoms,

Realizing that the individual, having duties to other individuals and to the community to which he belongs, is under a responsibility to strive for the promotion and observance of the rights recognized in the present Covenant,

Agree upon the following articles:

PART I

Article 1

1. All peoples have the right of self-determination. By virtue of that right they freely determine their political status and freely pursue their economic, social and cultural development.

2. All peoples may, for their own ends, freely dispose of their natural wealth and resources without prejudice to any obligations arising out of in-

---

[1] In force since 3 January 1976.

ternational economic co-operation, based upon the principle of mutual benefit, and international law. In no case may a people be deprived of its own means of subsistence.

3. The States Parties to the present Covenant, including those having responsibility for the administration of Non-Self-Governing and Trust Territories, shall promote the realization of the right of self-determination, and shall respect that right, in conformity with the provisions of the Charter of the United Nations.

PART II

Article 2

1. Each State Party to the present Covenant undertakes to take steps, individually and through international assistance and co-operation, especially economic and technical, to the maximum of its available resources, with a view to achieving progressively the full realization of the rights recognized in the present Covenant by all appropriate means, including particularly the adoption of legislative measures.

2. The States Parties to the present Covenant undertake to guarantee that the rights enunciated in the present Covenant will be exercised without discrimination of any kind as to race, colour, sex, language, religion, political or other opinion, national or social origin, property, birth or other status.

3. Developing countries, with due regard to human rights and their national economy, may determine to what extent they would guarantee the economic rights recognized in the present Covenant to non-nationals.

Article 3

The States Parties to the present Covenant undertake to ensure the equal right of men and women to the enjoyment of all economic, social and cultural rights set forth in the present Covenant.

Article 4

The States Parties to the present Covenant recognize that, in the enjoyment of those rights provided by the State in conformity with the present Covenant, the State may subject such rights only to such limitations as are determined by law only in so far as this may be compatible with the nature of these rights and solely for the purpose of promoting the general welfare in a democratic society.

Article 5

1. Nothing in the present Covenant may be interpreted as implying for any State, group or person any right to engage in any activity or to perform any act aimed at the destruction of any of the rights or freedoms recognized

herein, or at their limitation to a greater extent than is provided for in the present Covenant.

2. No restriction upon or derogation from any of the fundamental human rights recognized or existing in any country in virtue of law, conventions, regulations or custom shall be admitted on the pretext that the present Covenant does not recognize such rights or that it recognizes them to a lesser extent.

PART III

Article 6

1. The States Parties to the present Covenant recognize the right to work, which includes the right of everyone to the opportunity to gain his living by work which he freely chooses or accepts, and will take appropriate steps to safeguard this right.

2. The steps to be taken by a State Party to the present Covenant to achieve the full realization of this right shall include technical and vocational guidance and training programmes, policies and techniques to achieve steady economic, social and cultural development and full and productive employment under conditions safeguarding fundamental political and economic freedoms to the individual.

Article 7

The States Parties to the present Covenant recognize the right of everyone to the enjoyment of just and favourable conditions of work which ensure, in particular:

(a) Remuneration which provides all workers, as a minimum, with:

(i) Fair wages and equal remuneration of work of equal value without distinction of any kind, in particular women being guaranteed conditions of work not inferior to those enjoyed by men, with equal pay for equal work;

(ii) A decent living for themselves and their families in accordance with the provisions of the present Covenant;

(b) Safe and healthy working conditions;

(c) Equal opportunity for everyone to be promoted in his employment to an appropriate higher level, subject to no considerations other than those of seniority and competence;

(d) Rest, leisure and reasonable limitation of working hours and periodic holidays with pay, as well as remuneration for public holidays.

Article 8

1. The States Parties to the present Covenant undertake to ensure:

(a) The right of everyone to form trade unions and join the trade union of his choice, subject only to the rules of the organization concerned, for the promotion and protection of his economic and social interests. No restrictions may be placed on the exercise of this right other than those prescribed by law and which are necessary in a democratic society in the interests of national security or public order or for the protection of the rights and freedoms of others;

(b) The right of trade unions to establish national federations or confederations and the right of the latter to form or join international trade-union organizations;

(c) The right of trade unions to function freely subject to no limitations other than those prescribed by law and which are necessary in a democratic society in the interests of national security or public order or for the protection of the rights and freedoms of others;

(d) The right to strike, provided that it is exercised in conformity with the laws of the particular country.

2. This article shall not prevent the imposition of lawful restrictions on the exercise of these rights by members of the armed forces or of the police or of the administration of the State.

3. Nothing in this article shall authorize States Parties to the International Labour Organisation Convention of 1948 concerning Freedom of Association and Protection of the Right to Organise to take legislative measures which would prejudice, or apply the law in such a manner as would prejudice, the guarantees provided for in that Convention.

Article 9

The States Parties to the present Covenant recognize the right of everyone to social security, including social insurance.

Article 10

The States Parties to the present Covenant recognize that:

1. The widest possible protection and assistance should be accorded to the family, which is the natural and fundamental group unit of society, particularly for its establishment and while it is responsible for the care and education of dependent children. Marriage must be entered into with the free consent of the intending spouses.

2. Special protection should be accorded to mothers during a reasonable period before and after childbirth. During such period working mothers should be accorded paid leave or leave with adequate social security benefits.

3. Special measures of protection and assistance should be taken on behalf of all children and young persons without any discrimination for reasons of parentage or other conditions. Children and young persons should be protected from economic and social exploitation. Their employment in work harmful to their morals or health or dangerous to life or likely to hamper their normal development should be punishable by law. States should also set age limits below which the paid employment of child labour should be prohibited and punishable by law.

Article 11

1. The States Parties to the present Covenant recognize the right of everyone to an adequate standard of living for himself and his family, including adequate food, clothing and housing, and to the continuous improvement of living conditions. The States Parties will take appropriate steps to ensure the realization of this right, recognizing to this effect the essential importance of international co-operation based on free consent.

2. The States Parties to the present Covenant, recognizing the fundamental right of everyone to be free from hunger, shall take, individually and through international co-operation, the measures, including specific programmes, which are needed:

(a) To improve methods of production, conservation and distribution of food by making full use of technical and scientific knowledge, by disseminating knowledge of the principles of nutrition and by developing or reforming agrarian systems in such a way as to achieve the most efficient development and utilization of natural resources;

(b) Taking into account the problems of both food-importing and food-exporting countries, to ensure an equitable distribution of world food supplies in relation to need.

Article 12

1. The States Parties to the present Covenant recognize the right of everyone to the enjoyment of the highest attainable standard of physical and mental health.

2. The steps to be taken by the States Parties to the present Covenant to achieve the full realization of this right shall include those necessary for:

(a) The provision for the reduction of the stillbirth-rate and of infant mortality and for the healthy development of the child;

(b) The improvement of all aspects of environmental and industrial hygiene;

(c) The prevention, treatment and control of epidemic, endemic, occupational and other diseases;

(d) The creation of conditions which would assure to all medical service and medical attention in the event of sickness.

Article 13

1. The States Parties to the present Covenant recognize the right of everyone to education. They agree that education shall be directed to the full development of the human personality and the sense of its dignity, and shall strengthen the respect for human rights and fundamental freedoms. They further agree that education shall enable all persons to participate effectively in a free society, promote understanding, tolerance and friendship among all nations and all racial, ethnic or religious groups, and further the activities of the United Nations for the maintenance of peace.

2. The States Parties to the present Covenant recognize that, with a view to achieving the full realization of this right:

(a) Primary education shall be compulsory and available free to all;

(b) Secondary education in its different forms, including technical and vocational secondary education, shall be made generally available and accessible to all by every appropriate means, and in particular by the progressive introduction of free education;

(c) Higher education shall be made equally accessible to all, on the basis of capacity, by every appropriate means, and in particular by the progressive introduction of free education;

(d) Fundamental education shall be encouraged or intensified as far as possible for those persons who have not received or completed the whole period of their primary education;

(e) The development of a system of schools at all levels shall be actively pursued, an adequate fellowship system shall be established, and the material conditions of teaching staff shall be continuously improved.

3. The States Parties to the present Covenant undertake to have respect for the liberty of parents and, when applicable, legal guardians to choose for their children schools, other than those established by the public authorities, which conform to such minimum educational standards as may be laid down or approved by the State and to ensure the religious and moral education of their children in conformity with their own convictions.

4. No part of this article shall be construed so as to interfere with the liberty of individuals and bodies to establish and direct educational institutions, subject always to the observance of the principles set forth in paragraph 1 of this article and to the requirement that the education given in such institutions shall conform to such minimum standards as may be laid down by the State.

Article 14

Each State Party to the present Covenant which, at the time of becoming a Party, has not been able to secure in its metropolitan territory or other territories under its jurisdiction compulsory primary education, free of charge, undertakes, within two years, to work out and adopt a detailed plan of action for the progressive implementation, within a reasonable number of years, to be fixed in the plan, of the principle of compulsory education free of charge for all.

Article 15

1. The States Parties to the present Covenant recognize the right of everyone:

(a) To take part in cultural life;

(b) To enjoy the benefits of scientific progress and its applications;

(c) To benefit from the protection of the moral and material interests resulting from any scientific, literary or artistic production of which he is the author.

2. The steps to be taken by the States Parties to the present Covenant to achieve the full realization of this right shall include those necessary for the conservation, the development and the diffusion of science and culture.

3. The States Parties to the present Covenant undertake to respect the freedom indispensable for scientific research and creative activity.

4. The States Parties to the present Covenant recognize the benefits to be derived from the encouragement and development of international contacts and co-operation in the scientific and cultural fields.

PART IV

Article 16

1. The States Parties to the present Covenant undertake to submit in conformity with this part of the Covenant reports on the measures which they have adopted and the progress made in achieving the observance of the rights recognized herein.

2. (a) All reports shall be submitted to the Secretary-General of the United Nations, who shall transmit copies to the Economic and Social Council for consideration in accordance with the provisions of the present Covenant;

(b) The Secretary-General of the United Nations shall also transmit to the specialized agencies copies of the reports, or any relevant parts therefrom, from States Parties to the present Covenant which are also members of these specialized agencies in so far as these reports, or parts therefrom, relate to any matters which fall within the responsibilities of the said agencies in accordance with their constitutional instruments.

Article 17

1. The States Parties to the present Covenant shall furnish their reports in stages, in accordance with a programme to be established by the Economic and Social Council within one year of the entry into force of the present Covenant after consultation with the States Parties and the specialized agencies concerned.

2. Reports may indicate factors and difficulties affecting the degree of fulfilment of obligations under the present Covenant.

3. Where relevant information has previously been furnished to the United Nations or to any specialized agency by any State Party to the present Covenant, it will not be necessary to reproduce that information, but a precise reference to the information so furnished will suffice.

Article 18

Pursuant to its responsibilities under the Charter of the United Nations in the field of human rights and fundamental freedoms, the Economic and Social Council may make arrangements with the specialized agencies in respect of their reporting to it on the progress made in achieving the observance of the provisions of the present Covenant falling within the scope of their activities. These reports may include particulars of decisions and recommendations on such implementation adopted by their competent organs.

Article 19

The Economic and Social Council may transmit to the Commission on Human Rights for study and general recommendation or, as appropriate, for information the reports concerning human rights submitted by States in accordance with articles 16 and 17, and those concerning human rights submitted by the specialized agencies in accordance with article 18.

Article 20

The States Parties to the present Covenant and the specialized agencies concerned may submit comments to the Economic and Social Council on any general recommendation under article 19 or reference to such general recommendation in any report of the Commission on Human Rights or any documentation referred to therein.

Article 21

The Economic and Social Council may submit from time to time to the General Assembly reports with recommendations of a general nature and a summary of the information received from the States Parties to the present Covenant and the specialized agencies on the measures taken and the progress made in achieving general observance of the rights recognized in the present Covenant.

Article 22

The Economic and Social Council may bring to the attention of other organs of the United Nations, their subsidiary organs and specialized agencies concerned with furnishing technical assistance any matters arising out of the reports referred to in this part of the present Covenant which may assist such bodies in deciding, each within its field of competence, on the advisability of international measures likely to contribute to the effective progressive implementation of the present Covenant.

Article 23

The States Parties to the present Covenant agree that international action for the achievement of the rights recognized in the present Covenant includes such methods as the conclusion of conventions, the adoption of recommendations, the furnishing of technical assistance and the holding of regional meetings and technical meetings for the purpose of consultation and study organized in conjunction with the Governments concerned.

Article 24

Nothing in the present Covenant shall be interpreted as impairing the provisions of the Charter of the United Nations and of the constitutions of the specialized agencies which define the respective responsibilities of the various organs of the United Nations and of the specialized agencies in regard to the matters dealt with in the present Covenant.

Article 25

Nothing in the present Covenant shall be interpreted as impairing the inherent right of all peoples to enjoy and utilize fully and freely their natural wealth and resources.

PART V

Article 26

1. The present Covenant is open for signature by any State Member of the United Nations or member of any of its specialized agencies, by any State Party to the Statute of the International Court of Justice, and by any other State which has been invited by the General Assembly of the United Nations to become a party to the present Covenant.
2. The present Covenant is subject to ratification. Instruments of ratification shall be deposited with the Secretary-General of the United Nations.
3. The present Covenant shall be open to accession by any State referred to in paragraph 1 of this article.
4. Accession shall be effected by the deposit of an instrument of accession with the Secretary-General of the United Nations.
5. The Secretary-General of the United Nations shall inform all States which have signed the present Covenant or acceded to it of the deposit of each instrument of ratification or accession.

Article 27

1. The present Covenant shall enter into force three months after the date of the deposit with the Secretary-General of the United Nations of the thirty-fifth instrument of ratification or instrument of accession.
2. For each State ratifying the present Covenant or acceding to it after the deposit of the thirty-fifth instrument of ratification or instrument of accession, the present Covenant shall enter into force three months after the date of the deposit of its own instrument of ratification or instrument of accession.

Article 28

The provisions of the present Covenant shall extend to all parts of federal States without any limitations or exceptions.

Article 29

1. Any State Party to the present Covenant may propose an amendment and file it with the Secretary-General of the United Nations. The Secretary-General shall thereupon communicate any proposed amendments to the States Parties to the present Covenant with a request that they notify him whether they favour a conference of States Parties for the purpose of considering and voting upon the proposals. In the event that at least one third of the States Parties favours such a conference, the Secretary-General shall convene the conference under the auspices of the United Nations. Any amendment adopted by a majority of the States Parties present and voting at the conference shall be submitted to the General Assembly of the United Nations for approval.

2. Amendments shall come into force when they have been approved by the General Assembly of the United Nations and accepted by a two-thirds majority of the States Parties to the present Covenant in accordance with their respective constitutional processes.

3. When amendments come into force they shall be binding on those States Parties which have accepted them, other States Parties still being bound by the provisions of the present Covenant and any earlier amendment which they have accepted.

Article 30

Irrespective of the notifications made under article 26, paragraph 5, the Secretary-General of the United Nations shall inform all States referred to in paragraph 1 of the same article of the following particulars:

(a) Signatures, ratifications and accessions under article 26;

(b) The date of the entry into force of the present Covenant under article 27 and the date of the entry into force of any amendments under article 29.

Article 31

1. The present Covenant, of which the Chinese, English, French, Russian and Spanish texts are equally authentic, shall be deposited in the archives of the United Nations.

2. The Secretary-General of the United Nations shall transmit certified copies of the present Covenant to all States referred to in article 26.

International Covenant on Civil and Political Rights [1]

PREAMBLE

The States Parties to the Present Covenant,

Considering that, in accordance with the principles proclaimed in the Charter of the United Nations, recognition of the inherent dignity and of the equal and inalienable rights of all members of the human family is the foundation of freedom, justice and peace in the world,

Recognizing that these rights derive from the inherent dignity of the human person,

Recognizing that, in accordance with the Universal Declaration of Human Rights, the ideal of free human beings enjoying civil and political freedom and freedom from fear and want can only be achieved if conditions are created whereby everyone may enjoy his civil and political rights, as well as his economic, social and cultural rights,

Considering the obligation of States under the Charter of the United Nations to promote universal respect for, and observance of, human rights and freedoms,

Realizing that the individual, having duties to other individuals and to the community to which he belongs, is under a responsibility to strive for the promotion and observance of the rights recognized in the present Covenant,

Agree upon the following articles:

PART I

Article 1

1. All peoples have the right of self-determination. By virtue of that right they freely determine their political status and freely pursue their economic, social and cultural development.

2. All peoples may, for their own ends, freely dispose of their natural wealth and resources without prejudice to any obligations arising out of international economic co-operation, based upon the principle of mutual ben-

---

[1] In force since 23 March 1976.

efit, and international law. In no case may a people be deprived of its own means of subsistence.

3. The States Parties to the present Covenant, including those having responsibility for the administration of Non-Self-Governing and Trust Territories, shall promote the realization of the right of self-determination, and shall respect that right, in conformity with the provisions of the Charter of the United Nations.

PART II

Article 2

1. Each State Party to the present Covenant undertakes to respect and to ensure to all individuals within its territory and subject to its jurisdiction the rights recognized in the present Covenant, without distinction of any kind, such as race, colour, sex, language, religion, political or other opinion, national or social origin, property, birth or other status.

2. Where not already provided for by existing legislative or other measures, each State Party to the present Covenant undertakes to take the necessary steps, in accordance with its constitutional processes and with the provisions of the present Covenant, to adopt such legislative or other measures as may be necessary to give effect to the rights recognized in the present Covenant.

3. Each State Party to the present Covenant untertakes:

(a) To ensure that any person whose rights or freedoms as herein recognized are violated shall have an effective remedy, notwithstanding that the violation has been committed by persons acting in an official capacity;

(b) To ensure that any person claiming such a remedy shall have his right thereto determined by competent judicial, administrative or legislative authorities, or by any other competent authority provided for by the legal system of the State, and to develop the possibilities of judicial remedy;

(c) To ensure that the competent authorities shall enforce such remedies when granted.

Article 3

The States Parties to the present Covenant undertake to ensure the equal right of men and women to the enjoyment of all civil and political rights set forth in the present Covenant.

Article 4

1. In time of public emergency which threatens the life of the nation and the existence of which is officially proclaimed, the States Parties to the present Covenant may take measures derogating from their obligations under the present Covenant to the extent strictly required by the exigencies of the situation, provided that such measures are not inconsistent with their other obli-

gations under international law and do not involve discrimination solely on the ground of race, colour, sex, language, religion or social origin.

2. No derogation from articles 6, 7, 8 (paragraphs 1 and 2), 11, 15, 16 and 18 may be made under this provision.

3. Any State Party to the present Covenant availing itself of the right of derogation shall immediately inform the other States Parties to the present Covenant, through the intermediary of the Secretary-General of the United Nations, of the provisions from which it has derogated and of the reasons by which it was actuated. A further communication shall be made, through the same intermediary, on the date on which it terminates such derogation.

Article 5

1. Nothing in the present Covenant may be interpreted as implying for any State, group or person any right to engage in any activity or perform any act aimed at the destruction of any of the rights and freedoms recognized herein or at their limitation to a greater extent than is provided for in the present Covenant.

2. There shall be no restriction upon or derogation from any of the fundamental human rights recognized or existing in any State Party to the present Covenant pursuant to law, conventions, regulations or custom on the pretext that the present Covenant does not recognize such rights or that it recognizes them to a lesser extent.

PART III

Article 6

1. Every human being has the inherent right to life. This right shall be protected by law. No one shall be arbitrarily deprived of his life.

2. In countries which have not abolished the death penalty, sentence of death may be imposed only for the most serious crimes in accordance with the law in force at the time of the commission of the crime and not contrary to the provisions of the present Covenant and to the Convention on the Prevention and Punishment of the Crime of Genocide. This penalty can only be carried out pursuant to a final judgement rendered by a competent court.

3. When deprivation of life constitutes the crime of genocide, it is understood that nothing in this article shall authorize any State Party to the present Covenant to derogate in any way from any obligation assumed under the provisions of the Convention on the Prevention and Punishment of the Crime of Genocide.

4. Anyone sentenced to death shall have the right to seek pardon or commutation of the sentence. Amnesty, pardon or commutation of the sentence of death may be granted in all cases.

5. Sentence of death shall not be imposed for crimes committed by persons below eighteen years of age and shall not be carried out on pregnant women.

6. Nothing in this article shall be invoked to delay or to prevent the abolition of capital punishment by any State Party to the present Covenant.

Article 7

No one shall be subjected to torture or to cruel, inhuman or degrading treatment or punishment. In particular, no one shall be subjected without his free consent to medical or scientific experimentation.

Article 8

1. No one shall be held in slavery; slavery and the slave-trade in all their forms shall be prohibited.

2. No one shall be held in servitude.

3. (a) No one shall be required to perform forced or compulsory labour;

(b) Paragraph 3 (a) shall not be held to preclude, in countries where imprisonment with hard labour may be imposed as a punishment for a crime, the performance of hard labour in pursuance of a sentence to such punishment by a competent court;

(c) For the purpose of this paragraph the term "forced or compulsory labour" shall not include:

(i) Any work or service, not referred to in subparagraph (b), normally required of a person who is under detention in consequence of a lawful order of a court, or of a person during conditional release from such detention;

(ii) Any service of a military character and, in countries where conscientious objection is recognized, any national service required by law of conscientious objectors;

(iii) Any service exacted in cases of emergency or calamity threatening the life or well-being of the community;

(iv) Any work or service which forms part of normal civil obligations.

Article 9

1. Everyone has the right to liberty and security of person. No one shall be subjected to arbitrary arrest or detention. No one shall be deprived of his liberty except on such grounds and in accordance with such procedure as are established by law.

2. Anyone who is arrested shall be informed, at the time of arrest, of the reasons for his arrest and shall be promptly informed of any charges against him.

3. Anyone arrested or detained on a criminal charge shall be brought promptly before a judge or other officer authorized by law to exercise judicial power and shall be entitled to trial within a reasonable time or to release. It shall not be the general rule that persons awaiting trial shall be detained in custody, but release may be subject to guarantees to appear for trial, at any

other stage of the judicial proceedings, and, should occasion arise, for execution of the judgement.

4. Anyone who is deprived of his liberty by arrest or detention shall be entitled to take proceedings before a court, in order that that court may decide without delay on the lawfulness of his detention and order his release if the detention is not lawful.

5. Anyone who has been the victim of unlawful arrest or detention shall have an enforceable right to compensation.

Article 10

1. All persons deprived of their liberty shall be treated with humanity and with respect for the inherent dignity of the human person.

2. (a) Accused persons shall, save in exceptional circumstances, be segregated from convicted persons and shall be subject to separate treatment appropriate to their status as unconvicted persons;

(b) Accused juvenile persons shall be separated from adults and brought as speedily as possible for adjudication.

3. The penitentiary system shall comprise treatment of prisoners the essential aim of which shall be their reformation and social rehabilitation. Juvenile offenders shall be segregated from adults and be accorded treatment appropriate to their age and legal status.

Article 11

No one shall be imprisoned merely on the ground of inability to fulfil a contractual obligation.

Article 12

1. Everyone lawfully within the territory of a State shall, within that territory, have the right to liberty of movement and freedom to choose his residence.

2. Everyone shall be free to leave any country, including his own.

3. The above-mentioned rights shall not be subject to any restrictions except those which are provided by law, are necessary to protect national security, public order (*ordre public*), public health or morals or the rights and freedoms of others, and are consistent with the other rights recognized in the present Covenant.

4. No one shall be arbitrarily deprived of the right to enter his own country.

Article 13

An alien lawfully in the territory of a State Party to the present Covenant may be expelled therefrom only in pursuance of a decision reached in accordance with law and shall, except where compelling reasons of national security otherwise require, be allowed to submit the reasons against his expulsion and to have his case reviewed by, and be presented for the purpose before, the competent authority or a person or persons especially designated by the competent authority.

Article 14

1. All persons shall be equal before the courts and tribunals. In the determination of any criminal charge against him, or of his rights and obligations in a suit at law, everyone shall be entitled to a fair and public hearing by a competent, independent and impartial tribunal established by law. The Press and the public may be excluded from all or part of a trial for reasons of morals, public order (*ordre public*) or national security in a democratic society, or when the interest of the private lives of the parties so requires, or to the extent strictly necessary in the opinion of the court in special circumstances where publicity would prejudice the interests of justice; but any judgement rendered in a criminal case or in a suit at law shall be made public except where the interest of juvenile persons otherwise requires or the proceedings concern matrimonial disputes or the guardianship of children.

2. Everyone charged with a criminal offence shall have the right to be presumed innocent until proved guilty according to law.

3. In the determination of any criminal charge against him, everyone shall be entitled to the following minimum guarantees, in full equality:

(a) To be informed promptly and in detail in a language which he understands of the nature and cause of the charge against him;

(b) To have adequate time and facilities for the preparation of his defence and to communicate with counsel of his own choosing;

(c) To be tried without undue delay;

(d) To be tried in his presence, and to defend himself in person or through legal assistance of his own choosing; to be informed, if he does not have legal assistance, of this right; and to have legal assistance assigned to him, in any case where the interests of justice so require, and without payment by him in any such case if he does not have sufficient means to pay for it;

(e) To examine, or have examined, the witnesses against him and to obtain the attendance and examination of witnesses on his behalf under the same conditions as witnesses against him;

(f) To have the free assistance of an interpreter if he cannot understand or speak the language used in court;

(g) Not to be compelled to testify against himself or to confess guilt.

4. In the case of juvenile persons, the procedure shall be such as will take account of their age and the desirability of promoting their rehabilitation.

5. Everyone convicted of a crime shall have the right to his conviction and sentence being reviewed by a higher tribunal according to law.

6. When a person has by a final decision been convicted of a criminal offence and when subsequently his conviction has been reversed or he has been pardoned on the ground that a new or newly discovered fact shows conclusively that there has been a miscarriage of justice, the person who has suffered punishment as a result of such conviction shall be compensated according to law, unless it is proved that the non-disclosure of the unknown fact in time is wholly or partly attributable to him.

7. No one shall be liable to be tried or punished again for an offence for which he has already been finally convicted or acquitted in accordance with the law and penal procedure of each country.

Article 15

1. No one shall be held guilty of any criminal offence on account of any act or omission which did not constitute a criminal offence, under national or international law, at the time when it was committed. Nor shall a heavier penalty be imposed than the one that was applicable at the time when the criminal offence was committed. If, subsequent to the commission of the offence, provision is made by law for the imposition of a lighter penalty, the offender shall benefit thereby.

2. Nothing in this article shall prejudice the trial and punishment of any person for any act or omission which, at the time when it was committed, was criminal according to the general principles of law recognized by the community of nations.

Article 16

Everyone shall have the right to recognition everywhere as a person before the law.

Article 17

1. No one shall be subjected to arbitrary or unlawful interference with his privacy, family, home or correspondence, nor to unlawful attacks on his honour and reputation.

2. Everyone has the right to the protection of the law against such interference or attacks.

Article 18

1. Everyone shall have the right to freedom of thought, conscience and religion. This right shall include freedom to have or to adopt a religion or belief of his choice, and freedom, either individually or in community with others and in public or private, to manifest his religion or belief in worship, observance, practice and teaching.

2. No one shall be subject to coercion which would impair his freedom to have or to adopt a religion or belief of his choice.

3. Freedom to manifest one's religion or beliefs may be subject only to such limitations as are prescribed by law and are necessary to protect public safety, order, health, or morals or the fundamental rights and freedoms of others.

4. The States Parties to the present Covenant undertake to have respect for the liberty of parents and, when applicable, legal guardians to ensure the religious and moral education of their children in conformity with their own convictions.

Article 19

1. Everyone shall have the right to hold opinions without interference.

2. Everyone shall have the right to freedom of expression; this right shall include freedom to seek, receive and impart information and ideas of all kinds, regardless of frontiers, either orally, in writing or in print, in the form of art, or through any other media of his choice.

3. The exercise of the rights provided for in paragraph 2 of this article carries with it special duties and responsibilities. It may therefore be subject to certain restrictions, but these shall only be such as are provided by law and are necessary:

(a) For respect of the rights or reputations of others;

(b) For the protection of national security or of public order (*ordre public*), or of public health or morals.

Article 20

1. Any propaganda for war shall be prohibited by law.

2. Any advocacy of national, racial or religious hatred that constitutes incitement to discrimination, hostility or violence shall be prohibited by law.

Article 21

The right of peaceful assembly shall be recognized. No restrictions may be placed on the exercise of this right other than those imposed in conformity with the law and which are necessary in a democratic society in the interests of national security or public safety, public order (*ordre public*), the protection of public health or morals or the protection of the rights and freedoms of others.

Article 22

1. Everyone shall have the right to freedom of association with others, including the right to form and join trade unions for the protection of his interests.

2. No restrictions may be placed on the exercise of this right other than those which are prescribed by law and which are necessary in a democratic society in the interests of national security or public safety, public order (*ordre public*), the protection of public health or morals or the protection of

the rights and freedoms of others. This article shall not prevent the imposition of lawful restrictions on members of the armed forces and of the police in their exercise of this right.

3. Nothing in this article shall authorize States Parties to the International Labour Organisation Convention of 1948 concerning Freedom of Association and Protection of the Right to Organise to take legislative measures which would prejudice, or to apply the law in such a manner as to prejudice, the guarantees provided for in that Convention.

Article 23

1. The family is the natural and fundamental group unit of society and is entitled to protection by society and the State.

2. The right of men and women of marriageable age to marry and to found a family shall be recognized.

3. No marriage shall be entered into without the free and full consent of the intending spouses.

4. States Parties to the present Covenant shall take appropriate steps to ensure equality of rights and responsibilities of spouses as to marriage, during marriage and at its dissolution. In the case of dissolution, provision shall be made for the necessary protection of any children.

Article 24

1. Every child shall have, without any discrimination as to race, colour, sex, language, religion, national or social origin, property or birth, the right to such measures of protection as are required by his status as a minor, on the part of his family, society and the State.

2. Every child shall be registered immediately after birth and shall have a name.

3. Every child has the right to acquire a nationality.

Article 25

Every citizen shall have the right and the opportunity, without any of the distinctions mentioned in article 2 and without unreasonable restrictions:

(a) To take part in the conduct of public affairs, directly or through freely chosen representatives;

(b) To vote and to be elected at genuine periodic elections which shall be by universal and equal suffrage and shall be held by secret ballot, guaranteeing the free expression of the will of the electors;

(c) To have access, on general terms of equality, to public service in his country.

Article 26

All persons are equal before the law and are entitled without any discrimination to the equal protection of the law. In this respect, the law shall prohibit any discrimination and guarantee to all persons equal and effective protection against discrimination on any ground such as race, colour, sex, language, religion, political or other opinion, national or social origin, property, birth or other status.

Article 27

In those States in which ethnic, religious or linguistic minorities exist, persons belonging to such minorities shall not be denied the right, in community with the other members of their group, to enjoy their own culture, to profess and practise their own religion, or to use their own language.

PART IV

Article 28

1. There shall be established a Human Rights Committee (hereafter referred to in the present Covenant as the Committee). It shall consist of eighteen members and shall carry out the functions hereinafter provided.

2. The Committee shall be composed of nationals of the States Parties to the present Covenant who shall be persons of high moral character and recognized competence in the field of human rights, consideration being given to the usefulness of the participation of some persons having legal experience.

3. The members of the Committee shall be elected and shall serve in their personal capacity.

Article 29

1. The members of the Committee shall be elected by secret ballot from a list of persons possessing the qualifications prescribed in article 28 and nominated for the purpose by the States Parties to the present Covenant.

2. Each State Party to the present Covenant may nominate not more than two persons. These persons shall be nationals of the nominating State.

3. A person shall be eligible for renomination.

Article 30

1. The initial election shall be held no later than six months after the date of the entry into force of the present Covenant.

2. At least four months before the date of each election to the Committee, other than an election to fill a vacancy declared in accordance with article 34, the Secretary-General of the United Nations shall address a written invitation to the States Parties to the present Covenant to submit their nominations for membership of the Committee within three months.

3. The Secretary-General of the United Nations shall prepare a list in alphabetical order of all the persons thus nominated, with an indication of the States Parties which have nominated them, and shall submit it to the States

Parties to the present Covenant no later than one month before the date of each election.

4. Elections of the members of the Committee shall be held at a meeting of the States Parties to the present Covenant convened by the Secretary-General of the United Nations at the Headquarters of the United Nations. At that meeting, for which two thirds of the States Parties to the present Covenant shall constitute a quorum, the persons elected to the Committee shall be those nominees who obtain the largest number of votes and an absolute majority of the votes of the representatives of States Parties present and voting.

Article 31

1. The Committee may not include more than one national of the same State.

2. In the election of the Committee, consideration shall be given to equitable geographical distribution of membership and to the representation of the different forms of civilization and of the principal legal systems.

Article 32

1. The members of the Committee shall be elected for a term of four years. They shall be eligible for re-election if renominated. However, the terms of nine of the members elected at the first election shall expire at the end of two years; immediately after the first election, the names of these nine members shall be chosen by lot by the Chairman of the meeting referred to in article 30, paragraph 4.

2. Elections at the expiry of office shall be held in accordance with the preceding articles of this part of the present Covenant.

Article 33

1. If, in the unanimous opinion of the other members, a member of the Committee has ceased to carry out his functions for any cause other than absence of a temporary character, the Chairman of the Committee shall notify the Secretary-General of the United Nations, who shall then declare the seat of that member to be vacant.

2. In the event of the death or the resignation of a member of the Committee, the Chairman shall immediately notify the Secretary-General of the United Nations, who shall declare the seat vacant from the date of death or the date on which the resignation takes effect.

Article 34

1. When a vacancy is declared in accordance with article 33 and if the term of office of the member to be replaced does not expire within six months of the declaration of the vacancy, the Secretary-General of the United Nations shall notify each of the States Parties to the present Covenant, which

may within two months submit nominations in accordance with article 29 for the purpose of filling the vacancy.

2. The Secretary-General of the United Nations shall prepare a list in alphabetical order of the persons thus nominated and shall submit it to the States Parties to the present Covenant. The election to fill the vacancy shall then take place in accordance with the relevant provisions of this part of the present Covenant.

3. A member of the Committee elected to fill a vacancy declared in accordance with article 33 shall hold office for the remainder of the term of the member who vacated the seat on the Committee under the provisions of that article.

Article 35

The members of the Committee shall, with the approval of the General Assembly of the United Nations, receive emoluments from United Nations resources on such terms and conditions as the General Assembly may decide, having regard to the importance of the Committee's responsibilities.

Article 36

The Secretary-General of the United Nations shall provide the necessary staff and facilities for the effective performance of the functions of the Committee under the present Covenant.

Article 37

1. The Secretary-General of the United Nations shall convene the initial meeting of the Committee at the Headquarters of the United Nations.

2. After its initial meeting, the Committee shall meet at such times as shall be provided in its rules of procedure.

3. The Committee shall normally meet at the Headquarters of the United Nations or at the United Nations Office at Geneva.

Article 38

Every member of the Committee shall, before taking up his duties, make a solemn declaration in open committee that he will perform his functions impartially and conscientiously.

Article 39

1. The Committee shall elect its officers for a term of two years. They may be re-elected.

2. The Committee shall establish its own rules of procedure, but these rules shall provide, *inter alia,* that:

(a) Twelve members shall constitute a quorum;

(b) Decisions of the Committee shall be made by a majority vote of the members present.

Article 40

1. The States Parties to the present Covenant undertake to submit reports on the measures they have adopted which give effect to the rights recognized herein and on the progress made in the enjoyment of those rights:

(a) Within one year of the entry into force of the present Covenant for the States Parties concerned;

(b) Thereafter whenever the Committee so requests.

2. All reports shall be submitted to the Secretary-General of the United Nations, who shall transmit them to the Committee for consideration. Reports shall indicate the factors and difficulties, if any, affecting the implementation of the present Covenant.

3. The Secretary-General of the United Nations may, after consultation with the Committee, transmit to the specialized agencies concerned copies of such parts of the reports as may fall within their field of competence.

4. The Committee shall study the reports submitted by the States Parties to the present Covenant. It shall transmit its reports, and such general comments as it may consider appropriate, to the States Parties. The Committee may also transmit to the Economic and Social Council these comments along with the copies of the reports it has received from States Parties to the present Covenant.

5. The States Parties to the present Covenant may submit to the Committee observations on any comments that may be made in accordance with paragraph 4 of this article.

Article 41

1. A State Party to the present Covenant may at any time declare under this article that it recognizes the competence of the Committee to receive and consider communications to the effect that a State Party claims that another State Party is not fulfilling its obligations under the present Covenant. Communications under this article may be received and considered only if submitted by a State Party which has made a declaration recognizing in regard to itself the competence of the Committee. No communication shall be received by the Committee if it concerns a State Party which has not made such a declaration. Communications received under this article shall be dealt with in accordance with the following procedure:

(a) If a State Party to the present Covenant considers that another State Party is not giving effect to the provisions of the present Covenant, it may, by written communication, bring the matter to the attention of that State Party. Within three months after the receipt of the communication, the receiving State shall afford the State which sent the communication an explanation or any other statement in writing clarifying the matter, which should include, to the extent possible and pertinent, reference to domestic procedures and remedies taken, pending, or available in the matter.

(b) If the matter is not adjusted to the satisfaction of both States Parties concerned within six months after the receipt by the receiving State of the initial communication, either State shall have the right to refer the matter to the Committee, by notice given to the Committee and to the other State.

(c) The Committee shall deal with a matter referred to it only after it has ascertained that all available domestic remedies have been invoked and exhausted in the matter, in conformity with the generally recognized principles of international law. This shall not be the rule where the application of the remedies is unreasonably prolonged.

(d) The Committee shall hold closed meetings when examining communications under this article.

(e) Subject to the provisions of subparagraph (c), the Committee shall make available its good offices to the States Parties concerned with a view to a friendly solution of the matter on the basis of respect for human rights and fundamental freedoms as recognized in the present Covenant.

(f) In any matter referred to it, the Committee may call upon the States Parties concerned, referred to in subparagraph (b), to supply any relevant information.

(g) The States Parties concerned, referred to in subparagraph (b), shall have the right to be represented when the matter is being considered in the Committee and to make submissions orally and/or in writing.

(h) The Committee shall, within twelve months after the date of receipt of notice under subparagraph (b), submit a report:

(i) If a solution within the terms of subparagraph (e) is reached, the Committee shall confine its report to a brief statement of the facts and of the solution reached;

(ii) If a solution within the terms of subparagraph (e) is not reached, the Committee shall confine its report to a brief statement of the facts; the written submissions and record of the oral submissions made by the States Parties concerned shall be attached to the report.

In every matter, the report shall be communicated to the States Parties concerned.

2. The provisions of this article shall come into force when ten States Parties to the present Covenant have made declarations under paragraph 1 of this article. Such declarations shall be deposited by the States Parties with the Secretary-General of the United Nations, who shall transmit copies thereof to the other States Parties. A declaration may be withdrawn at any time by notification to the Secretary-General. Such a withdrawal shall not prejudice the consideration of any matter which is the subject of a communication already transmitted under this article; no further communication by any State Party shall be received after the notification of withdrawal of the declaration has been received by the Secretary-General, unless the State Party concerned has made a new declaration.

Article 42

1. (a) If a matter referred to the Committee in accordance with article 41 is not resolved to the satisfaction of the States Parties concerned, the Committee may, with the prior consent of the States Parties concerned, appoint an *ad hoc* Conciliation Commission (hereinafter referred to as the Commission). The good offices of the Commission shall be made available to the States Parties concerned with a view to an amicable solution of the matter on the basis of respect for the present Covenant;

(b) The Commission shall consist of five persons acceptable to the States Parties concerned. If the States Parties concerned fail to reach agreement within three months on all or part of the composition of the Commission, the members of the Commission concerning whom no agreement has been reached shall be elected by secret ballot by a two-thirds majority vote of the Committee from among its members.

2. The members of the Commission shall serve in their personal capacity. They shall not be nationals of the States Parties concerned, or of a State not party to the present Covenant, or of a State Party which has not made a declaration under article 41.

3. The Commission shall elect its own Chairman and adopt its own rules of procedure.

4. The meetings of the Commission shall normally be held at the Headquarters of the United Nations or at the United Nations Office at Geneva. However, they may be held at such other convenient places as the Commission may determine in consultation with the Secretary-General of the United Nations and the States Parties concerned.

5. The secretariat provided in accordance with article 36 shall also service the commissions appointed under this article.

6. The information received and collated by the Committee shall be made available to the Commission and the Commission may call upon the States Parties concerned to supply any other relevant information.

7. When the Commission has fully considered the matter, but in any event not later than twelve months after having been seized of the matter, it shall submit to the Chairman of the Committee a report for communication to the States Parties concerned:

(a) If the Commission is unable to complete its consideration of the matter within twelve months, it shall confine its report to a brief statement of the status of its consideration of the matter;

(b) If an amicable solution to the matter on the basis of respect for human rights as recognized in the present Covenant is reached, the Commission shall confine its report to a brief statement of the facts and of the solution reached;

(c) If a solution within the terms of subparagraph (b) is not reached, the Commission's report shall embody its findings on all questions of fact relevant to the issues between the States Parties concerned, and its views on the possibilities of an amicable solution of the matter. This report shall also contain the written submissions and a record of the oral submissions made by the States Parties concerned.

(d) If the Commission's report is submitted under subparagraph (c), the States Parties concerned shall, within three months of the receipt of the report, notify the Chairman of the Committee whether or not they accept the contents of the report of the Commission.

8. The provisions of this article are without prejudice to the responsibilities of the Committee under article 41.

9. The States Parties concerned shall share equally all the expenses of the members of the Commission in accordance with estimates to be provided by the Secretary-General of the United Nations.

10. The Secretary-General of the United Nations shall be empowered to pay the expenses of the members of the Commission, if necessary, before reimbursement by the States Parties concerned, in accordance with paragraph 9 of this article.

Article 43

The members of the Committee, and of the *ad hoc* conciliation commissions which may be appointed under article 42, shall be entitled to the facilities, privileges and immunities of experts on mission for the United Nations as laid down in the relevant sections of the Convention on the Privileges and Immunities of the United Nations.

Article 44

The provisions for the implementation of the present Covenant shall apply without prejudice to the procedures prescribed in the field of human rights by or under the constituent instruments and the conventions of the United Nations and of the specialized agencies and shall not prevent the States Parties to the present Covenant from having recourse to other procedures for settling a dispute in accordance with general or special international agreements in force between them.

Article 45

The Committee shall submit to the General Assembly of the United Nations, through the Economic and Social Council, and annual report on its activities.

PART V

Article 46

Nothing in the present Covenant shall be interpreted as impairing the provisions of the Charter of the United Nations and of the constitutions of the specialized agencies which define the respective responsibilities of the various organs of the United Nations and of the specialized agencies in regard to the matters dealt with in the present Covenant.

Article 47

Nothing in the present Covenant shall be interpreted as impairing the inherent right of all peoples to enjoy and utilize fully and freely their natural wealth and resources.

PART VI

Article 48

1. The present Covenant is open for signature by any State Member of the United Nations or member of any of its specialized agencies, by any State Party to the Statute of the International Court of Justice, and by any other State which has been invited by the General Assembly of the United Nations to become a party to the present Covenant.
2. The present Covenant is subject to ratification. Instruments of ratification shall be deposited with the Secretary-General of the United Nations.
3. The present Covenant shall be open to accession by any State referred to in paragraph 1 of this article.
4. Accession shall be effected by the deposit of an instrument of accession with the Secretary-General of the United Nations.
5. The Secretary-General of the United Nations shall inform all States which have signed this Covenant or acceded to it of the deposit of each instrument of ratification or accession.

Article 49

1. The present Covenant shall enter into force three months after the date of the deposit with the Secretary-General of the United Nations of the thirty-fifth instrument of ratification or instrument of accession.
2. For each State ratifying the present Covenant or acceding to it after the deposit of the thirty-fifth instrument of ratification or instrument of accession, the present Covenant shall enter into force three months after the date of the deposit of its own instrument of ratification or instrument of accession.

Article 50

The provisions of the present Covenant shall extend to all parts of federal States without any limitations or exceptions.

Article 51

1. Any State Party to the present Covenant may propose an amendment and file it with the Secretary-General of the United Nations. The Secretary-General of the United Nations shall thereupon communicate any proposed

amendments to the States Parties to the present Covenant with a request that they notify him whether they favour a conference of States Parties for the purpose of considering and voting upon the proposals. In the event that at least one third of the States Parties favours such a conference, the Secretary-General shall convene the conference under the auspices of the United Nations. Any amendment adopted by a majority of the States Parties present and voting at the conference shall be submitted to the General Assembly of the United Nations for approval.

2. Amendments shall come into force when they have been approved by the General Assembly of the United Nations and accepted by a two-thirds majority of the States Parties to the present Covenant in accordance with their respective constitutional processes.

3. When amendments come into force, they shall be binding on those States Parties which have accepted them, other States Parties still being bound by the provisions of the present Covenant and any earlier amendment which they have accepted.

Article 52

Irrespective of the notifications made under article 48, paragraph 5, the Secretary-General of the United Nations shall inform all States referred to in paragraph 1 of the same article of the following particulars:

(a) Signatures, ratifications and accessions under article 48;

(b) The date of the entry into force of the present Covenant under article 49 and the date of the entry into force of any amendments under article 51.

Article 53

1. The present Covenant, of which the Chinese, English, French, Russian and Spanish texts are equally authentic, shall be deposited in the archives of the United Nations.

2. The Secretary-General of the United Nations shall transmit certified copies of the present Covenant to all States referred to in article 48.

Optional Protocol to the International Covenant on Civil and Political Rights[1]

The States Parties to the Present Protocol,

Considering that in order further to achieve the purposes of the Covenant on Civil and Political Rights (hereinafter referred to as the Covenant) and the implementation of its provisions it would be appropriate to enable the Human Rights Committee set up in part IV of the Covenant (hereinafter referred to as the Committee) to receive and consider, as provided in the present Protocol, communications from individuals claiming to be victims of violations of any of the rights set forth in the Covenant,

Have agreed as follows:

Article 1

A State Party to the Covenant that becomes a party to the present Protocol recognizes the competence of the Committee to receive and consider communications from individuals subject to its jurisdiction who claim to be victims of a violation by that State Party of any of the rights set forth in the Covenant. No communication shall be received by the Committee if it concerns a State Party to the Covenant which is not a party to the present Protocol.

Article 2

Subject to the provisions of article 1, individuals who claim that any of their rights enumerated in the Covenant have been violated and who have exhausted all available domestic remedies may submit a written communication to the Committee for consideration.

Article 3

The Committee shall consider inadmissible any communication under the present Protocol which is anonymous, or which it considers to be an abuse of the right of submission of such communications or to be incompatible with the provisions of the Covenant.

---

[1] In force since 23 March 1976.

Article 4

1. Subject to the provisions of article 3, the Committee shall bring any communications submitted to it under the present Protocol to the attention of the State Party to the present Protocol alleged to be violating any provision of the Covenant.

2. Within six months, the receiving State shall submit to the Committee written explanations or statements clarifying the matter and the remedy, if any, that may have been taken by that State.

Article 5

1. The Committee shall consider communications received under the present Protocol in the light of all written information made available to it by the individual and by the State Party concerned.

2. The Committee shall not consider any communication from an individual unless it has ascertained that:

(a) The same matter is not being examined under another procedure of international investigation of settlement;

(b) The individual has exhausted all available domestic remedies. This shall not be the rule where the application of the remedies is unreasonably prolonged.

3. The Committee shall hold closed meetings when examining communications under the present Protocol.

4. The Committee shall forward its views to the State Party concerned and to the individual.

Article 6

The Committee shall include in its annual report under article 45 of the Covenant a summary of its activities under the present Protocol.

Article 7

Pending the achievement of the objectives of resolution 1514 (XV) adopted by the General Assembly of the United Nations on 14 December 1960 concerning the Declaration on the Granting of Independence to Colonial Countries and Peoples, the provisions of the present Protocol shall in no way limit the right of petition granted to these peoples by the Charter of the United Nations and other international conventions and instruments under the United Nations and its specialized agencies.

Article 8

1. The present Protocol is open for signature by any State which has signed the Covenant.

2. The present Protocol is subject to ratification by any State which has ratified or acceded to the Covenant. Instruments of ratification shall be deposited with the Secretary-General of the United Nations.

3. The present Protocol shall be open to accession by any State which has ratified or acceded to the Covenant.

4. Accession shall be effected by the deposit of an instrument of accession with the Secretary-General of the United Nations.

5. The Secretary-General of the United Nations shall inform all States which have signed the present Protocol or acceded to it of the deposit of each instrument of ratification or accession.

Article 9

1. Subject to the entry into force of the Covenant, the present Protocol shall enter into force three months after the date of the deposit with the Secretary-General of the United Nations of the tenth instrument of ratification or instrument of accession.

2. For each State ratifying the present Protocol or acceding to it after the deposit of the tenth instrument of ratification or instrument of accession, the present Protocol shall enter into force three months after the date of the deposit of its own instrument of ratification or instrument of accession.

Article 10

The provisions of the present Protocol shall extend to all parts of federal States without any limitations or exceptions.

Article 11

1. Any State Party to the present Protocol may propose an amendment and file it with the Secretary-General of the United Nations. The Secretary-General shall thereupon communicate any proposed amendments to the States Parties to the present Protocol with a request that they notify him whether they favour a conference of States Parties for the purpose of considering and voting upon the proposal. In the event that at least one third of the States Parties favours such a conference, the Secretary-General shall convene the conference under the auspices of the United Nations. Any amendment adopted by a majority of the States Parties present and voting at the conference shall be submitted to the General Assembly of the United Nations for approval.

2. Amendments shall come into force when they have been approved by the General Assembly of the United Nations and accepted by a two-thirds majority of the States Parties to the present Protocol in accordance with their respective constitutional processes.

3. When amendments come into force, they shall be binding on those States Parties which have accepted them, other States Parties still being bound by the provisions of the present Protocol and any earlier amendment which they have accepted.

Article 12

1. Any State Party may denounce the present Protocol at any time by written notification addressed to the Secretary-General of the United Nations. Denunciation shall take effect three months after the date of receipt of the notification by the Secretary-General.

2. Denunciation shall be without prejudice to the continued application of the provisions of the present Protocol to any communication submitted under article 2 before the effective date of denunciation.

Article 13

Irrespective of the notifications made under article 8, paragraph 5, of the present Protocol, the Secretary-General of the United Nations shall inform all States referred to in article 48, paragraph 1, of the Covenant of the following particulars:

(a) Signatures, ratifications and accessions under article 8;

(b) The date of the entry into force of the present Protocol under article 9 and the date of the entry into force of any amendments under article 11;

(c) Denunciations under article 12.

Article 14

1. The present Protocol, of which the Chinese, English, French, Russian and Spanish texts are equally authentic, shall be deposited in the archives of the United Nations.

2. The Secretary-General of the United Nations shall transmit certified copies of the present Protocol to all States referred to in article 48 of the Covenant.

European Convention for the Protection of Human Rights and Fundamental Freedoms[1]

The Governments signatory hereto, being Members of the Council of Europe,

Considering the Universal Declaration of Human Rights proclaimed by the General Assembly of the United Nations on 10th December 1948;

Considering that this Declaration aims at securing the universal and effective recognition and observance of the Rights therein declared;

Considering that the aim of the Council of Europe is the achievement of greater unity between its Members and that one of the methods by which that aim is to be pursued is the maintenance and further realisation of Human Rights and Fundamental Freedoms;

Reaffirming their profound belief in those Fundamental Freedoms which are the foundation of justice and peace in the world and are best maintained on the one hand by an effective political democracy and on the other by a common understanding and observance of the Human Rights upon which they depend;

Being resolved, as the Governments of European countries which are like-minded and have a common heritage of political traditions, ideals, freedom and the rule of law, to take the first steps for the collective enforcement of certain of the Rights stated in the Universal Declaration;

Have agreed as follows:

Article 1

The High Contracting Parties shall secure to everyone within their jurisdiction the rights and freedoms defined in Section I of this Convention.

SECTION I

Article 2

1. Everyone's right to life shall be protected by law. No one shall be deprived of his life intentionally save in the execution of a sentence of a court following his conviction of a crime for which this penalty is provided by law.

---

[1] In force since 3 September 1953.

2. Deprivation of life shall not be regarded as inflicted in contravention of this Article when it results from the use of force which is no more than absolutely necessary:

(a) in defence of any person from unlawful violence;

(b) in order to effect a lawful arrest or to prevent the escape of a person lawfully detained;

(c) in action lawfully taken for the purpose of quelling a riot or insurrection.

Article 3

No one shall be subjected to torture or to inhuman or degrading treatment of punishment.

Article 4

1. No one shall be held in slavery or servitude.

2. No one shall be required to perform forced or compulsory labour.

3. For the purpose of this Article the term "forced or compulsory labour" shall not include:

(a) any work required to be done in the ordinary course of detention imposed according to the provisions of Article 5 of this Convention or during conditional release from such detention;

(b) any service of a military character or, in case of conscientious objectors in countries where they are recognised, service exacted instead of compulsory military service;

(c) any service exacted in case of an emergency or calamity threatening the life or well-being of the community;

(d) any work or service which forms part of normal civic obligations.

Article 5

1. Everyone has the right to liberty and security of person. No one shall be deprived of his liberty save in the following cases and in accordance with a procedure prescribed by law:

(a) the lawful detention of a person after conviction by a competent court;

(b) the lawful arrest or detention of a person for non-compliance with the lawful order of a court or in order to secure the fulfilment of any obligation prescribed by law;

(c) the lawful arrest or detention of a person effected for the purpose of bringing him before the competent legal authority on reasonable suspicion of having committed an offence or when it is reasonably considered necessary to prevent his committing an offence or fleeing after having done so;

(d) the detention of a minor by lawful order for the purpose of educational supervision or his lawful detention for the purpose of bringing him before the competent legal authority;

(e) the lawful detention of persons for the prevention of the spreading of infectious diseases, of persons of unsound mind, alcoholics or drug addicts or vagrants:

(f) the lawful arrest or detention of a person to prevent his effecting an unauthorised entry into the country or of a person against whom action is being taken with a view to deportation or extradition.

2. Everyone who is arrested shall be informed promptly, in a language which he understands, of the reasons for his arrest and of any charge against him.

3. Everyone arrested or detained in accordance with the provisions of paragraph 1 (c) of this Article shall be brought promptly before a judge or other officer authorised by law to exercise judicial power and shall be entitled to trial within a reasonable time or to release pending trial. Release may be conditioned by guarantees to appear for trial.

4. Everyone who is deprived of his liberty by arrest or detention shall be entitled to take proceedings by which the lawfulness of his detention shall be decided speedily by a court and his release ordered if the detention is not lawful.

5. Everyone who has been the victim of arrest or detention in contravention of the provisions of this Article shall have an enforceable right to compensation.

Article 6

1. In the determination of his civil rights and obligations or of any criminal charge against him, everyone is entitled to a fair and public hearing within a reasonable time by an independent and impartial tribunal established by law. Judgment shall be pronounced publicly but the press and public may be excluded from all or part of the trial in the interests of morals, public order or national security in a democratic society, where the interests of juveniles or the protection of the private life of the parties so require, or to the extent strictly necessary in the opinion of the court in special circumstances where publicity would prejudice the interests of justice.

2. Everyone charged with a criminal offence shall be presumed innocent until proved guilty according to law.

3. Everyone charged with a criminal offence has the following minimum rights:

(a) to be informed promptly, in a language which he understands and in detail, of the nature and cause of the accusation against him;

(b) to have adequate time and facilities for the preparation of his defence;

(c) to defend himself in person or through legal assistance of his own choosing or, if he has not sufficient means to pay for legal assistance, to be given it free when the interests of justice so require;

(d) to examine or have examined witnesses against him and to obtain the attendance and examination of witnesses on his behalf under the same conditions as witnesses against him;

(e) to have the free assistance of an interpreter if he cannot understand or speak the language used in court.

Article 7

1. No one shall be held guilty of any criminal offence on account of any act or omission which did not constitute a criminal offence under national or international law at the time when it was committed. Nor shall a heavier penalty be imposed than the one that was applicable at the time the criminal offence was committed.

2. This Article shall not prejudice the trial and punishment of any person for any act or omission which, at the time when it was committed, was criminal according to the general principles of law recognised by civilised nations.

Article 8

1. Everyone has the right to respect for his private and family life, his home and his correspondence.

2. There shall be no interference by a public authority with the exercise of this right except such as is in accordance with the law and is necessary in a democratic society in the interests of national security, public safety or the economic well-being of the country, for the prevention of disorder or crime, for the protection of health or morals, or for the protection of the rights and freedoms of others.

Article 9

1. Everyone has the right to freedom of thought, conscience and religion; this right includes freedom to change his religion or belief and freedom, either alone or in community with others and in public or private, to manifest his religion or belief, in worship, teaching, practice and observance.

2. Freedom to manifest one's religion or beliefs shall be subject only to such limitations as are prescribed by law and are necessary in a democratic society in the interests of public safety, for the protection of public order, health or morals, or for the protection of the rights and freedoms of others.

Article 10

1. Everyone has the right to freedom of expression. This right shall include freedom to hold opinions and to receive and impart information and ideas without interference by public authority and regardless of frontiers. This Article shall not prevent States from requiring the licensing of broadcasting, television or cinema enterprises.

2. The exercise of these freedoms, since it carries with it duties and responsibilities, may be subject to such formalities, conditions, restrictions or penalties as are prescribed by law and are necessary in a democratic society, in the interests of national security, territorial integrity or public safety, for the prevention of disorder or crime, for the protection of health or morals, for the protection of the reputation or rights of others, for preventing the disclosure of information received in confidence, or for maintaining the authority and impartiality of the judiciary.

Article 11

1. Everyone has the right to freedom of peaceful assembly and to freedom of association with others, including the right to form and to join trade unions for the protection of his interests.

2. No restrictions shall be placed on the exercise of these rights other than such as are prescribed by law and are necessary in a democratic society in the interests of national security or public safety, for the prevention of disorder or crime, for the protection of health or morals or for the protection of the rights and freedoms of others. This Article shall not prevent the imposition of lawful restrictions on the exercise of these rights by members of the armed forces, of the police or of the administration of the State.

Article 12

Men and women of marriageable age have the right to marry and to found a family, according to the national laws governing the exercise of this right.

Article 13

Everyone whose rights and freedoms as set forth in this Convention are violated shall have an effective remedy before a national authority notwithstanding that the violation has been committed by persons acting in an official capacity.

Article 14

The enjoyment of the rights and freedoms set forth in this Convention shall be secured without discrimination on any ground such as sex, race, colour, language, religion, political or other opinion, national or social origin, association with a national minority, property, birth or other status.

Article 15

1. In time of war or other public emergency threatening the life of the nation any High Contracting Party may take measures derogating from its obligations under this Convention to the extent strictly required by the exigencies of the situation, provided that such measures are not inconsistent with its other obligations under international law.

2. No derogation from Article 2, except in respect of deaths resulting from lawful acts of war, or from Articles 3, 4 (paragraph 1) and 7 shall be made under this provision.

3. Any High Contracting Party availing itself of this right of derogation shall keep the Secretary-General of the Council of Europe fully informed of the measures which it has taken and the reasons therefore. It shall also inform the Secretary-General of the Council of Europe when such measures have ceased to operate and the provisions of the Convention are again being fully executed.

Article 16

Nothing in Articles 10, 11 and 14 shall be regarded as preventing the High Contracting Parties from imposing restrictions on the political activity of aliens.

Article 17

Nothing in this Convention may be interpreted as implying for any State, group or person any right to engage in any activity or perform any act aimed at the destruction of any of the rights and freedoms set forth herein or at their limitation to a greater extent than is provided for in the Convention.

Article 18

The restrictions permitted under this Convention to the said rights and freedoms shall not be applied for any purpose other than those for which they have been prescribed.

SECTION II

Article 19

To ensure the observance of the engagements undertaken by the High Contracting Parties in the present Convention, there shall be set up:

(1) A European Commission of Human Rights hereinafter referred to as "the Commission";

(2) A European Court of Human Rights, hereinafter referred to as "the Court".

SECTION III

Article 20

The Commission shall consist of a number of members equal to that of the High Contracting Parties. No two members of the Commission may be nationals of the same State.

Article 21

1. The members of the Commission shall be elected by the Committee of Ministers by an absolute majority of votes, from a list of names drawn up by the Bureau of the Consultative Assembly; each group of the Representatives of the High Contracting Parties in the Consultative Assembly shall put forward three candidates, of whom two at least shall be its nationals.

2. As far as applicable, the same procedure shall be followed to complete the Commission in the event of other States subsequently becoming Parties to this Convention, and in filling casual vacancies.

Article 22

1. The members of the Commission shall be elected for a period of six years. They may be re-elected. However, of the members elected at the first election, the terms of seven members shall expire at the end of three years.

2. The members whose terms are to expire at the end of the initial period of three years shall be chosen by lot by the Secretary-General of the Council of Europe immediately after the first election has been completed.

3. In order to ensure that, as far as possible, one half of the membership of the Commission shall be renewed every three years, the Committee of Ministers may decide, before proceeding to any subsequent election, that the term or terms of office of one or more members to be elected shall be for a period other than six years but not more than nine and not less than three years.

4. In cases where more than one term of office is involved and the Committee of Ministers applies the preceding paragraph, the allocation of the terms of office shall be effected by the drawing of lots by the Secretary-General, immediately after the election.

5. A member of the Commission elected to replace a member whose term of office has not expired shall hold office for the remainder of his predecessor's term.

6. The members of the Commission shall hold office until replaced. After having been replaced, they shall continue to deal with such cases as they already have under consideration.

Article 23

The members of the Commission shall sit on the Commission in their individual capacity.

Article 24

Any High Contracting Party may refer to the Commission, through the Secretary-General of the Council of Europe, any alleged breach of the provisions of the Convention by another High Contracting Party.

Article 25

1. The Commission may receive petitions addressed to the Secretary-General of the Council of Europe from any person, non-governmental organisation or group of individuals claiming to be the victim of a violation by one of the High Contracting Parties of the rights set forth in this Convention, provided that the High Contracting Party against which the complaint has been lodged has declared that it recognises the competence of the Commission to receive such petitions. Those of the High Contracting Parties who have made such a declaration undertake not to hinder in any way the effective exercise of this right.

2. Such declarations may be made for a specific period.

3. The declarations shall be deposited with the Secretary-General of the Council of Europe who shall transmit copies thereof to the High Contracting Parties and publish them.

4. The Commission shall only exercise the powers provided for in this Article when at least six High Contracting Parties are bound by declarations made in accordance with the preceding paragraphs.

Article 26

The Commission may only deal with the matter after all domestic remedies have been exhausted, according to the generally recognised rules of international law, and within a period of six months from the date on which the final decision was taken.

Article 27

1. The Commission shall not deal with any petition submitted under Article 25 which

(a) is anonymous, or

(b) is substantially the same as a matter which has already been examined by the Commission or has already been submitted to another procedure of international investigation or settlement and if it contains no relevant new information.

2. The Commission shall consider inadmissible any petition submitted under Article 25 which it considers incompatible with the provisions of the present Convention, manifestly ill-founded, or an abuse of the right of petition.

3. The Commission shall reject any petition referred to it which it considers inadmissible under Article 26.

Article 28

In the event of the Commission accepting a petition referred to it:

(a) it shall, with a view to ascertaining the facts, undertake together with the representatives of the parties an examination of the petition and, if need be, an investigation, for the effective conduct of which the States concerned shall furnish all necessary facilities, after an exchange of views with the Commission;

(b) it shall place itself at the disposal of the parties concerned with a view to securing a friendly settlement of the matter on the basis of respect for Human Rights as defined in this Convention.

Article 29

After it has accepted a petition submitted under Article 25, the Commission may nevertheless decide unanimously to reject the petition if, in the course of its examination, it finds that the existence of one of the grounds for non-acceptance provided for in Article 27 has been established.

In such a case, the decision shall be communicated to the parties.

Article 30

If the Commission succeeds in effecting a friendly settlement in accordance with Article 28, it shall draw up a Report which shall be sent to the States concerned, to the Committee of Ministers and to the Secretary-General of the Council of Europe for publication. This Report shall be confined to a brief statement of the facts and of the solution reached.

Article 31

1. If a solution is not reached, the Commission shall draw up a Report on the facts and state its opinion as to whether the facts found disclose a breach by the State concerned of its obligations under the Convention. The opinions of all the members of the Commission on this point may be stated in the Report.

2. The Report shall be transmitted to the Committee of Ministers. It shall also be transmitted to the States concerned, two shall not be at liberty to publish it.

3. In transmitting the Report to the Committee of Ministers the Commission may make such proposals as it thinks fit.

Article 32

1. If the question is not referred to the Court in accordance with Article 48 of this Convention within a period of three months from the date of the transmission of the Report to the Committee of Ministers, the Committee of Ministers shall decide by a majority of two-thirds of the members entitled to sit on the Committee whether there has been a violation of the Convention.

2. In the affirmative case the Committee of Ministers shall prescribe a period during which the High Contracting Party concerned must take the measures required by the decision of the Committee of Ministers.

3. If the High Contracting Party concerned has not taken satisfactory measures within the prescribed period, the Committee of Ministers shall de-

cide by the majority provided for in paragraph (1) above what effect shall be given to its original decision and shall publish the Report.

4. The High Contracting Parties undertake to regard as binding on them any decision which the Committee of Ministers may take in application of the preceding paragraphs.

Article 33

The Commission shall meet in camera.

Article 34

Subject to the provisions of Article 29, the Commission shall take its decisions by a majority of the Members present and voting.

Article 35

The Commission shall meet as the circumstances require. The meetings shall be convened by the Secretary General of the Council of Europe.

Article 36

The Commission shall draw up its own rules of procedure.

Article 37

The secretariat of the Commission shall be provided by the Secretary-General of the Council of Europe.

SECTION IV

Article 38

The European Court of Human Rights shall consist of a number of judges equal to that of the Members of the Council of Europe. No two judges may be nationals of the same State.

Article 39

1. The members of the Court shall be elected by the Consultative Assembly by a majority of the votes cast from a list of persons nominated by the Members of the Council of Europe; each Member shall nominate three candidates, of whom two at least shall be its nationals.

2. As far as applicable, the same procedure shall be followed to complete the Court in the event of the admission of new Members of the Council of Europe, and in filling casual vacancies.

3. The candidates shall be of high moral character and must either possess the qualifications required for appointment to high judicial office or be jurisconsults of recognised competence.

Article 40

1. The members of the Court shall be elected for a period of nine years. They may be re-elected. However, of the members elected at the first election the terms of four members shall expire at the end of three years, and the terms of four more members shall expire at the end of six years.

2. The members whose terms are to expire at the end of the initial periods of three and six years shall be chosen by lot by the Secretary-General immediately after the first election has been completed.

3. In order to ensure that, as far as possible, one third of the membership of the Court shall be renewed every three years, the Consultative Assembly may decide, before proceeding to any subsequent election, that the term or terms of office of one or more members to be elected shall be for a period other than nine years but not more than twelve and not less than six years.

4. In cases where more than one term of office is involved and the Consultative Assembly applies the preceding paragraph, the allocation of the terms of office shall be effected by the drawing of lots by the Secretary-General immediately after the election.

5. A member of the Court elected to replace a member whose term of office has not expired shall hold office for the remainder of his predecessor's term.

6. The members of the Court shall hold office until replaced. After having been replaced, they shall continue to deal with such cases as they already have under consideration.

Article 41

The Court shall elect its President and Vice-President for a period of three years. They may be re-elected.

Article 42

The members of the Court shall receive for each day of duty a compensation to be determined by the Committee of Ministers.

Article 43

For the consideration of each case brought before it the Court shall consist of a Chamber composed of seven judges. There shall sit as an ex officio member of the Chamber the judge who is a national of any State party concerned, or, if there is none, a person of its choice who shall sit in the capacity of judge; the names of the other judges shall be chosen by lot by the President before the opening of the case.

Article 44

Only the High Contracting Parties and the Commission shall have the right to bring a case before the Court.

Article 45

The jurisdiction of the Court shall extend to all cases concerning the interpretation and application of the present Convention which the High Contracting Parties or the Commission shall refer to it in accordance with Article 48.

Article 46

1. Any of the High Contracting Parties may at any time declare that it recognises as compulsory *ipso facto* and without special agreement the jurisdiction of the Court in all matters concerning the interpretation and application of the present Convention.

2. The declarations referred to above may be made unconditionally or on condition of reciprocity on the part of several or certain other High Contracting Parties or for a specified period.

3. These declarations shall be deposited with the Secretary-General of the Council of Europe who shall transmit copies thereof to the High Contracting Parties.

Article 47

The Court may only deal with a case after the Commission has acknowledged the failure of efforts for a friendly settlement and within the period of three months provided for in Article 32.

Article 48

The following may bring a case before the Court, provided that the High Contracting Party concerned, if there is only one, or the High Contracting Parties concerned, if there is more than one, are subject to the compulsory jurisdiction of the Court or, failing that, with the consent of the High Contracting Party concerned, if there is only one, or of the High Contracting Parties concerned if there is more than one:

(a) the Commission;

(b) a High Contracting Party whose national is alleged to be a victim;

(c) a High Contracting Party which referred the case to the Commission;

(d) a High Contracting Party against which the complaint has been lodged.

Article 49

In the event of dispute as to whether the Court has jurisdiction, the matter shall be settled by the decision of the Court.

Article 50

If the Court finds that a decision or a measure taken by a legal authority or any other authority of a High Contracting Party is completely or partially in conflict with the obligations arising from the present Convention, and if the internal law of the said Party allows only partial reparation to be made for the consequences of this decision or measure, the decision of the Court shall, if necessary, afford just satisfaction to the injured party.

Article 51

1. Reasons shall be given for the judgment of the Court.
2. If the judgment does not represent in whole or in part the unanimous opinion of the judges, any judge shall be entitled to deliver a separate opinion.

Article 52

The judgment of the Court shall be final.

Article 53

The High Contracting Parties undertake to abide by the decision of the Court in any case to which they are parties.

Article 54

The judgment of the Court shall be transmitted to the Committee of Ministers which shall supervise its execution.

Article 55

The Court shall draw up its own rules and shall determine its own procedure.

Article 56

1. The first election of the members of the Court shall take place after the declarations by the High Contracting Parties mentioned in Article 46 have reached a total of eight.
2. No case can be brought before the Court before this election.

SECTION V

Article 57

On receipt of a request from the Secretary-General of the Council of Europe any High Contracting Party shall furnish an explanation of the manner in which its internal law ensures the effective implementation of any of the provisions of this Convention.

Article 58

The expenses of the Commission and the Court shall be borne by the Council of Europe.

Article 59

The members of the Commission and of the Court shall be entitled, during the discharge of their functions, to the privileges and immunities provided for in Article 40 of the Statute of the Council of Europe and in the agreements made thereunder.

Article 60

Nothing in this Convention shall be construed as limiting or derogating from any of the human rights and fundamental freedoms which may be ensured under the laws of any High Contracting Party or under any other agreement to which it is a Party.

Article 61

Nothing in this Convention shall prejudice the powers conferred on the Committee of Ministers by the Statute of the Council of Europe.

Article 62

The High Contracting Parties agree that, except by special agreement, they will not avail themselves of treaties, conventions or declarations in force between them for the purpose of submitting, by way of petition, a dispute arising out of the interpretation or application of this Convention to a means of settlement other than those provided for in this Convention.

Article 63

1. Any State may at the time of its ratification or at any time thereafter declare by notification addressed to the Secretary-General of the Council of Europe that the present Convention shall extend to all or any of the territories for whose international relations it is responsible.

2. The Convention shall extend to the territory or territories named in the notification as from the thirtieth day after the receipt of this notification by the Secretary-General of the Council of Europe.

3. The provisions of this Convention shall be applied in such territories with due regard, however, to local requirements.

4. Any State which has made a declaration in accordance with paragraph 1 of this Article may at any time thereafter declare on behalf of one or more of the territories to which the declaration relates that it accepts the competence of the Commission to receive petitions from individuals, non-governmental organisations or groups of individuals in accordance with Article 25 of the present Convention.

Article 64

1. Any State may, when signing this Convention or when depositing its instrument of ratification, make a reservation in respect of any particular provision of the Convention to the extent that any law then in force in its terri-

tory is not in conformity with the provision. Reservations of a general character shall not be permitted under this Article.

2. Any reservation made under this Article shall contain a brief statement of the law concerned.

Article 65

1. A High Contracting Party may denounce the present Convention only after the expiry of five years from the date on which it became a Party to it and after six months' notice contained in a notification addressed to the Secretary-General of the Council of Europe, who shall inform the other High Contracting Parties.

2. Such a denunciation shall not have the effect of releasing the High Contracting Party concerned from its obligations under this Convention in respect of any act which, being capable of constituting a violation of such obligations, may have been performed by it before the date at which the denunciation became effective.

3. Any High Contracting Party which shall cease to be a Member of the Council of Europe shall cease to be a Party to this Convention under the same conditions.

4. The Convention may be denounced in accordance with the provisions of the preceding paragraphs in respect of any territory to which it has been declared to extend under the terms of Article 63.

Article 66

1. This Convention shall be open to the signature of the Members of the Council of Europe. It shall be ratified. Ratifications shall be deposited with the Secretary-General of the Council of Europe.

2. The present Convention shall come into force after the deposit of ten instruments of ratification.

3. As regards any signatory ratifying subsequently, the Convention shall come into force at the date of the deposit of its instrument of ratification.

4. The Secretary-General of the Council of Europe shall notify all the Members of the Council of Europe of the entry into force of the Convention, the names of the High Contracting Parties who have ratified it, and the deposit of all instruments of ratification which may be affected subsequently.

Done at Rome this 4th day of November 1950 in English and French, both texts being equally authentic, in a single copy which shall remain deposited in the archives of the Council of Europe. The Secretary General shall transmit certified copies to each of the signatories.

Additional Protocols[1]

Protocol (No. 1) to the Convention for the Protection of Human Rights and Fundamental Freedoms[2]

The Governments signatory hereto, being Members of the Council of Europe,

Being resolved to take steps to ensure the collective enforcement of certain rights and freedoms other than those already included in Section I of the Convention for the Protection of Human Rights and Fundamental Freedoms signed at Rome on 4th November, 1950 (hereinafter referred to as "the Convention"),

Have agreed as follows:

Article 1

Every natural or legal person is entitled to the peaceful enjoyment of his possessions. No one shall be deprived of his possessions except in the public interest and subject to the conditions provided for by law and by the general principles of international law.

The preceding provisions shall not, however, in any way impair the right of a State to enforce such laws as it deems necessary to control the use of property in accordance with the general interest or to secure the payment of taxes or other contributions or penalties.

Article 2

No person shall be denied the right to education. In the exercise of any functions which it assumes in relation to education and to teaching, the State shall respect the right of parents to ensure such education and teaching in conformity with their own religious and philosophical convictions.

Article 3

The High Contracting Parties undertake to hold free elections at reasonable intervals by secret ballot, under conditions which will ensure the free expression of the opinion of the people in the choice of the legislature.

Article 4

Any High Contracting Party may at the time of signature or ratification or at any time thereafter communicate to the Secretary-General of the Council of Europe a declaration stating the extent to which it undertakes that the

---

[1] Protocols 3, 5 and 8 concern amendments to the text of the Convention on Human Rights and have already been incorporated into the text printed here, with the exception of Protocol No. 8 which is not yet in force.

[2] In force since 18 May 1954.

provisions of the present Protocol shall apply to such of the territories for the international relations of which it is responsible as are named therein.

Any High Contracting Party which has communicated a declaration in virtue of the preceding paragraph may from time to time communicate a further declaration modifying the terms of any former declaration or terminating the application of the provisions of this Protocol in respect of any territory.

A declaration made in accordance with this Article shall be deemed to have been made in accordance with Paragraph (1) of Article 63 of the Convention.

Article 5

As between the High Contracting Parties the provisions of Articles 1, 2, 3 and 4 of this Protocol shall be regarded as additional Articles to the Convention and all the provisions of the Convention shall apply accordingly.

Article 6

This Protocol shall be open for signature by the Members of the Council of Europe, who are the signatories of the Convention; it shall be ratified at the same time as or after the ratification of the Convention. It shall enter into force after the deposit of ten instruments of ratification. As regards any signatory ratifying subsequently, the Protocol shall enter into force at the date of the deposit of its instrument of ratification.

The instruments of ratification shall be deposited with the Secretary-General of the Council of Europe, who will notify all Members of the names of those who have ratified.

Done at Paris on the 20th day of March 1952, in English and French, both texts being equally authentic, in a single copy which shall remain deposited in the archives of the Council of Europe. The Secretary General shall transmit certified copies to each of the signatory Governments.

Protocol No. 2 to the Convention for the Protection of Human Rights and Fundamental Freedoms Conferring upon the European Court of Human Rights Competence to Give Advisory Opinions[1]

The member States of the Council of Europe signatory hereto:

Having regard to the provisions of the Convention for the Protection of Human Rights and Fundamental Freedoms signed at Rome on 4th November 1950 (hereinafter referred to as "the Convention") and, in particular, Article 19 instituting, among other bodies, a European Court of Human Rights (hereinafter referred to as "the Court");

[1] In force since 21 September 1970.

Considering that it is expedient to confer upon the Court competence to give advisory opinions subject to certain conditions;

Have agreed as follows:

Article 1

1. The Court may, at the request of the Committee of Ministers, give advisory opinions on legal questions concerning the interpretation of the Convention and the Protocols thereto.

2. Such opinions shall not deal with any question relating to the content or scope of the rights or freedoms defined in Section 1 of the Convention and in the Protocols thereto, or with any other question which the Commission, the Court or the Committee of Ministers might have to consider in consequence of any such proceedings as could be instituted in accordance with the Convention.

3. Decisions of the Committee of Ministers to request an advisory opinion of the Court shall require a two-thirds majority vote of the representatives entitled to sit on the Committee.

Article 2

The Court shall decide whether a request for an advisory opinion submitted by the Committee of Ministers is within its consultative competence as defined in Article 1 of this Protocol.

Article 3

1. For the consideration of requests for an advisory opinion, the Court shall sit in plenary session.

2. Reasons shall be given for advisory opinions of the Court.

3. If the advisory opinion does not represent in whole or in part the unanimous opinion of the judges, any judge shall be entitled to deliver a separate opinion.

4. Advisory opinions of the Court shall be communicated to the Committee of Ministers.

Article 4

The powers of the Court under Article 55 of the Convention shall extend to the drawing up of such rules and the determination of such procedure as the Court may think necessary for the purposes of this Protocol.

Article 5

1. This Protocol shall be open to signature by member States of the Council of Europe, signatories to the Convention, who may become Parties to it by:

(a) signature without reservation in respect of ratification or acceptance;

(b) signature with reservation in respect of ratification or acceptance, followed by ratification or acceptance.

Instruments of ratification or acceptance shall be deposited with the Secretary-General of the Council of Europe.

2. This Protocol shall enter into force as soon as all States Parties to the Convention shall have become Parties to the Protocol, in accordance with the provisions of paragraph 1 of this Article.

3. From the date of the entry into force of this Protocol, Articles 1 to 4 shall be considered an integral part of the Convention.

4. The Secretary-General of the Council of Europe shall notify the member States of the Council of:

(a) any signature without reservation in respect of ratification or acceptance;

(b) any signature with reservation in respect of ratification or acceptance;

(c) the deposit of any instrument of ratification or acceptance;

(d) the date of entry into force of this Protocol in accordance with paragraph 2 of this Article.

In witness whereof, the undersigned, being duly authorised thereto, have signed this Protocol.

Done at Strasbourg, this 6th day of May 1963, in English and French, both texts being equally authoritative, in a single copy which shall remain deposited in the archives of the Council of Europe. The Secretary General shall transmit certified copies to each of the signatory States.

Protocol No. 4 to the Convention for the Protection of Human Rights and Fundamental Freedoms, Securing Certain Rights and Freedoms Other than those already Included in the Convention and in the First Protocol thereto[1]

The Governments signatory hereto, being Members of the Council of Europe,

Being resolved to take steps to ensure the collective enforcement of certain rights and freedoms other than those already included in Section I of the Convention for the Protection of Human Rights and Fundamental Freedoms signed at Rome on 4th November, 1950 (hereinafter referred to as "the Convention") and in Articles 1 to 3 of the First Protocol to the Convention, signed at Paris on 20th March, 1952,

Have agreed as follows:

Article 1

No one shall be deprived of his liberty merely on the ground of inability to fulfil a contractual obligation.

[1] In force since 2 May 1968.

Article 2

1. Everyone lawfully within the territory of a State shall, within that territory have the right to liberty of movement and freedom to choose his residence.

2. Everyone shall be free to leave any country, including his own.

3. No restrictions shall be placed on the exercise of these rights other than such as are in accordance with law and are necessary in a democratic society in the interests of national security or public safety, for the maintenance of "ordre public", for the prevention of crime, for the protection of health or morals, or for the protection of the rights and freedoms of others.

4. The rights set forth in paragraph 1 may also be subject, in particular areas, to restrictions imposed in accordance with law and justified by the public interest in a democratic society.

Article 3

1. No one shall be expelled, by means either of an individual or of a collective measure, from the territory of the State of which he is a national.

2. No one shall be deprived of the right to enter the territory of the State of which he is a national.

Article 4

Collective expulsion of aliens is prohibited.

Article 5

1. Any High Contracting Party may, at the time of signature or ratification of this Protocol, or at any time thereafter, communicate to the Secretary-General of the Council of Europe a declaration stating the extent to which it undertakes that the provisions of this Protocol shall apply to such of the territories for the international relations of which it is responsible as are named therein.

2. Any High Contracting Party which has communicated a declaration in virtue of the preceding paragraph may, from time to time, communicate a further declaration modifying the terms of any former declaration or terminating the application of the provisions of this Protocol in respect of any territory.

3. A declaration made in accordance with this Article shall be deemed to have been made in accordance with paragraph 1 of Article 63 of the Convention.

4. The territory of any State to which this Protocol applies by virtue of ratification or acceptance by that State, and each territory to which this Protocol is applied by virtue of a declaration by that State under this Article, shall be treated as separate territories for the purpose of the references in Articles 2 and 3 to the territory of a State.

Article 6

1. As between the High Contracting Parties the provisions of Articles 1 to 5 of this Protocol shall be regarded as additional Articles to the Convention, and all the provisions of the Convention shall apply accordingly.

2. Nevertheless, the right of individual recourse recognised by a declaration made under Article 25 of the Convention, or the acceptance of the compulsory jurisdiction of the Court by a declaration made under Article 46 of the Convention, shall not be effective in relation to this Protocol unless the High Contracting Party concerned has made a statement recognising such right, or accepting such jurisdiction, in respect of all or any of Articles 1 to 4 of the Protocol.

Article 7

1. This Protocol shall be open for signature by the Members of the Council of Europe who are the signatories of the Convention; it shall be ratified at the same time as or after the ratification of the Convention. It shall enter into force after the deposit of five instruments of ratification. As regards any signatory ratifying subsequently the Protocol shall enter into force at the date of the deposit of its instrument of ratification.

2. The instruments of ratification shall be deposited with the Secretary-General of the Council of Europe, who will notify all Members of the names of those who have ratified.

In witness whereof, the undersigned, being duly authorised thereto, have signed this Protocol.

Done at Strasbourg, this 16th day of September 1963, in English and in French, both texts being equally authoritative, in a single copy which shall remain deposited in the archives of the Council of Europe. The Secretary General shall transmit certified copies to each of the signatory States.

Protocol No. 6 to the Convention for the Protection of Human Rights and Fundamental Freedoms Concerning the Abolition of the Death Penalty [1]

The member States of the Council of Europe, signatory to this Protocol to the Convention for the Protection of Human Rights and Fundamental Freedoms, signed at Rome on 4 November 1950 (hereinafter referred to as "the Convention"),

Considering that the evolution that has occurred in several member States of the Council of Europe expresses a general tendency in favour of abolition of the death penalty,

Have agreed as follows:

---

[1] In force since 1 March 1985.

Article 1

The death penalty shall be abolished. No one shall be condemned to such penalty or executed.

Article 2

A State may make provision in its law for the death penalty in respect of acts committed in time of war or of imminent threat of war; such penalty shall be applied only in the instances laid down in the law and in accordance with its provisions. The State shall communicate to the Secretary General of the Council of Europe the relevant provisions of that law.

Article 3

No derogation from the provisions of this Protocol shall be made under Article 15 of the Convention.

Article 4

No reservation may be made under Article 64 of the Convention in respect of the provisions of this Protocol.

Article 5

1. Any State may at the time of signature or when depositing its instrument of ratification, acceptance or approval, specify the territory or territories to which this Protocol shall apply.

2. Any State may at any later date, by a declaration addressed to the Secretary General of the Council of Europe, extend the application of this Protocol to any other territory specified in the declaration. In respect of such territory the Protocol shall enter into force on the first day of the month following the date of receipt of such a declaration by the Secretary General.

3. Any declaration made under the two preceding paragraphs may, in respect of any territory specified in such declaration, be withdrawn by a notification addressed to the Secretary General. The withdrawal shall become effective on the first day of the month following the date of receipt of such notification by the Secretary General.

Article 6

As between the States Parties the provisions of Articles 1 to 5 of this Protocol shall be regarded as additional articles to the Convention and all the provisions of the Convention shall apply accordingly.

Article 7

This Protocol shall be open for signature by the member States of the Council of Europe, signatories to the Convention. It shall be subject to ratification, acceptance or approval. A member State of the Council of Europe may not ratify, accept or approve this Protocol unless it has, simultaneously or previously, ratified the Convention. Instruments of ratification, acceptance or approval shall be deposited with the Secretary General of the Council of Europe.

Article 8

1. This Protocol shall enter into force on the first day of the month following the date on which five member States of the Council of Europe have expressed their consent to be bound by the Protocol in accordance with the provisions of Article 7.

2. In respect of any member State which subsequently expresses its consent to be bound by it, the Protocol shall enter into force on the first day of the month following the date of the deposit of the instrument of ratification, acceptance or approval.

Article 9

The Secretary General of the Council of Europe shall notify the member States of the Council of:

(a) any signature;

(b) the deposit of any instrument of ratification, acceptance or approval;

(c) any date of entry into force of this Protocol in accordance with Articles 5 and 8;

(d) any other act, notification or communication relating to this Protocol.

In witness whereof the undersigned, being duly authorised thereto, have signed this Protocol.

Done at Strasbourg, the twenty-eighth April one thousand nine hundred and eighty-three, in English and French, both texts being equally authentic, in a single copy which shall be deposited in the archives of the Council of Europe. The Secretary General of the Council of Europe shall transmit certified copies to each member State of the Council of Europa.

Protocol No. 7 to the Convention for the Protection of Human Rights and Fundamental Freedoms [1]

The member States of the Council of Europe signatory hereto,

Being resolved to take further steps to ensure the collective enforcement of certain rights and freedoms by means of the Convention for the Protection of Human Rights and Fundamental Freedoms signed at Rome on 4 November 1950 (hereinafter referred to as "the Convention");

Have agreed as follows:

[1] Not yet in force.

Article 1

1. An alien lawfully resident in the territory of a State shall not be expelled therefrom except in pursuance of a decision reached in accordance with law and shall be allowed:

(a) to submit reasons against his expulsion,

(b) to have his case reviewed, and

(c) to be represented for these purposes before the competent authority or a person or persons designated by that authority.

2. An alien may be expelled before the exercise of his rights under paragraph 1 (a), (b) and (c) of this Article, when such expulsion is necessary in the interests of public order or is grounded on reasons of national security.

Article 2

1. Everyone convicted of a criminal offence by a tribunal shall have the right to have conviction or sentence reviewed by a higher tribunal. The exercise of this right, including the grounds on which it may be exercised, shall be governed by law.

2. This right may be subject to exceptions in regard to offences of a minor character, as prescribed by law, or in cases in which the person concerned was tried in the first instance by the highest tribunal or was convicted following an appeal against acquittal.

Article 3

When a person has by a final decision been convicted of a criminal offence and when subsequently his conviction has been reversed, or he has been pardoned, on the ground that a new or newly discovered fact shows conclusively that there has been a miscarriage of justice, the person who has suffered punishment as a result of such conviction shall be compensated according to the law or the practice of the State concerned, unless it is proved that the non-disclosure of the unknown fact in time is wholly or partly attributable to him.

Article 4

1. No one shall be liable to be tried or punished again in criminal proceedings under the jurisdiction of the same State for an offence for which he has already been finally acquitted or convicted in accordance with the law and penal procedure of that State.

2. The provisions of the preceding paragraph shall not prevent the reopening of the case in accordance with the law and penal procedure of the State concerned, if there is evidence of new or newly discovered facts, or if there has been a fundamental defect in the previous proceedings, which could affect the outcome of the case.

3. No derogation from this Article shall be made under Article 15 of the Convention.

Article 5

1. Spouses shall enjoy equality of rights and responsibilities of a private law character between them, and in their relations with their children, as to marriage, during marriage and in the event of its dissolution. This Article shall not prevent States from taking such measures as are necessary in the interests of the children.

Article 6

1. Any State may at the time of signature or when depositing its instrument of ratification, acceptance or approval, specify the territory or territories to which this Protocol shall apply and state the extent to which it undertakes that the provisions of this Protocol shall apply to this or these territories.

2. Any State may at any later date, by a declaration addressed to the Secretary General of the Council of Europe, extend the application of this Protocol to any other territory specified in the declaration. In respect of such territory the Protocol shall enter into force on the first day of the month following the expiration of a period of two months after the date of receipt by the Secretary General of such declaration.

3. Any declaration made under the two preceding paragraphs may, in respect of any territory specified in such declaration, be withdrawn or modified by a notification addressed to the Secretary General. The withdrawal or modification shall become effective on the first day of the month following the expiration of a period of two months after the date of receipt of such notification by the Secretary General.

4. A declaration made in accordance with this Article shall be deemed to have been made in accordance with paragraph 1 of Article 63 of the Convention.

5. The territory of any State to which this Protocol applies by virtue of ratification, acceptance or approval by that State, and each territory to which this Protocol is applied by virtue of a declaration by that State under this Article, may be treated as separate territories for the purpose of the reference in Article 1 to the territory of a State.

Article 7

1. As between the States Parties, the provisions of Articles 1 to 6 of this Protocol shall be regarded as additional Articles to the Convention, and all the provisions of the Convention shall apply accordingly.

2. Nevertheless, the right of individual recourse recognised by a declaration made under Article 25 of the Convention, or the acceptance of the compulsory jurisdiction of the Court by a declaration made under Article 46 of the Convention, shall not be effective in relation to this Protocol unless the State concerned has made a statement recognising such right, or accepting such jurisdiction in respect of Articles 1 to 5 of this Protocol.

Article 8

This Protocol shall be open for signature by member States of the Council of Europe which have signed the Convention. It is subject to ratification, acceptance or approval. A member State of the Council of Europe may not ratify, accept or approve this Protocol without previously or simultaneously ratifying the Convention. Instruments of ratification, acceptance or approval shall be deposited with the Secretary General of the Council of Europe.

Article 9

1. This Protocol shall enter into force on the first day of the month following the expiration of a period of two months after the date on which seven member States of the Council of Europe have expressed their consent to be bound by the Protocol in accordance with the provisions of Article 8.

2. In respect of any member State which subsequently expresses its consent to be bound by it, the Protocol shall enter into force on the first day of the month following the expiration of a period of two months after the date of the deposit of the instrument of ratification, acceptance or approval.

Article 10

The Secretary General of the Council of Europe shall notify all the member States of the Council of:

(a) any signature;

(b) the deposit of any instrument of ratification, acceptance or approval;

(c) any date of entry into force of this Protocol in accordance with Articles 6 and 9;

(d) any other act, notification or declaration relating to this Protocol.

In witness whereof the undersigned, being duly authorised thereto, have signed this Protocol.

Done at Strasbourg, the twenty-two November one thousand nine hundred and eighty four, in English and French, both texts being equally authentic, in a single copy which shall be deposited in the archives of the Council of Europe shall transmit certified copies to each member State of the Council.

American Convention on Human Rights[1]

PREAMBLE

The American states signatory to the present Convention,

Reaffirming their intention to consolidate in this hemisphere, within the framework of democratic institutions, a system of personal liberty and social justice based on respect for the essential rights of man;

Recognizing that the essential rights of man are not derived from one's being a national of a certain state, but are based upon attributes of the human personality, and that they therefore justify international protection in the form of a convention reinforcing or complementing the protection provided by the domestic law of the American states;

Considering that these principles have been set forth in the Charter of the Organization of American States, in the American Declaration of the Rights and Duties of Man, and in the Universal Declaration of Human Rights, and that they have been reaffirmed and refined in other international instruments, worldwide as well as regional in scope;

Reiterating that, in accordance with the Universal Declaration of Human Rights, the ideal of free men enjoying freedom from fear and want can be achieved only if conditions are created whereby everyone may enjoy his economic, social, and cultural rights, as well as his civil and political rights; and

Considering that the Third Special Inter-American Conference (Buenos Aires, 1967) approved the incorporation into the Charter of the Organization itself of broader standards with respect to economic, social, and educational rights and resolved that an inter-American convention on human rights should determine the structure, competence, and procedure of the organs responsible for these matters,

Have agreed upon the following:

[1] In force since 18 July 1978.

PART I. STATE OBLIGATIONS AND RIGHTS PROTECTED

Chapter I. General Obligations

Article 1. Obligation to Respect Rights

1. The States Parties to this Convention undertake to respect the rights and freedoms recognized herein and to ensure to all persons subject to their jurisdiction the free and full exercise of those rights and freedoms, without any discrimination for reasons of race, color, sex, language, religion, political or other opinion, national or social origin, economic status, birth, or any other social condition.

2. For the purposes of this Convention, "person" means every human being.

Article 2. Domestic Legal Effects

Where the exercise of any of the rights or freedoms referred to in Article 1 is not already ensured by legislative or other provisions, the States Parties undertake to adopt, in accordance with their constitutional processes and the provisions of this Convention, such legislative or other measures as may be necessary to give effect to those rights or freedoms.

Chapter II. Civil and Political Rights

Article 3. Right to Juridical Personality

Every person has the right to recognition as a person before the law.

Article 4. Right to Life

1. Every person has the right to have his life respected. This right shall be protected by law and, in general, from the moment of conception. No one shall be arbitrarily deprived of his life.

2. In countries that have not abolished the death penalty, it may be imposed only for the most serious crimes and pursuant to a final judgment rendered by a competent court and in accordance with a law establishing such punishment, enacted prior to the commission of the crime. The application of such punishment shall not be extended to crimes to which it does not presently apply.

3. The death penalty shall not be reestablished in states that have abolished it.

4. In no case shall capital punishment be inflicted for political offenses or related common crimes.

5. Capital punishment shall not be imposed upon persons who, at the time the crime was committed, were under 18 years of age or over 70 years of age; nor shall it be applied to pregnant women.

6. Every person condemned to death shall have the right to apply for amnesty, pardon, or commutation of sentence, which may be granted in all

cases. Capital punishment shall not be imposed while such a petition is pending decision by the competent authority.

Article 5. Right to Humane Treatment

1. Every person has the right to have his physical, mental, and moral integrity respected.

2. No one shall be subjected to torture or to cruel, inhuman, or degrading punishment or treatment. All persons deprived of their liberty shall be treated with respect for the inherent dignity of the human person.

3. Punishment shall not be extended to any person other than the criminal.

4. Accused persons shall, save in exceptional circumstances, be segregated from convicted persons, and shall be subject to separate treatment appropriate to their status as unconvicted persons.

5. Minors while subject to criminal proceedings shall be separated from adults and brought before specialized tribunals, as speedily as possible, so that they may be treated in accordance with their status as minors.

6. Punishments consisting of deprivation of liberty shall have as an essential aim the reform and social readaptation of the prisoners.

Article 6. Freedom from Slavery

1. No one shall be subject to slavery or to involuntary servitude, which are prohibited in all their forms, as are the slave trade and traffic in women.

2. No one shall be required to perform forced or compulsory labor. This provision shall not be interpreted to mean that, in those countries in which the penalty established for certain crimes is deprivation of liberty at forced labor, the carrying out of such a sentence imposed by a competent court is prohibited. Forced labor shall not adversely affect the dignity or the physical or intellectual capacity of the prisoner.

3. For the purposes of this article, the following do not constitute forced or compulsory labor:

(a) work or service normally required of a person imprisoned in execution of a sentence or formal decision passed by the competent judicial authority. Such work or service shall be carried out under the supervision and control of public authorities, and any persons performing such work or service shall not be placed at the disposal of any private party, company, or juridical person;

(b) military service and, in countries in which conscientious objectors are recognized, national service that the law may provide for in lieu of military service;

(c) service exacted in time of danger or calamity that threatens the existence or the well-being of the community; or

(d) work or service that forms part of normal civic obligations.

Article 7. Right to Personal Liberty

1. Every person has the right to personal liberty and security.

2. No one shall be deprived of his physical liberty except for the reasons and under the conditions established beforehand by the constitution of the State Party concerned or by a law established pursuant thereto.

3. No one shall be subject to arbitrary arrest or imprisonment.

4. Anyone who is detained shall be informed of the reasons for his detention and shall be promptly notified of the charge or charges against him.

5. Any person detained shall be brought promptly before a judge or other officer authorized by law to exercise judicial power and shall be entitled to trial within a reasonable time or to be released without prejudice to the continuation of the proceedings. His release may be subject to guarantees to assure his appearance for trial.

6. Anyone who is deprived of his liberty shall be entitled to recourse to a competent court, in order that the court may decide without delay on the lawfulness of his arrest or detention and order his release if the arrest or detention is unlawful. In States Parties whose laws provide that anyone who believes himself to be threatened with deprivation of his liberty is entitled to recourse to a competent court in order that it may decide on the lawfulness of such threat, this remedy may not be restricted or abolished. The interested party or another person in his behalf is entitled to seek these remedies.

7. No one shall be detained for debt. This principle shall not limit the orders of a competent judicial authority issued for non-fulfillment of duties of support.

Article 8. Right to a Fair Trial

1. Every person has the right to a hearing, with due guarantees and within a reasonable time, by a competent, independent, and impartial tribunal, previously established by law, in the substantiation of any accusation of a criminal nature made against him or for the determination of his rights and obligations of a civil, labor, fiscal, or any other nature.

2. Every person accused of a criminal offense has the right to be presumed innocent so long as his guilt has not been proven according to law. During the proceedings, every person is entitled, with full equality, to the following minimum guarantees:

(a) the right of the accused to be assisted without charge by a translator or interpreter, if he does not understand or does not speak the language of the tribunal or court;

(b) prior notification in detail to the accused of the charges against him;

(c) adequate time and means for the preparation of his defense;

(d) the right of the accused to defend himself personally or to be assisted by legal counsel of his own choosing, and to communicate freely and privately with his counsel;

(e) the inalienable right to be assisted by counsel provided by the state, paid or not as the domestic law provides, if the accused does not defend himself personally or engage his own counsel within the time period established by law;

(f) the right of the defense to examine witnesses present in the court and to obtain the appearance, as witnesses, of experts or other persons who may throw light on the facts;

(g) the right not to be compelled to be a witness against himself or to plead guilty; and

(h) the right to appeal the judgment to a higher court.

3. A confession of guilt by the accused shall be valid only if it is made without coercion of any kind.

4. An accused person acquitted by a nonappealable judgment shall not be subjected to a new trial for the same cause.

5. Criminal proceedings shall be public, except insofar as may be necessary to protect the interests of justice.

Article 9. Freedom from Ex Post Facto Laws

No one shall be convicted of any act or omission that did not constitute a criminal offense, under the applicable law, at the time it was committed. A heavier penalty shall not be imposed than the one that was applicable at the time the criminal offense was committed. If subsequent to the commission of the offense the law provides for the imposition of a lighter punishment, the guilty person shall benefit therefrom.

Article 10. Right to Compensation

Every person has the right to be compensated in accordance with the law in the event he has been sentenced by a final judgment through a miscarriage of justice.

Article 11. Right to Privacy

1. Everyone has the right to have his honor respected and his dignity recognized.

2. No one may be the object of arbitrary or abusive interference with his private life, his family, his home, or his correspondence, or of unlawful attacks on his honor or reputation.

3. Everyone has the right to the protection of the law against such interference or attacks.

Article 12. Freedom of Conscience and Religion

1. Everyone has the right to freedom of conscience and of religion. This right includes freedom to maintain or to change one's religion or beliefs, and freedom to profess or disseminate one's religion or beliefs, either individually or together with others, in public or in private.

2. No one shall be subject to restrictions that might impair his freedom to maintain or to change his religion or beliefs.

3. Freedom to manifest one's religion and beliefs may be subject only to the limitations prescribed by law that are necessary to protect public safety, order, health, or morals, or the rights or freedoms of others.

4. Parents or guardians, as the case may be, have the right to provide for the religious and moral education of their children or wards that is in accord with their own convictions.

Article 13. Freedom of Thought and Expression

1. Everyone has the right to freedom of thought and expression. This right includes freedom to seek, receive, and impart information and ideas of all kinds, regardless of frontiers, either orally, in writing, in print, in the form of art, or through any other medium of one's choice.

2. The exercise of the right provided for in the foregoing paragraph shall not be subject to prior censorship but shall be subject to subsequent imposition of liability, which shall be expressly established by law to the extent necessary to ensure:

(a) respect for the rights or reputations of others; or

(b) the protection of national security, public order, or public health or morals.

3. The right of expression may not be restricted by indirect methods or means, such as the abuse of government or private controls over newsprint, radio broadcasting frequencies, or equipment used in the dissemination of information, or by any other means tending to impede the communication and circulation of ideas and opinions.

4. Notwithstanding the provisions of paragraph 2 above, public entertainments may be subject by law to prior censorship for the sole purpose of regulating access to them for the moral protection of childhood and adolescence.

5. Any propaganda for war and any advocacy of national, racial, or religious hatred that constitute incitements to lawless violence or to any other similar illegal action against any person or group of persons on any grounds including those of race, color, religion, language, or national origin shall be considered as offenses punishable by law.

Article 14. Right of Reply

1. Anyone injured by inaccurate or offensive statements or ideas disseminated to the public in general by a legally regulated medium of communication has the right to reply or to make a correction using the same communications outlet, under such conditions as the law may establish.

2. The correction or reply shall not in any case remit other legal liabilities that may have been incurred.

3. For the effective protection of honor and reputation, every publisher, and every newspaper, motion picture, radio, and television company, shall have a person responsible who is not protected by immunities or special privileges.

Article 15. Right of Assembly

The right of peaceful assembly, without arms, is recognized. No restrictions may be placed on the exercise of this right other than those imposed in conformity with the law and necessary in a democratic society in the interest of national security, public safety or public order, or to protect public health or morals or the rights or freedoms of others.

Article 16. Freedom of Association

1. Everyone has the right to associate freely for ideological, religious, political, economic, labor, social, cultural, sports, or other purposes.

2. The exercise of this right shall be subject only to such restrictions established by law as may be necessary in a democratic society, in the interest of national security, public safety or public order, or to protect public health or morals or the rights and freedoms of others.

3. The provisions of this article do not bar the imposition of legal restrictions, including even deprivation of the exercise of the right of association, on members of the armed forces and the police.

Article 17. Rights of the Family

1. The family is the natural and fundamental group unit of society and is entitled to protection by society and the state.

2. The right of men and women of marriageable age to marry and to raise a family shall be recognized, if they meet the conditions required by domestic laws, insofar as such conditions do not affect the principle of nondiscrimination established in this Convention.

3. No marriage shall be entered into without the free and full consent of the intending spouses.

4. The States Parties shall take appropriate steps to ensure the equality of rights and the adequate balancing of responsibilities of the spouses as to marriage, during marriage, and in the event of its dissolution. In case of dissolution, provision shall be made for the necessary protection of any children solely on the basis of their own best interests.

5. The law shall recognize equal rights for children born out of wedlock and those born in wedlock.

Article 18. Right to a Name

Every person has the right to a given name and to the surnames of his parents or that of one of them. The law shall regulate the manner in which this right shall be ensured for all, by the use of assumed names if necessary.

Article 19. Rights of the Child

Every minor child has the right to the measures of protection required by his condition as a minor on the part of his family, society, and the state.

Article 20. Right to Nationality

1. Every person has the right to a nationality.

2. Every person has the right to the nationality of the state in whose territory he was born if he does not have the right to any other nationality.

3. No one shall be arbitrarily deprived of his nationality or of the right to change it.

Article 21. Right to Property

1. Everyone has the right to the use and enjoyment of his property. The law may subordinate such use and enjoyment to the interest of society.

2. No one shall be deprived of his property except upon payment of just compensation, for reasons of public utility or social interest, and in the cases and according to the forms established by law.

3. Usury and any other form of exploitation of man by man shall be prohibited by law.

Article 22. Freedom of Movement and Residence

1. Every person lawfully in the territory of a State Party has the right to move about in it, and to reside in it subject to the provisions of the law.

2. Every person has the right to leave any country freely, including his own.

3. The exercise of the foregoing rights may be restricted only pursuant to a law to the extent necessary in a democratic society to prevent crime or to protect national security, public safety, public order, public morals, public health, or the rights or freedoms of others.

4. The exercise of the rights recognized in paragraph 1 may also be restricted by law in designated zones for reasons of public interest.

5. No one can be expelled from the territory of the state of which he is a national or be deprived of the right to enter it.

6. An alien lawfully in the territory of a State Party to this Convention may be expelled from it only pursuant to a decision reached in accordance with law.

7. Every person has the right to seek and be granted asylum in a foreign territory, in accordance with the legislation of the state and international conventions, in the event he is being pursued for political offenses or related common crimes.

8. In no case may an alien be deported or returned to a country, regardless of whether or not it is his country of origin, if in that country his right to life or personal freedom is in danger of being violated because of his race, nationality, religion, social status, or political opinions.

9. The collective expulsion of aliens is prohibited.

Article 23. Right to Participate in Government

1. Every citizen shall enjoy the following rights and opportunities:

(a) to take part in the conduct of public affairs, directly or through freely chosen representatives;

(b) to vote and to be elected in genuine periodic elections, which shall be by universal and equal suffrage and by secret ballot that guarantees the free expression of the will of the voters; and

(c) to have access, under general conditions of equality, to the public service of his country.

2. The law may regulate the exercise of the rights and opportunities referred to in the preceding paragraph only on the basis of age, nationality, residence, language, education, civil and mental capacity, or sentencing by a competent court in criminal proceedings.

Article 24. Right to Equal Protection

All persons are equal before the law. Consequently, they are entitled, without discrimination, to equal protection of the law.

Article 25. Right to Judicial Protection

1. Everyone has the right to simple and prompt recourse, or any other effective recourse, to a competent court or tribunal for protection against acts that violate his fundamental rights recognized by the constitution or laws of the state concerned or by this Convention, even though such violation may have been committed by persons acting in the course of their official duties.

2. The States Parties undertake:

(a) to ensure that any person claiming such remedy shall have his rights determined by the competent authority provided for by the legal system of the state;

(b) to develop the possibilities of judicial remedy; and

(c) to ensure that the competent authorities shall enforce such remedies when granted.

Chapter III. Economic, Social, and Cultural Rights

Article 26. Progressive Development

The States Parties undertake to adopt measures, both internally and through international cooperation, especially those of an economic and technical nature, with a view to achieving progressively, by legislation or other appropriate means, the full realization of the rights implicit in the economic, social, educational, scientific, and cultural standards set forth in the Charter of the Organization of American States as amended by the Protocol of Buenos Aires.

Chapter IV. Suspension of Guarantees, Interpretation, and Application

Article 27. Suspension of Guarantees

1. In time of war, public danger, or other emergency that threatens the independence or security of a State Party, it may take measures derogating from its obligations under the present Convention to the extent and for the period of time strictly required by the exigencies of the situation, provided that such measures are not inconsistent with its other obligations under international law and do not involve discrimination on the ground of race, color, sex, language, religion, or social origin.

2. The foregoing provision does not authorize any suspension of the following articles: Article 3 (Right to Juridical Personality), Article 4 (Right to Life), Article 5 (Right to Humane Treatment), Article 6 (Freedom from Slavery), Article 9 (Freedom from *Ex Post Facto* Laws), Article 12 (Freedom of Conscience and Religion), Article 17 (Rights of the Family), Article 18 (Right to a Name), Article 19 (Rights of the Child), Article 20 (Right to Nationality), and Article 23 (Right to Participate in Government), or of the judicial guarantees essential for the protection of such rights.

3. Any State Party availing itself of the right of suspension shall immediately inform the other States Parties, through the Secretary General of the Organization of American States, of the provisions the application of which it has suspended, the reasons that gave rise to the suspension, and the date set for the termination of such suspension.

Article 28. Federal Clause

1. Where a State Party is constituted as a federal state, the national government of such State Party shall implement all the provisions of the Convention over whose subject matter it exercises legislative and judicial jurisdiction.

2. With respect to the provisions over whose subject matter the constituent units of the federal state have jurisdiction, the national government shall immediately take suitable measures, in accordance with its constitution and its laws, to the end that the competent authorities of the constituent units may adopt appropriate provisions for the fulfillment of this Convention.

3. Whenever two or more States Parties agree to form a federation or other type of association, they shall take care that the resulting federal or other compact contains the provisions necessary for continuing and rendering effective the standards of this Convention in the new state that is organized.

Article 29. Restrictions Regarding Interpretation

No provision of this Convention shall be interpreted as:

(a) permitting any State Party, group, or person to suppress the enjoyment or exercise of the rights and freedoms recognized in this Convention or to restrict them to a greater extent than is provided for herein;

(b) restricting the enjoyment or exercise of any right or freedom recognized by virtue of the laws of any State Party or by virtue of another convention to which one of the said states is a party;

(c) precluding other rights or guarantees that are inherent in the human personality or derived from representative democracy as a form of government; or

(d) excluding or limiting the effect that the American Declaration of the Rights and Duties of Man and other international acts of the same nature may have.

Article 30. Scope of Restrictions

The restrictions that, pursuant to this Convention, may be placed on the enjoyment or exercise of the rights or freedoms recognized herein may not be applied except in accordance with laws enacted for reasons of general interest and in accordance with the purpose for which such restrictions have been established.

Article 31. Recognition of Other Rights

Other rights and freedoms recognized in accordance with the procedures established in Articles 76 and 77 may be included in the system of protection of this Convention.

Chapter V. Responsibilities

Article 32. Relationship between Duties and Rights

1. Every person has responsibilities to his family, his community, and mankind.

2. The rights of each person are limited by the rights of others, by the security of all, and by the just demands of the general welfare, in a democratic society.

PART II. MEANS OF PROTECTION

Chapter VI. Competent Organs

Article 33

The following organs shall have competence with respect to matters relating to the fulfillment of the commitments made by the States Parties to this Convention:

(a) the Inter-American Commission on Human Rights, referred to as "The Commission"; and

(b) the Inter-American Court of Human Rights, referred to as "The Court."

Chapter VII. Inter-American Commission on Human Rights

Section 1. Organization

Article 34

The Inter-American Commission on Human Rights shall be composed of seven members, who shall be persons of high moral character and recognized competence in the field of human rights.

Article 35

The Commission shall represent all the member countries of the Organization of American States.

Article 36

1. The members of the Commission shall be elected in a personal capacity by the General Assembly of the Organization from a list of candidates proposed by the governments of the member states.

2. Each of those governments may propose up to three candidates, who may be nationals of the states proposing them or of any other member state of the Organization of American States. When a slate of three is proposed, at least one of the candidates shall be a national of a state other than the one proposing the slate.

Article 37

1. The members of the Commission shall be elected for a term of four years and may be reelected only once, but the terms of three of the members chosen in the first election shall expire at the end of two years. Immediately following that election the General Assembly shall determine the names of those three members by lot.

2. No two nationals of the same state may be members of the Commission.

Article 38

Vacancies that may occur on the Commission for reasons other than the normal expiration of a term shall be filled by the Permanent Council of the Organization in accordance with the provisions of the Statute of the Commission.

Article 39

The Commission shall prepare its Statute, which it shall submit to the General Assembly for approval. It shall establish its own Regulations.

Article 40

Secretariat services for the Commission shall be furnished by the appropriate specialized unit of the General Secretariat of the Organization. This unit shall be provided with the resources required to accomplish the tasks assigned to it by the Commission.

Section 2. Functions

Article 41

The main function of the Commission shall be to promote respect for and defense of human rights. In the exercise of its mandate, it shall have the following functions and powers:

(a) to develop an awareness of human rights among the peoples of America;

(b) to make recommendations to the governments of the member states, when it considers such action advisable, for the adoption of progressive measures in favor of human rights within the framework of their domestic law and constitutional provisions as well as appropriate measures to further the observance of those rights;

(c) to prepare such studies or reports as it considers advisable in the performance of its duties;

(d) to request the governments of the member states to supply it with information on the measures adopted by them in matters of human rights;

(e) to respond, through the General Secretariat of the Organization of American States, to inquiries made by the member states on matters related to human rights and, within the limits of its possibilities, to provide those states with the advisory services they request;

(f) to take action on petitions and other communications pursuant to its authority under the provisions of Articles 44 through 51 of this Convention; and

(g) to submit an annual report to the General Assembly of the Organization of American States.

Article 42

The States Parties shall transmit to the Commission a copy of each of the reports and studies that they submit annually to the Executive Committees of the Inter-American Economic and Social Council and the Inter-American Council for Education, Science, and Culture, in their respective fields, so that the Commission may watch over the promotion of the rights implicit in the economic, social, educational, scientific, and cultural standards set forth in the Charter of the Organization of American States as amended by the Protocol of Buenos Aires.

Article 43

The States Parties undertake to provide the Commission with such information as it may request of them as to the manner in which their domestic law ensures the effective application of any provisions of this Convention.

Section 3. Competence

Article 44

Any person or group of persons, or any nongovernmental entity legally recognized in one or more member states of the Organization, may lodge petitions with the Commission containing denunciations or complaints of violation of this Convention by a State Party.

Article 45

1. Any State Party may, when it deposits its instrument of ratification of or adherence to this Convention, or at any later time, declare that it recognizes the competence of the Commission to receive and examine communications in which a State Party alleges that another State Party has committed a violation of a human right set forth in this Convention.

2. Communications presented by virtue of this article may be admitted and examined only if they are presented by a State Party that has made a declaration recognizing the aforementioned competence of the Commission. The Commission shall not admit any communication against a State Party that has not made such a declaration.

3. A declaration concerning recognition of competence may be made to be valid for an indefinite time, for a specified period, or for a specific case.

4. Declarations shall be deposited with the General Secretariat of the Organization of American States, which shall transmit copies thereof to the member states of that Organization.

Article 46

1. Admission by the Commission of a petition or communication lodged in accordance with Articles 44 or 45 shall be subject to the following requirements:

(a) that the remedies under domestic law have been pursued and exhausted in accordance with generally recognized principles of international law;

(b) that the petition or communication is lodged within a period of six months from the date on which the party alleging violation of his rights was notified of the final judgment;

(c) that the subject of the petition or communication is not pending in another international proceeding for settlement; and

(d) that, in the case of Article 44, the petition contains the name, nationality, profession, domicile, and signature of the person or persons or of the legal representative of the entity lodging the petition.

2. The provisions of paragraphs 1 (a) and 1 (b) of this article shall not be applicable when:

(a) the domestic legislation of the state concerned does not afford due process of law for the protection of the right or rights that have allegedly been violated;

(b) the party alleging violation of his rights has been denied access to the remedies under domestic law or has been prevented from exhausting them; or

(c) there has been unwarranted delay in rendering a final judgment under the aforementioned remedies.

Article 47

The Commission shall consider inadmissible any petition or communication submitted under Articles 44 or 45 if:

(a) any of the requirements indicated in Article 46 has not been met;

(b) the petition or communication does not state facts that tend to establish a violation of the rights guaranteed by this Convention;

(c) the statements of the petitioner or of the state indicate that the petition or communication is manifestly groundless or obviously out of order; or

(d) the petition or communication is substantially the same as one previously studied by the Commission or by another international organization.

Section 4. Procedure

Article 48

1. When the Commission receives a petition or communication alleging violation of any of the rights protected by this Convention, it shall proceed as follows:

(a) If it considers the petition or communication admissible, it shall request information from the government of the state indicated as being responsible for the alleged violations and shall furnish that government a transcript of the pertinent portions of the petition or communication. This information shall be submitted within a reasonable period to be determined by the Commission in accordance with the circumstances of each case.

(b) After the information has been received, or after the period established has elapsed and the information has not been received, the Commission shall ascertain whether the grounds for the petition or communication still exist. If they do not, the Commission shall order the record to be closed.

(c) The Commission may also declare the petition or communication inadmissible or out of order on the basis of information or evidence subsequently received.

(d) If the record has not been closed, the Commission shall, with the knowledge of the parties, examine the matter set forth in the petition or communication in order to verify the facts. If necessary and advisable, the Commission shall carry out an investigation, for the effective conduct of which it shall request, and the states concerned shall furnish to it, all necessary facilities.

(e) The Commission may request the states concerned to furnish any pertinent information and, if so requested, shall hear oral statements or receive written statements from the parties concerned.

(f) The Commission shall place itself at the disposal of the parties concerned with a view to reaching a friendly settlement of the matter on the basis of respect for the human rights recognized in this Convention.

2. However, in serious and urgent cases, only the presentation of a petition or communication that fulfills all the formal requirements of admissibility shall be necessary in order for the Commission to conduct an investigation with the prior consent of the state in whose territory a violation has allegedly been committed.

Article 49

If a friendly settlement has been reached in accordance with paragraph 1 (f) of Article 48, the Commission shall draw up a report, which shall be transmitted to the petitioner and to the States Parties to this Convention, and shall then be communicated to the Secretary General of the Organization of American States for publication. This report shall contain a brief statement of the facts and of the solution reached. If any party in the case so requests, the fullest possible information shall be provided to it.

Article 50

1. If a settlement is not reached, the Commission shall, within the time limit established by its Statute, draw up a report setting forth the facts and stating its conclusions. If the report, in whole or in part, does not represent the unanimous agreement of the members of the Commission, any member may attach to it a separate opinion. The written and oral statements made by the parties in accordance with paragraph 1 (e) of Article 48 shall also be attached to the report.

2. The report shall be transmitted to the states concerned, which shall not be at liberty to publish it.

3. In transmitting the report, the Committee may make such proposals and recommendations as it sees fit.

Article 51

1. If, within a period of three months from the date of the transmittal of the report of the Commission to the states concerned, the matter has not either been settled or submitted by the Commission or by the state concerned to the Court and its jurisdiction accepted, the Commission may, by the vote of an absolute majority of its members, set forth its opinion and conclusions concerning the question submitted for its consideration.

2. Where appropriate, the Commission shall make pertinent recommendations and shall prescribe a period within which the state is to take the measures that are incumbent upon it to remedy the situation examined.

3. When the prescribed period has expired, the Commission shall decide by the vote of an absolute majority of its members whether the state has taken adequate measures and whether to publish its report.

Chapter VIII. Inter-American Court of Human Rights

Section 1. Organization

Article 52

1. The Court shall consist of seven judges, nationals of the member states of the Organization, elected in an individual capacity from among jurists of the highest moral authority and of recognized competence in the field of human rights, who possess the qualifications required for the exercise of the highest judicial functions in conformity with the law of the state of which they are nationals or of the state that proposes them as candidates.

2. No two judges may be nationals of the same state.

Article 53

1. The judges of the Court shall be elected by secret ballot by an absolute majority vote of the States Parties to the Convention, in the General Assembly of the Organization, from a panel of candidates proposed by those states.

2. Each of the States Parties may propose up to three candidates, nationals of the state that proposes them or of any other member state of the Organization of American States. When a slate of three is proposed, at least one of the candidates shall be a national of a state other than the one proposing the slate.

Article 54

1. The judges of the Court shall be elected for a term of six years and may be reelected only once. The term of three of the judges chosen in the first election shall expire at the end of three years. Immediately after the election, the names of the three judges shall be determined by lot in the General Assembly.

2. A judge elected to replace a judge whose term has not expired shall complete the term of the latter.

3. The judges shall continue in office until the expiration of their term. However, they shall continue to serve with regard to cases that they have begun to hear and that are still pending, for which purposes they shall not be replaced by the newly elected judges.

Article 55

1. If a judge is a national of any of the States Parties to a case submitted to the Court, he shall retain his right to hear that case.

2. If one of the judges called upon to hear a case should be a national of one of the States Parties to the case, any other State Party in the case may appoint a person of its choice to serve on the Court as an *ad hoc* judge.

3. If among the judges called upon to hear a case none is a national of any of the States Parties to the case, each of the latter may appoint an *ad hoc* judge.

4. An *ad hoc* judge shall possess the qualifications indicated in Article 52.

5. If several States Parties to the Convention should have the same interest in a case, they shall be considered as a single party for purposes of the above provisions. In case of doubt, the Court shall decide.

Article 56

Five judges shall constitute a quorum for the transaction of business by the Court.

Article 57

The Commission shall appear in all cases before the Court.

Article 58

1. The Court shall have its seat at the place determined by the States Parties to the Convention in the General Assembly of the Organization; however, it may convene in the territory of any member state of the Organization of American States when a majority of the Court consider it desirable, and with the prior consent of the state concerned. The seat of the Court may be changed by the States Parties to the Convention in the General Assembly by a two-thirds vote.

2. The Court shall appoint its own Secretary.

3. The Secretary shall have his office at the place where the Court has its seat and shall attend the meetings that the Court may hold away from its seat.

Article 59

The Court shall establish its Secretariat, which shall function under the direction of the Secretary of the Court, in accordance with the administrative standards of the General Secretariat of the Organization in all respect not incompatible with the independence of the Court. The staff of the Court's Secretariat shall be appointed by the Secretary General of the Organization, in consultation with the Secretary of the Court.

Article 60

The Court shall draw up its Statute which it shall submit to the General Assembly for approval. It shall adopt its own Rules of Procedure.

Section 2. Jurisdiction and Functions

Article 61

1. Only the States Parties and the Commission shall have the right to submit a case to the Court.

2. In order for the Court to hear a case, it is necessary that the procedures set forth in Articles 48 to 50 shall have been completed.

Article 62

1. A State Party may, upon depositing its instrument of ratification or adherence to this Convention, or at any subsequent time, declare that it recognizes as binding, *ipso facto,* and not requiring special agreement, the jurisdiction of the Court on all matters relating to the interpretation or application of this Convention.

2. Such declaration may be made unconditionally, on the condition of reciprocity, for a specified period, or for specific cases. It shall be presented to the Secretary General of the Organization, who shall transmit copies thereof to the other member states of the Organization and to the Secretary of the Court.

3. The jurisdiction of the Court shall comprise all cases concerning the interpretation and application of the provisions of this Convention that are submitted to it, provided that the States Parties to the case recognize or have recognized such jurisdiction, whether by special declaration pursuant to the preceding paragraphs, or by a special agreement.

Article 63

1. If the Court finds that there has been a violation of a right or freedom protected by this Convention, the Court shall rule that the injured party be ensured the enjoyment of his right or freedom that was violated. It shall also rule, if appropriate, that the consequences of the measure or situation that constituted the breach of such right or freedom be remedied and that fair compensation be paid to the injured party.

2. In cases of extreme gravity and urgency, and when necessary to avoid irreparable damage to persons, the Court shall adopt such provisional measures as it deems pertinent in matters it has under consideration. With respect to a case not yet submitted to the Court, it may act at the request of the Commission.

Article 64

1. The member states of the Organization may consult the Court regarding the interpretation of this Convention or of other treaties concerning the protection of human rights in the American states. Within their spheres of competence, the organs listed in Chapter X of the Charter of the Organization of American States, as amended by the Protocol of Buenos Aires, may in like manner consult the Court.

2. The Court, at the request of a member state of the Organization, may provide that state with opinions regarding the compatibility of any of its domestic laws with the aforesaid international instruments.

Article 65

To each regular session of the General Assembly of the Organization of American States the Court shall submit, for the Assembly's consideration, a report on its work during the previous year. It shall specify, in particular, the cases in which a state has not complied with its judgments, making any pertinent recommendations.

Section 3. Procedure

Article 66

1. Reasons shall be given for the judgment of the Court.
2. If the judgment does not represent in whole or in part the unanimous opinion of the judges, any judge shall be entitled to have his dissenting or separate opinion attached to the judgment.

Article 67

The judgment of the Court shall be final and not subject to appeal. In case of disagreement as to the meaning or scope of the judgment, the Court shall interpret it at the request of any of the parties, provided the request is made within ninety days from the date of notification of the judgment.

Article 68

1. The States Parties to the Convention undertake to comply with the judgment of the Court in any case to which they are parties.
2. That part of a judgment that stipulates compensatory damages may be executed in the country concerned in accordance with domestic procedure governing the execution of judgments against the state.

Article 69

The parties to the case shall be notified of the judgment of the Court and it shall be transmitted to the States Parties to the Convention.

Chapter IX. Common provisions

Article 70

1. The judges of the Court and the members of the Commission shall enjoy, from the moment of their election and throughout their term of office, the immunities extended to diplomatic agents in accordance with international law. During the exercise of their official function they shall, in ad-

dition, enjoy the diplomatic privileges necessary for the performance of their duties.

2. At no time shall the judges of the Court or the members of the Commission be held liable for any decisions or opinions issued in the exercise of their functions.

Article 71

The position of judge of the Court or member of the Commission is incompatible with any other activity that might affect the independence or impartiality of such judge or member, as determined in the respective statutes.

Article 72

The judges of the Court and the members of the Commission shall receive emoluments and travel allowances in the form and under the conditions set forth in their statutes, with due regard for the importance and independence of their office. Such emoluments and travel allowances shall be determined in the budget of the Organization of American States, which shall also include the expenses of the Court and its Secretariat. To this end, the Court shall draw up its own budget and submit it for approval to the General Assembly through the General Secretariat. The latter may not introduce any changes in it.

Article 73

The General Assembly may, only at the request of the Commission or the Court, as the case may be, determine sanctions to be applied against members of the Commission or judges of the Court when there are justifiable grounds for such action as set forth in the respective statutes. A vote of a two-thirds majority of the member states of the Organization shall be required for a decision in the case of members of the Commission and, in the case of judges of the Court, a two-thirds majority vote of the States Parties to the Convention shall also be required.

PART III. GENERAL AND TRANSITORY PROVISIONS

Chapter X. Signature, Ratification, Reservations, Amendments, Protocols, and Denunciation

Article 74

1. This Convention shall be open for signature and ratification by or adherence of any member state of the Organization of American States.

2. Ratification of or adherence to this Convention shall be made by the deposit of an instrument of ratification or adherence with the General Secretariat of the Organization of American States. As soon as eleven states have deposited their instruments of ratification or adherence, the Convention shall

enter into force. With respect to any state that ratifies or adheres thereafter, the Convention shall enter into force on the date of the deposit of its instrument of ratification or adherence.

3. The Secretary General shall inform all member states of the Organization of the entry into force of the Convention.

Article 75

This Convention shall be subject to reservations only in conformity with the provisions of the Vienna Convention on the Law of Treaties signed on May 23, 1969.

Article 76

1. Proposals to amend this Convention may be submitted to the General Assembly for the action it deems appropriate by any State Party directly, and by the Commission or the Court through the Secretary General.

2. Amendments shall enter into force for the states ratifying them on the date when two-thirds of the States Parties to this Convention have deposited their respective instruments of ratification. With respect to the other States Parties, the amendments shall enter into force on the dates on which they deposit their respective instruments of ratification.

Article 77

1. In accordance with Article 31, any State Party and the Commission may submit proposed protocols to this Convention for consideration by the States Parties at the General Assembly with a view to gradually including other rights and freedoms within its system of protection.

2. Each protocol shall determine the manner of its entry into force and shall be applied only among the States Parties to it.

Article 78

1. The States Parties may denounce this Convention at the expiration of a five-year period starting from the date of its entry into force and by means of notice given one year in advance. Notice of the denunciation shall be addressed to the Secretary General of the Organization, who shall inform the other States Parties.

2. Such a denunciation shall not have the effect of releasing the State Party concerned from the obligations contained in this Convention with respect to any act that may constitute a violation of those obligations and that has been taken by that state prior to the effective date of denunciation.

Chapter XI. Transitory Provisions

Section 1. Inter-American Commission on Human Rights

Article 79

Upon the entry into force of this Convention, the Secretary General shall, in writing, request each member state of the Organization to present, within ninety days, its candidates for membership on the Inter-American Commission on Human Rights. The Secretary General shall prepare a list in alphabetical order of the candidates presented, and transmit it to the member states of the Organization at least thirty days prior to the next session of the General Assembly.

Article 80

The members of the Commission shall be elected by secret ballot of the General Assembly from the list of candidates referred to in Article 79. The candidates who obtain the largest number of votes and an absolute majority of the votes of the representatives of the member states shall be declared elected. Should it become necessary to have several ballots in order to elect all the members of the Commission, the candidates who receive the smallest number of votes shall be eliminated successively, in the manner determined by the General Assembly.

Section 2. Inter-American Court of Human Rights

Article 81

Upon the entry into force of this Convention, the Secretary General shall, in writing, request each State Party to present, within ninety days, its candidates for membership on the Inter-American Court of Human Rights. The Secretary General shall prepare a list in alphabetical order of the candidates presented and transmit it to the States Parties at least thirty days prior to the next session of the General Assembly.

Article 82

The judges of the Court shall be elected from the list of candidates referred to in Article 81, by secret ballot of the States Parties to the Convention in the General Assembly. The candidates who obtain the largest number of votes and an absolute majority of the votes of the representatives of the States Parties shall be declared elected. Should it become necessary to have several ballots in order to elect all the judges of the Court, the candidates who receive the smallest number of votes shall be eliminated successively, in the manner determined by the States Parties.

STATEMENTS AND RESERVATIONS

Statement of Chile

The Delegation of Chile signs this Convention, subject to its subsequent parliamentary approval and ratification, in accordance with the constitutional rules in force.

Statement of Ecuador

The Delegation of Ecuador has the honor of signing the American Convention on Human Rights. It does not believe that it is necessary to make any specific reservation at this time, without prejudice to the general power set forth in the Convention itself that leaves the governments free to ratify it or not.

Reservation of Uruguay

Article 80.2 of the Constitution of Uruguay provides that citizenship is suspended for a person indicted according to law in a criminal prosecution that may result in a sentence of imprisonment in a penitentiary. This restriction on the exercise of the rights recognized in Article 23 of the Convention is not envisaged among the circumstances provided for in this respect by paragraph 2 of Article 23, for which reason the Delegation of Uruguay expresses a reservation on this matter.

In witness whereof, the undersigned Plenipotentiaries, whose full powers were found in good and due form, sign this Convention, which shall be called "PACT ON SAN JOSE, COSTA RICA", (in the city of San José, Costa Rica, this twenty-second day of November, nineteen hundred and sixty-nine).

African Charter on Human and Peoples' Rights [1]

PREAMBLE

The African States members of the Organization of African Unity, parties to the present convention entitled "African Charter on Human and Peoples' Rights",

Recalling Decision 115 (XVI) of the Assembly of Heads of State and Government at its Sixteenth Ordinary Session held in Monrovia, Liberia, from 17 to 20 July 1979 on the preparation of a "preliminary draft on an African Charter on Human and Peoples' Rights providing *inter alia* for the establishment of bodies to promote and protect human and peoples' rights";

Considering the Charter of the Organization of African Unity, which stipulates that "freedom, equality, justice and dignity are essential objectives for the achievement of the legitimate aspirations of the African peoples";

Reaffirming the pledge they solemnly made in Article 2 of the said Charter to eradicate all forms of colonialism from Africa, to coordinate and intensify their cooperation and efforts to achieve a better life for the peoples of Africa and to promote international cooperation having due regard to the Charter of the United Nations and the Universal Declaration of Human Rights;

Taking into consideration the virtues of their historical tradition and the values of African civilization which should inspire and characterize their reflection on the concept of human and peoples' rights;

Recognizing on the one hand, that fundamental human rights stem from the attributes of human beings, which justifies their national and international protection and on the other hand that the reality and respect of peoples rights should necessarily guarantee human rights;

Considering that the enjoyment of rights and freedoms also implies the performance of duties on the part of everyone;

Convinced that it is henceforth essential to pay a particular attention to the right to development and that civil and political rights cannot be dissociated from economic, social and cultural rights in their conception as well

[1] In force since 21 October 1986.

as universality and that the satisfaction of economic, social and cultural rights is a guarantee for the enjoyment of civil and political rights;

Conscious of their duty to achieve the total liberation of Africa, the peoples of which are still struggling for their dignity and genuine independence, and undertaking to eliminate colonialism, neo-colonialism, apartheid, zionism and to dismantle aggressive foreign military bases and all forms of discrimination, particularly those based on race, ethnic group, color, sex, language, religion or political opinions;

Reaffirming their adherence to the principles of human and peoples' rights and freedoms contained in the declarations, conventions and other instruments adopted by the Organization of African Unity, the Movement of Non-Aligned Countries and the United Nations;

Firmly convinced of their duty to promote and protect human and peoples' rights and freedoms taking into account the importance traditionally attached to these rights and freedoms in Africa;

Have agreed as follows:

PART I. RIGHTS AND DUTIES

Chapter I. Human and Peoples' Rights

Article 1

The Member States of the Organization of African Unity parties to the present Charter shall recognize the rights, duties and freedoms enshrined in this Charter and shall undertake to adopt legislative or other measures to give effect to them.

Article 2

Every individual shall be entitled to the enjoyment of the rights and freedoms recognized and guaranteed in the present Charter without distinction of any kind such as race, ethnic group, color, sex, language, religion, political or any other opinion, national and social origin, fortune, birth or other status.

Article 3

1. Every individual shall be equal before the law.
2. Every individual shall be entitled to equal protection of the law.

Article 4

Human beings are inviolable. Every human being shall be entitled to respect for his life and the integrity of his person. No one may be arbitrarily deprived of this right.

Article 5

Every individual shall have the right to the respect of the dignity inherent in a human being and to the recognition of his legal status. All forms of exploitation and degradation of man particularly slavery, slave trade, torture, cruel, inhuman or degrading punishment and treatment shall be prohibited.

Article 6

Every individual shall have the right to liberty and to the security of his person. No one may be deprived of his freedom except for reasons and conditions previously laid down by law. In particular, no one may be arbitrarily arrested or detained.

Article 7

1. Every individual shall have the right to have his cause heard. This comprises:

(a) the right to an appeal to competent national organs against acts of violating his fundamental rights as recognized and guaranteed by conventions, laws, regulations and customs in force;

(b) the right to be presumed innocent until proved guilty by a competent court or tribunal;

(c) the right to defence, including the right to be defended by counsel of his choice;

(d) the right to be tried within a reasonable time by an impartial court or tribunal.

2. No one may be condemned for an act or omission which did not constitute a legally punishable offence at the time it was committed. No penalty may be inflicted for an offence for which no provision was made at the time it was committed. Punishment is personal and can be imposed only on the offender.

Article 8

Freedom of conscience, the profession and free practice of religion shall be guaranteed. No one may, subject to law and order, be submitted to measures restricting the exercise of these freedoms.

Article 9

1. Every individual shall have the right to receive information.

2. Every individual shall have the right to express and disseminate his opinions within the law.

Article 10.

1. Every individual shall have the right to free association provided that he abides by the law.

2. Subject to the obligation of solidarity provided for in Article 29 no one may be compelled to join an association.

Article 11

Every individual shall have the right to assemble freely with others. The exercise of this right shall be subject only to necessary restrictions provided for by law in particular those enacted in the interest of national security, the safety, health, ethics and rights and freedoms of others.

Article 12

1. Every individual shall have the right to freedom of movement and residence within the borders of a State provided he abides by the law.

2. Every individual shall have the right to leave any country including his own, and to return to his country. This right may only be subject to restrictions, provided for by law for the protection of national security, law and order, public health or morality.

3. Every individual shall have the right, when persecuted, to seek and obtain asylum in other countries in accordance with laws of those countries and international conventions.

4. A non-national legally admitted in a territory of a State Party to the present Charter, may only be expelled from it by virtue of a decision taken in accordance with the law.

5. The mass expulsion of non-nationals shall be prohibited. Mass expulsion shall be that which is aimed at national, racial, ethnic or religious groups.

Article 13

1. Every citizen shall have the right to participate freely in the government of his country, either directly or through freely chosen representatives in accordance with the provisions of the law.

2. Every citizen shall have the right of equal access to the public service of his country.

3. Every individual shall have the right of access to public property and services in strict equality of all persons before the law.

Article 14

The right to property shall be guaranteed. It may only be encroached upon in the interest of public need or in the general interest of the community and in accordance with the provisions of appropriate laws.

Article 15

Every individual shall have the right to work under equitable and satisfactory conditions, and shall receive equal pay for equal work.

Article 16

1. Every individual shall have the right to enjoy the best attainable state of physical and mental health.

2. States parties to the present Charter shall take the necessary measures to protect the health of their people and to ensure that they receive medical attention when they are sick.

Article 17

1. Every individual shall have the right to education.

2. Every individual may freely, take part in the cultural life of his community.

3. The promotion and protection of morals and traditional values recognized by the community shall be the duty of the State.

Article 18

1. The family shall be the natural unit and basis of society. It shall be protected by the State which shall take care of its physical health and moral.

2. The State shall have the duty to assist the family which is the custodian of morals and traditional values recognized by the community.

3. The State shall ensure the elimination of every discrimination against women and also censure the protection of the rights of the woman and the child as stipulated in international declarations and conventions.

4. The aged and the disabled shall also have the right to special measures of protection in keeping with their physical or moral needs.

Article 19

All peoples shall be equal; they shall enjoy the same respect and shall have the same rights. Nothing shall justify the domination of a people by another.

Article 20

1. All peoples shall have the right to existence. They shall have the unquestionable and inalienable right to self-determination. They shall freely determine their political status and shall pursue their economic and social development according to the policy they have freely chosen.

2. Colonized or oppressed peoples shall have the right to free themselves from the bonds of domination by resorting to any means recognized by the international community.

3. All peoples shall have the right to the assistance of the States parties to the present Charter in their liberation struggle against foreign domination, be it political, economic or cultural.

Article 21

1. All peoples shall freely dispose of their wealth and natural resources. This right shall be exercised in the exclusive interest of the people. In no case shall a people be deprived of it.

2. In case of spoliation the dispossessed people shall have the right to the lawful recovery of its property as well as to an adequate compensation.

3. The free disposal of wealth and natural resources shall be exercised without prejudice to the obligation of promoting international economic cooperation based on mutual respect, equitable exchange and the principles of international law.

4. States parties to the present Charter shall individually and collectively exercise the right to free disposal of their wealth and natural resources with a view to strengthening African unity and solidarity.

5. States parties to the present Charter shall undertake to eliminate all forms of foreign economic exploitation particularly that practiced by international monopolies so as to enable their peoples to fully benefit from the advantages derived from their national resources.

Article 22

1. All peoples shall have the right to their economic, social and cultural development with due regard to their freedom and identity and in the equal enjoyment, of the common heritage of mankind.

2. States shall have the duty, individually or collectively, to ensure the exercise of the right to development.

Article 23

1. All peoples shall have the right to national and international peace and security. The principles of solidarity and friendly relations implicitly affirmed by the Charter of the United Nations and reaffirmed by that of the Organization of African Unity shall govern relations between States.

2. For the purpose of strengthening peace, solidarity and friendly relations, States parties to the present Charter shall ensure that:

(a) any individual enjoying the right of asylum under Article 12 of the present Charter shall not engage in subversive activities against his country of origin or any other State party to the present Charter;

(b) their territories shall not be used as bases for subversive or terrorist activities against the people of any other State party to the present Charter.

Article 24

All peoples shall have the right to a general satisfactory environment favorable to their development.

Article 25

States parties to the present Charter shall have the duty to promote and ensure through teaching, education and publication, the respect of the rights and freedoms contained in the present Charter and to see to it that these freedoms and rights as well as corresponding obligations and duties are understood.

Article 26

States parties to the present Charter shall have the duty to guarantee the independence of the Courts and shall allow the establishment and improvement of appropriate national institutions entrusted with the promotion and protection of the rights and freedoms guaranteed by the present Charter.

Chapter II. Duties

Article 27

1. Every individual shall have duties towards his family and society, the State and other legally recognized communities and the international community.

2. The rights and freedoms of each individual shall be exercised with due regard to the rights of others, collective security, morality and common interest.

Article 28

Every individual shall have the duty to respect and consider his fellow beings without discrimination, and to maintain relations aimed at promoting, safeguarding and reinforcing mutual respect and tolerance.

Article 29

The individual shall also have the duty:

1. To preserve the harmonious development of the family and to work for the cohesion and respect of the family; to respect his parents at all times, to maintain them in case of need;

2. To serve his national community by placing his physical and intellectual abilities at its service;

3. Not to compromise the security of the State whose national or resident he is;

4. To preserve and strengthen social and national solidarity, particularly when the latter is threatened;

5. To preserve and strengthen the national independence and the territorial integrity of his country and to contribute to its defence in accordance with the law;

6. To work to the best of his abilities and competence, and to pay taxes imposed by law in the interest of the society;

7. To preserve and strengthen positive African cultural values in his relations with other members of the society, in the spirit of tolerance, dialogue

and consultation and, in general, to contribute to the promotion of the moral well being of society;

8. To contribute to the best of his abilities, at all times and at all levels, to the promotion and achievement of African unity.

PART II. MEASURES OF SAFEGUARD

Chapter I. Establishment and Organization of the African Commission on Human and Peoples' Rights

Article 30

An African Commission on Human and Peoples' Rights, hereinafter called "the Commission", shall be established within the Organization of African Unity to promote human and peoples' rights and ensure their protection in Africa.

Article 31

1. The Commission shall consist of eleven members chosen from amongst African personalities of the highest reputation, known for their high morality, integrity, impartiality and competence in matters of human and peoples' rights; particular consideration being given to persons having legal experience.

2. The members of the Commission shall serve in their personal capacity.

Article 32

The Commission shall not include more than one national of the same State.

Article 33

The members of the Commission shall be elected by secret ballot by the Assembly of Heads of State and Government, from a list of persons nominated by the States parties to the present Charter.

Article 34

Each State party to the present Charter may not nominate more than two candidates. The candidates must have the nationality of one of the States parties to the present Charter. When two candidates are nominated by a State, one of them may not be a national of that State.

Article 35

1. The Secretary General of the Organization of African Unity shall invite States parties to the present Charter at least four months before the elections to nominate candidates;

2. The Secretary General of the Organization of African Unity shall make an alphabetical list of the persons thus nominated and communicate it to the Heads of State and Government at least one month before the elections.

Article 36

The members of the Commission shall be elected for a six year period and shall be eligible for re-election. However, the term of office of four of the members elected at the first election shall terminate after two years and the term of office of the three others, at the end of four years.

Article 37

Immediately after the first election, the Chairman of the Assembly of Heads of State and Government of the Organization of African Unity shall draw lots to decide the names of those members referred to in Article 36.

Article 38

After their election, the members of the Commission shall make a solemn declaration to discharge their duties impartially and faithfully.

Article 39

1. In case of death or resignation of a member of the Commission, the Chairman of the Commission shall immediately inform the Secretary General of the Organization of African Unity, who shall declare the seat vacant from the date of death or from the date on which the resignation takes effect.

2. If, in the unanimous opinion of other members of the Commission, a member has stopped discharging his duties for any reason other than a temporary absence, the Chairman of the Commission shall inform the Secretary General of the Organization of African Unity, who shall then declare the seat vacant.

3. In each of the cases anticipated above, the Assembly of Heads of State and Government shall replace the member whose seat became vacant for the remaining period of his term unless the period is less than six months.

Article 40

Every member of the Commission shall be in office until the date his successor assumes office.

Article 41

The Secretary General of the Organization of African Unity shall appoint the Secretary of the Commission. He shall also provide the staff and services necessary for the effective discharge of the duties of the Commission. The Organization of African Unity shall bear the costs of the staff and services.

Article 42

1. The Commission shall elect its Chairman and Vice Chairman for a two year period. They shall be eligible for re-election.

2. The Commission shall lay down its rules of procedure.

3. Seven members shall form a quorum.

4. In case of an equality of votes, the Chairman shall have a casting vote.

5. The Secretary General may attend the meetings of the Commission. He shall neither participate in deliberations nor shall he be entitled to vote. The Chairman of the Commission may, however, invite him to speak.

Article 43

In discharging their duties, members of the Commission shall enjoy diplomatic privileges and immunities provided for in the General Convention on the Privileges and Immunities of the Organization of African Unity.

Article 44

Provision shall be made for the emoluments and allowances of the members of the Commission in the Regular Budget of the Organization of African Unity.

Chapter II. Mandate of the Commission

Article 45

The functions of the Commission shall be:

1. To promote Human and Peoples' Rights and in particular:

(a) to collect documents, undertake studies and researches on African problems in the field of human and peoples' rights, organize seminars, symposia and conferences, disseminate information, encourage national and local institutions concerned with human and peoples' rights, and should the case arise, give its views or make recommendations to Governments.

(b) to formulate and lay down, principles and rules aimed at solving legal problems relating to human and peoples' rights and fundamental freedoms upon which African Governments may base their legislations.

(c) co-operate with other African and international institutions concerned with the promotion and protection of human and peoples' rights.

2. Ensure the protection of human and peoples' rights under conditions laid down by the present Charter.

3. Interpret all the provisions of the present Charter at the request of a State party, an institution of the OAU or an African Organization recognized by the OAU.

4. Perform any other tasks which may be entrusted to it by the Assembly of Heads of State and Government.

Chapter III. Procedure of the Commission

Article 46

The Commission may resort to any appropriate method of investigation; it may hear from the Secretary General of the Organization of African Unity or any other person capable of enlightening it.

Communication from States

Article 47

If a State party to the present Charter has good reasons to believe that another State party to this Charter has violated the provisions of the Charter, it may draw, by written communication, the attention of that State to the matter. This communication shall also be addressed to the Secretary General of the OAU and to the Chairman of the Commission. Within three months of the receipt of the communication, the State to which the communication is addressed shall give the enquiring State, written explanation or statement elucidating the matter. This should include as much as possible relevant information relating to the laws and rules of procedure applied and applicable, and the redress already given or course of action available.

Article 48

If within three months from the date on which the original communication is received by the State to which it is addressed, the issue is not settled to the satisfaction of the two States involved through bilateral negotiation or by any other peaceful procedure, either State shall have the right to submit the matter to the Commission through the Chairman and shall notify the other States involved.

Article 49

Notwithstanding the provisions of Article 47, if a State party to the present Charter considers that another State party has violated the provisions of the Charter, it may refer the matter directly to the Commission by addressing a communication to the Chairman, to the Secretary General of the Organization of African Unity and the State concerned.

Article 50

The Commission can only deal with a matter submitted to it after making sure that all local remedies, if they exist, have been exhausted, unless it is obvious to the Commission that the procedure of achieving these remedies would be unduly prolonged.

Article 51

1. The Commission may ask the States concerned to provide it with all relevant information.

2. When the Commission is considering the matter, States concerned may be represented before it and submit written or oral representation.

Article 52

After having obtained from the States concerned and from other sources all the information it deems necessary and after having tried all appropriate means to reach an amicable solution based on the respect of Human and Peoples' Rights, the Commission shall prepare, within a reasonable period of time from the notification referred to in Article 48, a report stating the facts and its findings. This report shall be sent to the States concerned and communicated to the Assembly of Heads of State and Government.

Article 53

While transmitting its report, the Commission may make to the Assembly of Heads of State and Government such recommendations as it deems useful.

Article 54

The Commission shall submit to each ordinary Session of the Assembly of Heads of State and Government a report on its activities.

Other Communications

Article 55

1. Before each Session, the Secretary of the Commission shall make a list of the communications other than those of States parties to the present Charter and transmit them to the members of the Commission, who shall indicate which communications should be considered by the Commission.

2. A communication shall be considered by the Commission if a simple majority of its members so decide.

Article 56

Communications relating to human and peoples' rights referred to in Article 55 received by the Commission, shall be considered if they:

1. Indicate their authors even if the latter request anonymity,

2. Are compatible with the Charter of the Organization of African Unity or with the present Charter,

3. Are not written in disparaging or insulting language directed against the State concerned and its institutions or to the Organization of African Unity,

4. Are not based exclusively on news discriminated through the mass media,

5. Are sent after exhausting local remedies, if any, unless it is obvious that this procedure is unduly prolonged,

6. Are submitted within a reasonable period from the time local remedies are exhausted or from the date the Commission is seized of the matter, and

7. Do not deal with cases which have been settled by these States involved in accordance with the principles of the Charter of the United Nations, or the Charter of the Organization of African Unity or the provisions of the present Charter.

Article 57

Prior to any substantive consideration, all communications shall be brought to the knowledge of the State concerned by the Chairman of the Commission.

Article 58

1. When it appears after deliberations of the Commission that one or more communications apparently relate to special cases which reveal the existence of a series of serious or massive violations of human and peoples' rights, the Commission shall draw the attention of the Assembly of Heads of State and Government to these special cases.

2. The Assembly of Heads of State and Government may then request the Commission to undertake an in-depth study of these cases and make a factual report, accompanied by its findings and recommendations.

3. A case of emergency duly noticed by the Commission shall be submitted by the latter to the Chairman of the Assembly of Heads of State and Government who may request an in-depth study.

Article 59

1. All measures taken within the provisions of the present Chapter shall remain confidential until such a time as the Assembly of Heads of State and Government shall otherwise decide.

2. However, the report shall be published by the Chairman of the Commission upon the decision of the Assembly of Heads of State and Government.

3. The report on the activities of the Commission shall be published by its Chairman after it has been considered by the Assembly of Heads of State and Government.

Chapter IV. Applicable Principles

Article 60

The Commission shall draw inspiration from international law on human and peoples' rights, particularly from the provisions of various African instruments on human and peoples' rights, the Charter of the United Nations, the Charter of the Organization of African Unity, the Universal Declaration of Human Rights, other instruments adopted by the United Nations and by African countries in the field of human and peoples' rights as well as from the provisions of various instruments adopted within the Specialized Agencies of the United Nations of which the parties to the present Charter are members.

Article 61

The Commission shall also take into consideration, as subsidiary measures to determine the principles of law, other general or special international conventions, laying down rules expressly recognized by member states of the Organization of African Unity, African practices consistent with international norms on human and peoples' rights, customs generally accepted as law, general principles of law recognized by African states as well as legal precedents and doctrine.

Article 62

Each state party shall undertake to submit every two years, from the date the present Charter comes into force, a report on the legislative or other measures taken with a view to giving effect to the rights and freedoms recognized and guaranteed by the present Charter.

Article 63

1. The present Charter shall be open to signature, ratification or adherence of the member states of the Organization of African Unity.
2. The instruments of ratification or adherence to the present Charter shall be deposited with the Secretary General of the Organization of African Unity.
3. The present Charter shall come into force three months after the reception by the Secretary General of the instruments of ratification or adherence of a simple majority of the member states of the Organization of African Unity.

PART III. GENERAL PROVISIONS

Article 64

1. After the coming into force of the present Charter, members of the Commission shall be elected in accordance with the relevant Articles of the present Charter.
2. The Secretary General of the Organization of African Unity shall convene the first meeting of the Commission at the Headquarters of the Organization within three months of the constitution of the Commission. Thereafter, the Commission shall be convened by its Chairman whenever necessary but at least once a year.

Article 65

For each of the States that will ratify or adhere to the present Charter after its coming into force, the Charter shall take effect three months after the date of the deposit by that State of its instrument of ratification or adherence.

Article 66

Special protocols or agreements may, if necessary, supplement the provisions of the present Charter.

Article 67

The Secretary General of the Organization of African Unity shall inform member states of the Organization of the deposit of each instrument of ratification or adherence.

Article 68

The present Charter may be amended if a State party makes a written request to that effect to the Secretary General of the Organization of African Unity. The Assembly of Heads of State and Government may only consider the draft amendment after all the States parties have been duly informed of it and the Commission has given its opinion on it at the request of the sponsoring State. The amendment shall be approved by a simple majority of the States parties. It shall come into force for each State which has accepted it in accordance with its constitutional procedure three months after the Secretary General has received notice of the acceptance.

Adopted by the eighteenth Assembly of Heads of State and Government – June 1981 – Nairobi, Kenya

Max-Planck-Institut für ausländisches öffentliches Recht und Völkerrecht

Beiträge zum ausländischen öffentlichen Recht und Völkerrecht

Hrsg.: R. Bernhardt, K. Doehring, J. A. Frowein

Bde. 27–59 erschienen im Carl Heymanns Verlag KG Köln, Berlin (Bestellung an: Max-Planck-Institut für Völkerrecht, Berliner Str. 48, 6900 Heidelberg 1);
ab Band 60 im Springer-Verlag Berlin, Heidelberg, New York, Tokyo

92 Juliane *Kokott:* **Das interamerikanische System zum Schutz der Menschenrechte.** 1986. XII, 166 Seiten (6 Seiten English Summary). Geb. 78,– DM

91 Rolf *Kühner:* **Vorbehalte zu multilateralen völkerrechtlichen Verträgen.** 1986. XI, 307 Seiten (6 Seiten English Summary). Geb. 98,– DM

90 Daniel *Thürer:* **Bund und Gemeinden.** Eine rechtsvergleichende Untersuchung zu den unmittelbaren Beziehungen zwischen Bund und Gemeinden in der Bundesrepublik Deutschland, den Vereinigten Staaten von Amerika und der Schweiz. 1986. XVII, 352 Seiten (7 Seiten English Summary). Geb. 118,– DM

89 Helmut *Damian:* **Staatenimmunität und Gerichtszwang.** Grundlagen und Grenzen der völkerrechtlichen Freiheit fremder Staaten von inländischer Gerichtsbarkeit in Verfahren der Zwangsvollstreckung oder Anspruchssicherung. 1985. XV, 261 Seiten (11 Seiten English Summary). Geb. 78,– DM

88 Rudolf *Dolzer:* **Eigentum, Enteignung und Entschädigung im geltenden Völkerrecht.** 1985. XIII, 331 Seiten (3 Seiten English Summary). Geb. 118,– DM

87 Norbert *Wühler:* **Die internationale Schiedsgerichtsbarkeit in der völkerrechtlichen Praxis der Bundesrepublik Deutschland.** 1985. XIII, 239 Seiten (5 Seiten English Summary). Geb. 88,– DM

86 Peter *Malanczuk:* **Region und unitarische Struktur in Großbritannien.** Die verfassungsrechtliche und verwaltungsorganisatorische Bedeutung der Region in England, Wales und Schottland. 1984. XIII, 296 Seiten (5 Seiten English Summary). Geb. 98,– DM

85 Rüdiger *Wolfrum:* **Die Internationalisierung staatsfreier Räume.** Die Entwicklung einer internationalen Verwaltung für Antarktis, Weltraum, Hohe See und Meeresboden. 1984. XX, 757 Seiten (11 Seiten English Summary). Geb. 198,– DM

84 Wolfram *Karl:* **Vertrag und spätere Praxis im Völkerrecht.** Zum Einfluß der Praxis auf Inhalt und Bestand völkerrechtlicher Verträge. 1983. XX, 438 Seiten (17 Seiten English Summary). Geb. 98,– DM.

83 Lothar *Gündling:* **Die 200 Seemeilen-Wirtschaftszone.** Entstehung eines neuen Regimes des Meeresvölkerrechts. 1983. XIV, 370 Seiten (8 Seiten English Summary). Geb. 98,– DM

82 Torsten *Stein:* **Die Auslieferungsausnahme bei politischen Delikten.** Normative Grenzen, Anwendung in der Praxis und Versuch einer Neuformulierung. 1983. XII, 402 Seiten (5 Seiten English Summary). Geb. 116,– DM

81 **Völkerrecht als Rechtsordnung – Internationale Gerichtsbarkeit – Menschenrechte – Festschrift für Hermann Mosler 1983.** XIV, 1057 Seiten. Geb. DM 298,–

80 Jutta *Stoll:* **Vereinbarungen zwischen Staat und ausländischem Investor.** Rechtsnatur und Bestandsschutz. 1982. XI, 166 Seiten (6 Seiten English Summary). Geb. 49,– DM

79 Meinhard *Hilf:* **Die Organisationsstruktur der Europäischen Gemeinschaften.** Rechtliche Gestaltungsmöglichkeiten und Grenzen. 1982. XVIII, 442 Seiten (12 Seiten English Summary, 13 Seiten Résumé français). Geb. 98,– DM

78 Ludwig *Weber:* **Die Zivilluftfahrt im Europäischen Gemeinschaftsrecht.** 1981. XXVIII, 428 Seiten (6 Seiten English Summary). Geb. 114,– DM

77 Michael *Schaefer:* **Die Funktionsfähigkeit des Sicherheitsmechanismus der Vereinten Nationen.** 1981. XXI, 471 Seiten (10 Seiten English Summary). Geb. 105,– DM

76 Eckart *Klein:* **Statusverträge im Völkerrecht.** Rechtsfragen territorialer Sonderregime. 1980. XIV, 395 Seiten (10 Seiten English Summary). Geb. 86,– DM

75 **Die Koalitionsfreiheit des Arbeitnehmers/The Freedom of the Worker to Organize/ La liberté syndicale des salariés.** Rechtsvergleichung und Völkerrecht/Comparative Law and International Law/Droit comparé et droit international public. 1980, XLIX, 1536 Seiten. (In 2 Bänden, die nur zusammen abgegeben werden.) Geb. 360,– DM

74 Hans *Reinhard:* **Rechtsgleichheit und Selbstbestimmung der Völker in wirtschaftlicher Hinsicht.** Die Praxis der Vereinten Nationen. 1980. XIII, 373 Seiten. Geb. 86,– DM

73 Theodor *Schweisfurth:* **Sozialistisches Völkerrecht?** Darstellung – Analyse – Wertung der sowjetmarxistischen Theorie vom Völkerrecht „neuen Typs". 1979. XIV, 615 Seiten. Geb. 108,– DM

72 **Grundrechtsschutz in Europa.** Europäische Menschenrechts-Konvention und Europäische Gemeinschaften. Internationales Kolloquium, veranstaltet vom Max-Planck-Institut für ausländisches öffentliches Recht und Völkerrecht, Heidelberg 1976. 1977. VIII, 248 Seiten. Geb. 62,– DM

71 Georg *Ress:* **Die Rechtslage Deutschlands nach dem Grundlagenvertrag vom 21. Dezember 1972.** 1978. XIV, 436 Seiten. Geb. 66,– DM

70 Hans *Krück:* **Völkerrechtliche Verträge im Recht der Europäischen Gemeinschaften.** Abschlußkompetenzen – Bindungswirkung – Kollisionen. 1977. XIII, 210 Seiten. Geb. 78,– DM

69 Michael *Bothe:* **Die Kompetenzstruktur des modernen Bundesstaates in rechtsvergleichender Sicht.** 1977. XIV, 350 Seiten. Geb. 130,– DM

68 Ulf-Dieter *Klemm:* **Die seewärtige Grenze des Festlandsockels.** Geschichte, Entwicklung und lex lata eines seevölkerrechtlichen Grundproblems. 1976. XIV, 285 Seiten. Geb. 98,– DM

67 Torsten *Stein:* **Amtshilfe in auswärtigen Angelegenheiten.** 1975. XII, 193 Seiten. Geb. 78,– DM

66 Karin *Oellers-Frahm:* **Die einstweilige Anordnung in der internationalen Gerichtsbarkeit.** 1975. X, 168 Seiten. Geb. 72,– DM

65 Werner *Morvay:* **Souveränitätsübergang und Rechtskontinuität im Britischen Commonwealth.** Ein Beitrag zur Lehre von der Staatensukzession. 1974. VIII, 116 Seiten. Geb. 58,– DM

64 Hartmut *Schiedermair:* **Der völkerrechtliche Status Berlins nach dem Viermächte-Abkommen vom 3. September 1971.** 1975. VII, 223 Seiten. Geb. 67,– DM

63 Hans *von Mangoldt:* **Die Schiedsgerichtsbarkeit als Mittel internationaler Streitschlichtung.** Zur Beilegung von Rechtsstreitigkeiten auf der Grundlage der Achtung vor dem Rechte. 1974. XII, 214 Seiten. Geb. 60,– DM

62 **Judicial Settlement of International Disputes.** International Court of Justice. Other Courts and Tribunals. Arbitration and Conciliation. An International Symposium. 1974. XII, 572 Seiten. Geb. 94,– DM

MIX
Papier aus verantwortungsvollen Quellen
Paper from responsible sources
FSC® C105338

If you have any concerns about our products,
you can contact us on
ProductSafety@springernature.com

In case Publisher is established outside the EU,
the EU authorized representative is:
Springer Nature Customer Service Center GmbH
Europaplatz 3, 69115 Heidelberg, Germany

Printed by Libri Plureos GmbH
in Hamburg, Germany